interactive
music
handbook

the definitive guide
to Internet music strategies,
enhanced CD production,
and business development

by
jodi summers

edited by
jon samsel

ALLWORTH PRESS
NEW YORK

Published by Allworth Press
An imprint of Allworth Communications
10 East 23rd Street, New York, NY 10010
www.allworth.com

Author: Jodi Summers
Editor: John Samsel
Chapter 10: Written by John Samsel
Cover Design: Tim Neil
Copy Editors: James Carr, Nicole Potter

Acknowledgement is made to the following for permission to reproduce the material indicated:
MCA, for excerpts from *On the Road with B.B. King*, screenplay by Michael Shaun Conaway, © 1996; Philips Interactive Media and Michael Shaun Conaway, for the design proposal from *In Search of the Lost Chord*; David Greene for the Case Study for *Real McCoy—One More Time Enhanced CD*; J. Diane Brinson & Mark Radcliffe, for their *Web Site Development Agreement*, excerpted by permission from *Multimedia Law and Business Handbook* published by Ladera Press; Paul Palumbo for excerpts from the *Interactive Publishers Handbook*; Jon Samsel & Darryl Wimberley for excerpts from the *Interactive Writer's Handbook*.

ISBN: 1-58115-000-8
Printed in Canada
Library of Congress Catalog Card Number: 98-70404

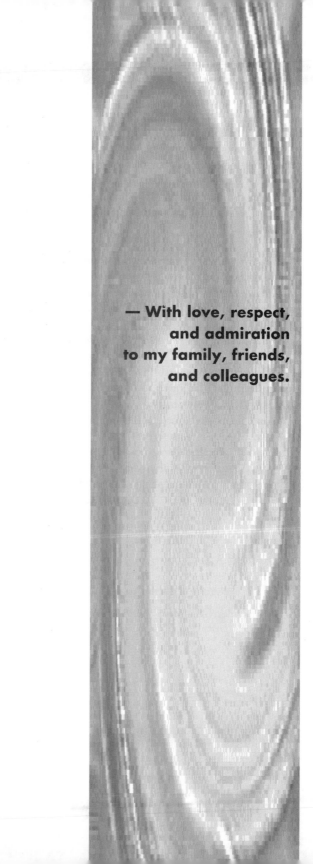

— With love, respect,
and admiration
to my family, friends,
and colleagues.

sponsor acknowledgments

Launched in 1995, **Music & Computers** is the only magazine dedicated to showing you how to make better music with your computer. It addresses three groups: newcomers, experienced computer users, and accomplished musicians. Through extensive tips and tutorials, detailed columns (the Fat Man on composing multimedia music, Jim Aikin on MIDI), and feature articles by luminaries like Craig Anderton, Julian Colbeck, and Bob Safir, *Music & Computers* teaches how to, not just about.

Music & Computers is available at bookstores, newsstands, music stores, and computer stores worldwide. For more background, visit *www.music-and-computers.com*. To subscribe (one year, six issues, $18.00) call (303) 678-0439. For advertising information, call Karin Becker at (415) 655-4119.

Sample Articles found in *Music & Computers:*
- Computer Game Music—How It's Done
- MOD Files: Do-It-Yourself Digital Sound
- Sampler Buyer's Guide
- Creating Killer Soundtracks
- Studio Secrets—Alternate MIDI Controllers
- Making Music on the Internet
- Inside the Computer Game Developers' Conference
- How to Get a Job in Multimedia Music
- Power-User Tips—Sequencing . . . Synth Programming . . . Sampling . . . MIDI Guitar . . . Drum Loops . . . Digital Recording and Editing . . . Mixing . . . Soundcards

The **APPLE MEDIA PROGRAM (AMP)** is the online media infomation source for technology, tools, resources, and the new media developer community. Designed for content developers and the creative community, AMP offers a breadth of resources and information to keep new media developers up-to-date on Apple's offerings for authoring and playback. AMP gives you access to some of the best minds and most successful members of the Interactive Media Community. Program features include the AMP Web Site and Members Only Area, Market Research Reports & Guidebooks, Apple Multimedia Information Mailing, Co-marketing Opportunities, Development Hardware Purchasing Privileges, Multimedia Events and Training Discounts, and Apple's Interactive Music Track.

Apple Media Program
Apple Computer, Inc.
One Infinite Loop
Cupertino, CA 95014
Voice: (408) 974-4897
www.amp.apple.com

Apple Computer's "MASTERS OF MEDIA" program educates customers on how to make and save money by leveraging their investments in their intellectual properties, and by managing the technology to more effectively communicate their ideas. For the creative or publisher, the equity is their content, for the production or pre-press company, color production and color fidelity, and for the corporation, the equity is their brand. "Masters of Media" is a comprehensive program for artists, designers, musicians, publishers, Web masters, advertising agencies, entertainment companies, and corporate communicators, providing the means to move and expand their content from one media to all media. Communications no longer have to be media-specific, but can now become media universal. Macintosh technologies allow everyone the power to visualize his ideas more easily, whether he wants to communicate across multiple media, in multiple languages, with consistent color, in 3-D, on the Internet, in virtual reality, or to automate the repetitive tasks of media creation. "Master The Media"

"Masters of Media"
Apple Computer, Inc.
One Infinite Loop
Cupertino, CA 95014
Voice: 1-800-776-2333 or (408) 996-1010
www.masters.media.apple.com or *www.apple.com*

The author would like to thank the numerous individuals and companies who helped make this book possible, including,

Deborah Anderson, New media marketing manager, Island Records

Paul Atkinson, President, Nu Millennia Records

James Baker, CEO, 21st Century Media

George Bartko, COO, Second Line Search

John Bates, New media consultant

Georgia Bergman, Vice president, creative enterprises, Warner Bros. Records

Nancy Berry, Chairman, Virgin Records America

Bryan Biniak, Director of business development, Harmonix Music Systems

David Bowie, One of the most innovative recording artists of the latter half of the 20th century

Ken Caillat, President, Highway One Media Entertainment

Vincent Castellucci, Adminstrator of licensing, The Harry Fox Agency, Inc.

Ted Cohen, Vice president multimedia music, Philips Interactive Media

Chris DeGarmo, Guitars, Queensryche

Thomas Dolby, Recording artist and video director, as well as president and CEO, Headspace

Kal Dolgin, Music consultant

Michael Dorf, President and CEO, Knit Media

Todd Fearn, CEO, REV Entertainment

Mike Gaffney, Vice president and general manager of Music, Navarre Corp.

Albhy Galuten, Vice president, interactive programming, Universal/MCA Entertainment Group

Marc Geiger, Chairman and CEO of ARTISTdirect and the Ultimate Band List

Mark Ghuneim, Vice president of Online and emerging technologies, Columbia Records/Sony Music

Robin Goodridge, Drums, Bush

Steve Gray, Vice president, Om Records

David Greene, President, Creative Spark

Bruce Hartley, Senior director of new media, Mercury Records

Liz Heller, Senior vice president of new media, Capitol Records

Jimmy Hotz, Vice president and chief technical officer, Hotz Corporation

Tony Kanal, Bass, No Doubt

TCR King III, Thanks for your passion, inspiration, and motivation throughout this project

Michael Leventhal, Multimedia attorney based in Santa Monica, California

Fay Schreibman McGrew, Marketing consultant, Second Line Search

Tom McGrew, President of GR8ideas and a really cool guy

John Mefford, Manager, multimedia marketing, Elektra Entertainment Group

Alex Melnyk, President, StoryWorks Interactive

Ted Mico, Special projects producer, Virgin Records

Dana DePuy Morgan, AMP program consultant, Apple Computer

Galia Linn Noy, Designer and developer, Hot Angels Multimedia

Oded Noy, Musican and system manager, Hot Angels Multimedia

Samantha Rawson, Operations coordinator, House of Blues New Media

Kelli Richards, Entertainment market consultant

Alex Rigopluos, President and CEO, Harmonix Music Systems, Inc.

Larry Rosen, Chairman and CEO, N2K Inc.

Leo Rossi, Vice president, Highway One Media Entertainment

Todd Rundgren (TR-i), Musician, multimedia artist and CEO of Waking Dreams

Jon Samsel, Editor and guiding light

Andy Secher, Editor, Hit Parader magazine, president of Titanium Records, and a dear friend

Cynthia Sexton, Vice president, multimedia, Virgin Records America

Sue Simone, Vice president, Myriad Entertainment

Nikke Slight, Online media, Atlantic Records

Christopher Smith, President, Om Records

David Stebbings, Senior vice president, technology, Recording Industry Association of America (RIAA)

Todd Steinman, Director of online and new media, Warner Bros. Records

Wim Stocks, Vice president and general manager of music, Digital Ent.

David Traub, New media visionary

Mark Waldrep, President, AIX Entertainment

Tony Winders, President, InterActive Agency

Part One: Enhanced CD Production

Part Three: Business Development

introduction by
todd rundgren

None of us remember a time before recorded music. We take for granted that we can have a listening experience at any socially tolerable instant and be assured of hearing the exact same performance as the last time. It's hard to imagine an ancient history when people could only enjoy (or otherwise) a musical presentation when musicians actually decided to get together and play. Or that each performance was a variation of the previous, almost never capturing the exact same essence as another rendition regardless of how the ensemble might strive. We just assume that music was meant to be recorded and any sound produced previous to that was simply evolutionary noodling.

This, of course, is not so. People still go to live performances expecting the unexpected, though they are usually drawn there by the previous experience of a recording. And just because a performance goes unrecorded does not mean that it is any less musical (conversely, there is no assumed musicality in simply being recorded).

But it must be granted that the gravity of recorded music and the industry that surrounds it distorts and eclipses the attitudes of listeners and performers alike. Though it is marketed the same as cars or lettuce or toothpaste, for most of us it means more than these elective commodities. It is a wonder drug, an inspiration, an unreplaceable necessity. It is a message from soul to soul. And it is an item on a shelf in a store in the mall. It comes in four-to-sixty-minute chunks that are priced uniformly regardless of quality. It got there through some chicken-and-egg process of interlocking commercial interests involved neither in making nor listening to it.

But all that is about change.

What if a giant metaphoric meteor took out the entire middle of the music distribution chain? What if there was nothing between an artist's lips and a listener's ear? Imagine, massive duplicating plants rusting away, printing presses and plastic molding machinery lying idle, trucks sold off for parts, and UPS and FedEx reporting record losses as "heavy sound" no longer moves along the highways and flyways. Record stores looking like demilitarized zones, radio program directors and independent promotion men holding hands as they leap from upper story windows, and MTV devoting an increasingly major part of its day to home shopping for leftover swag.

This ain't no party/disco/foolin' around. This scenario is possible right now and probable in the future. Right now I could put up a server in or close to my home, record to it, and devise my own method and economic model for distributing that recording. Moreover, I can revitalize that recorded performance with new ideas and update it nearly instantly to my listeners.

Wait, there's more! I can enhance the musical performance with a visual component to broaden the bandwidth of my message. I could even anticipate or incorporate input from the listeners and viewers so that I could better connect with them. I could even collaborate with other players and listeners in real-time and drag music back into the dark ages whence each performance was vital and unique.

Yes, this is the dreaded "Interactive Music" you've heard so many ghost stories about. Not simply a new disc format or a new commercial paradigm, it is a call to reevaluate the entire history of recorded sound, and especially the present. Music has always been a technology, one so subtle and complex that it thwarts the abilities of our most nimble thinking machines. But this problem (music) and this solution ("intera"connectivity) were made for each other and we are the beneficiaries.

As a listener I can look forward to hearing more of the music I like. And as an artist I can deliver music that, if it isn't live, is at least as fresh as milk and devoid of the prohibitions that physical duplication assumes. After all, since the advent of the CD it's all been bits anyway.

Between now and then I can compete better within the current distribution model by taking advantage of enhanced CD standards adopted by the industry. After all, everyone may someday have a computer (even if it's hidden inside the TV) but everyone has a CD player now.

As you can see, my range of options as an artist/entrepreneur have never been greater. I can stick with the old model or go for the new. I can help the industry make the transition to a relationship with the creators and consumers of music that emphasizes the experience instead of the marketing and distribution. Or I could smother the old order in its sleep and go directly to my audience, essentially become my own music industry. My choice.

I'm smiling.

—TR-i

> the artist formerly known as Todd Rundgren
> CEO, Waking Dreams
> *www.wakingdreams.com*

CD-ROM and Enhanced CDs are just a platform to provide a variety of information to people. Video, music, text, words; it's really a combination of approaches that can be melded into one presentation. On the surface, this new technology is not terribly different from television or video. What makes it interesting on the computer is that different angles can be designed to be explored by the user in whatever order they choose. Pieces of the presentation can be manipulated, which makes it different from passively watching a presentation that's already prepared. The ingredients are all laid out for you to ultimately get to the end of the recipe, but you can find your own path in a variety of ways at any given time.

What's great about this new technology is the ability to focus in on specific areas of interest. You can zoom in very quickly to an area of interest, as opposed to waiting for tape heads to rewind and fast forward. It's instant-active.

You can search and instantly get to where you need to go. Our *Promised Land* CD-ROM started as a documentation of the recording of *The Promised Land* album. We were talking about creating a documentary in a variety of formats. Enhanced CD and CD-ROM were potential platforms. That spurred discussion as to the other possibilities that exist with the CD-ROM platform—the combination of animation and video and all sorts of things together with a documentary.

From a musical standpoint, creating an interactive product was an opportunity for us to show people a different side of Queensryche. We write music, we record albums, we do live presentations. Now we're also able to provide people with insight into how we created this last album. The great thing about this insight is that it's interactive. The user can actually participate in a CD-ROM, and we felt that made it different.

What excited us most was the idea that people might be able to each have a different experience with this platform, while ultimately achieving the same end result. We thought some of our fans out there would find this approach interesting.

We were convinced of the viability of *The Promised Land* CD-ROM once we actually got talking to David Traub and some of the guys at MediaX that were going to be involved in designing this project. We saw some tremendous talent and felt that the combination of us working together would yield something unique: *Myst* goes to a concert.

The band had a lot of involvement in the project. We provided the foundation for the CD-ROM. We had chosen to record *The Promised Land* album at a log cabin up on an island, and that provided the backdrop. We got to talking about each one of us having our own little world that you could disappear into, and we contributed the details. Then we brainstormed together on the overall connection of the whole project; we created the framework of the documentary.

We were very involved in the preliminary stages and in the design stages, then we turned the artists loose with our input. We were involved right up until they started technically putting all the pieces together, at that point we stepped out of it.

We must also give tremendous credit to the artists who were involved. There were quite a few people who spent a lot of time and a lot of hours designing these images. We'd just dream them up, and then they made them a reality.

Our musical contribution was a lot of the incidental soundtrack and sounds for all kinds of special effects. It was fun.

CD-ROMs and Enhanced CDs are an amazing way to store and use information. There is a tremendous use for them. The data storage and compression capabilities are getting better and better, and pretty soon, you're going to be able to have an intense variety of information right at your fingertips. It can be the craziest things, music-related like our project, or a cookbook for that matter. When I was growing up the world was out there to discover. If you wanted to learn about it, you had the library, and really, that was it. Now you can sit there at your computer terminal at home and access anything. What's great about new technology is that it can give you instantaneous access to anything you want to find; just type in the word and go. It integrates really nicely into this idea of having the world at people's fingertips. It's the beginning of something really amazing. If I wasn't doing music and I didn't love it so much, I'd probably start a company doing new technology because I could think of a million things that you could do with Enhanced CDs and CD-ROMs.

The current delivery systems really allow the technology to shine. Ultimately, you know, the best creativity is still going to happen from people's real experiences, hands-on, in life. Technology just allows us all these tremendous new avenues to deliver those experiences to other people, and for them to actually witness, and experience other people's offerings.

—Chris DeGarmo
Queensryche

editor's note

Interactive music is perhaps the leading buzzword in the established music industry today. Everyone's in on the hype: record producers, recording artists, business managers, entertainment executives, Web designers, and multimedia developers alike. As a result, lots of money and resources are being devoted to this facinating new segment of the creative industry.

The *Interactive Music Handbook* was designed as a one-stop reference manual for new music enthusiasts worldwide. We've peppered the book with thought-provoking (and sometimes provocative) interviews, opinions, and case studies taken from professionals on the front lines of the interactive music scene.

As we gathered and analyzed the raw data for this book, we discovered that there were three specific areas of interest to explore and ultimately, deconstruct, when referring to the current interactive music scene.

The first subject area we tackle is Enhanced CD Production. Enhanced CD has been having a hard time finding its legs in the retail market. Confusing development standards, irregular packaging, and the lack of music industry marketing focus has perhaps softened the enthusiasm for this new medium. But complaints aside, Enhanced CD is an exciting product. It is the only product of the interactive music industry that can be quantified (in actual sales) as its own market. Record companies and publishers are devoting enormous resources to growing the Enhanced CD market beyond the traditional avenues of retail distribution. Enhanced CD, whatever your opinion of an individual title, improves upon traditional album liner notes.

The second area we explore is Internet Music. We specifically focus on the marketing issues, distribution models, and game plans for successful Web site broadcasting. Every professional we interviewed for this book held widely divergent opinions about the Internet's impact on music and the business models that will ultimately prevail. The good news is that as of this writing, they're all right.

The final topic we cover in this book is Business Development. Although many artists dislike reading contracts or securing content rights for a project, contracts and rights acquisition are perhaps the most important (and most overlooked) aspects of the music business.

After reading this book, we'd like to hear what you think about this business of interactive music. Take a few moments to visit our Web site at *www.allworth.com* and drop us a note. We'd like to hear from you!

part one

enhanced cd production

chapter 1

enhanced cd:
standards, tracks,
and digital facts

After a year of touring, we had loads of live footage shot with Super 8 cameras. We put that content on our Enhanced CDs to help break down a bit of the mystery behind the band. We gave our fans access.

—**Robin Goodridge** of Bush, a multiplatinum British
band that has released several Enhanced CDs

a brief history of music cds

As videos became an essential part of releasing an album in the eighties, Enhanced CDs and music-themed CD-ROMs are the hot music commodity of today, and perhaps into the next millennia. CD-ROMs and their cousins, Enhanced CDs, are the *fixed medium* most likely to be used to help musicians deliver their visual ideas to the consumer.

Music CD-ROMs first appeared on the market in 1993. Titles such as Peter Gabriel's *Xplora 1: Peter Gabriel's Secret World* and Todd Rundgren's *No World Order* broke new ground by boldly fusing the relationship between artist and computer. These stand-alone, music-themed multimedia CD-ROM discs were designed to play on computers as well as on traditional audio CD players. At $49.95 per title, not too many consumers purchased these titles solely for audio listening. The multimedia aspects of these discs made them appealing.

Then along came a new hybrid CD which included both audio and ROM data, allowing users to play a music selection, view text, receive audio and graphics information about the piece, genre or group, and get reviews or opinions. These innovative, interactive music titles (known as Enhanced CDs) can provide photographs of the artist, videos of a performance, bilingual translations of the lyrics (as in opera), music scores, computer generated music, games, biographical information, music theory, explanations of a song's symbolism, links to Internet Web sites, and other interpretations. The ability to cross-utilize assets (archived content and new material) is one of the biggest benefits of Enhanced CD technology.

"It's as far as you want to dream. All of that material that appears on the multimedia track is only limited by the developer and what somebody puts into code," notes Mark Waldrep, president of AIX Entertainment and producer of the Rolling Stones' *Stripped* Enhanced CD. "It simply opens up that extra area of the disc to whatever you want to put there."

cd standards

The term "CD-ROM" stands for Compact Disc Read Only Memory. CD-ROM is a massive information storage device that can be reproduced quickly and cheaply. A single CD-ROM can currently store 680 megabytes of data and is the mode of choice for the majority of consumer multimedia titles. Although there is a buzz that CD-ROM will be a transitional media, eventually being engulfed into the great void of the Internet, that sci-fi scenario is still quite a distance into the future. The entertainment industry recently agreed on a standard for the Digital Versatile Disc. The "DVD" is a five-inch disc which will hold something akin to six gigabytes of information. That's ten times the information that can be stored on a regular CD-ROM. Other than storage capacity, interactive media projects on CD-ROM have few limitations.

This content is stored in a uniform format and in a predefined location on all CD discs. It's a fine example of forethought. In the future, when we're playing with our CD-ROMs as often as we're listening to music, this standardization will permit for the introduction of smarter consumer CD players. For example, CD "aware" players will be able to display track information using the full title of each song rather than the track one, track two system that is currently used.

Since the average music album is still under an hour in length and a CD can hold about seventy-four minutes of music, there is typically between 100 and 200 megabytes of empty space on an audio CD which can be devoted to additional media.

What's confusing is the multiple number of competing CD-ROM formats for artists and record labels to choose from, almost all of which are noncompatible. Check out the shelves of your local retail outlet and you will find that there are several unique terms used to describe the various CD standards: Audio CDs, Enhanced CD, CD-I, CD-Plus, CD-Extra, Mac CD-ROM, DOS CD-ROM, Windows CD-ROM, etc. All CDs are the same physical size. Yet the discs vary in two significant ways:

- The way information is stored on the physical disc media

- The nature of the information that can be contained on them

All of the most popular CD technology has been developed by Sony and Philips. Each type of CD has a given set of parameters, or standards. These different types of CD standards are named after colors.

red book

The original disc: the audio CD conforms to the Red Book standard. Anything you play on your stereo is Red Book. The compact disc industry started in 1982 when Sony and Philips created the Compact Disc Digital Audio Standard, commonly known as the Red Book. Audio is the only type of data that can be stored with the technology. The Red Book standard allows for up to seventy-four minutes of stereo music using Pulse Code Modulation (PCM to compress two stereo channels into 640MB of space). Red Book organizes the audio to be stored into disc tracks with a fixed size and duration. Red for stereo.

yellow book

Computer CD-ROMs conform to the Yellow Book standard, also published by Sony and Philips. This standard defines the proper layout of the computer data on a disc. Yellow Book takes the basic Red Book standard and defines two new track types—computer data and compressed audio or picture data. The format also adds better error correction (necessary for computer data) and better random access capabilities.

mixed mode

When a CD has CD-ROM tracks and CD-Audio tracks it's called a "Mixed Mode" disc. To date, data cannot be read while sound is being played, so computer applications must use Mixed Mode in a staged manner. To get around these limitations and to obtain synchronization of multiple tracks, an interleafed style was added in the form of the CD-ROM/XA standard.

CD-ROM/XA (CD-ROM Extended Architecture) was proposed by Philips, Sony and Microsoft in 1988 as an extension to Yellow Book. This specification stretches the Yellow Book standard and adds the most interesting idea from Green Book (CD-I), interleaved audio. Before this time, audio was confined to one track at a time. Interleaved audio allows the sound to be divided and intermixed with other content.

The CD-ROM/XA drive needs special hardware to separate the channels. When it does, it gives the appearance of simultaneous synchronized media. Not only does CD-ROM/XA allow for intermixed sound, but it also provides various levels of fidelity and compression. CD-ROM/XA uses a more efficient technique of audio compression than the Red Book, allowing four to eight times more audio on the same disc.

These hybrid discs became known as Mixed Mode CDs. Mixed Mode CDs placed the ROM data on track one and audio on track two. And that seemed like an acceptable way to arrange the information on a disc at that time. The CD worked in a standard audio CD player (although the user had to manually skip track one) and the technology was designed to work with computer CD-ROM drives. Everything seems to be developing smoothly—until the music studios started screening the technology.

According to AIX president Waldrep, "Without exception, every single record company that I took these discs to, MCA and Geffen Records, A&M and the rest of them said, 'This is unacceptable. Our product is an audio product and should be flawless and completely identical to what people are currently receiving out of their Sam Goody and Tower Records stores. It starts with music on track one.' However, they liked the idea of putting multimedia and music on one disc."

"It was a software issue actually, not the hardware," notes Oded Noy, musician and system manager for the Hot Angels production team. "What happens is they put the data information on the first track and then the audio tracks afterward. When you put these discs in your regular CD player, 95 percent of the machines would automatically go to the audio track and start playing. Sometimes you would hear an incredibly obnoxious *eeekeeekeeeekeeek*, so in order to avoid that, the data track has to be on the last track."

blue book

Enhanced CD, CD-Plus and Multi-Session are all names for the Blue Book standard. In 1993/1994, Sony and Philips were busy propagating the name "CD-Plus," the name they coined to indicate the generic combination of multimedia material with audio CDs. That name quickly faded when Sony/Philips lost a court battle to market their CD-Plus product to music enthusiasts worldwide. It seems that a Canadian CD retailer already owned the Canadian trademark to the CD-Plus name, so Sony/Philips were precluded from selling product under that name. Sony and Philips next adopted the term "CD-Extra," which is the replacement name for CD-Plus. That name has flunked with developers and the general public.

For the record, the Recording Industry Association of America (RIAA) has officially dubbed this new technology "Enhanced CD." This new name for interactive music CDs has gained wide acceptance and is now the preferred term used to describe discs which contain both audio and ROM data.

"Enhanced CD is evolving," states Liz Heller, senior vice president of New Media for Capitol Records. "It's part of a long-term process of artists becoming much more involved with technology, and utilizing the tools of that technology to support their creative vision."

Jackson Browne's *Looking East* Enhanced CD features the evolution of a song. Soundgarden's *Alive In the Superunknown* has an autoplay mode which gives the title the feel of a cool screen saver.

Enhanced CD is a hybrid disc format which merges the audio-only characteristics of Red Book and the visual data of Yellow Book. (You'd think they'd call it Orange Book, but noooo.) With the Blue Book standard, the music is on the first track and the computer data is on the second track. Any user can take that CD and play it on any standard audio CD player, even though it is labeled CD-ROM. The disc will play without any difficulty, and won't have any squeaks because of computer data. It knows to handle both audio and computer data because there are two tracks, which is why Blue Book discs are called "Multi-Session" discs.

The record companies were pleased as punch with this new technology because it meant everything is absolutely identical to the audio Red Book discs. The upside is that you can now play your Enhanced CD on any stereo. The negative aspect is that you can't play it on all CD-ROM drives.

CD-ROM players are fairly unintelligent devices. If you have a single session CD-ROM player, meaning if you bought your drive before September 1994, you most probably can't play an Enhanced CD, because a single session driver isn't capable of reading a second session. Since Blue Book technology places the music on the first track and the computer data on the second track, a single session player—which reads only the first information session stored on a CD-ROM—cannot fully play a Multi-Session disc. If you have a single session CD-ROM driver on your computer, you would need to load new drivers in order to access that outside track, or the data track.

The modern Enhanced CD avoids the data track problem by specifying that all computer data be stored in a second session—one in which conventional audio CD players cannot access. In order for Enhanced CD discs to be properly recognized by a computer, there are prerequisites:

Your system must be equipped with a Multi-Session CD-ROM drive. If you purchased your system after late 1994, you probably have a Multi-Session drive, as well as a sound card.

Your CD-ROM firmware must support CD player discs. Depending on the rigidity of your CD-ROM firmware, your drive may or may not recognize Enhanced CD discs properly. The firmware included

in some drivers is inflexible to the point that they cannot accommodate the different data layout contained on Enhanced CD discs.
In some cases, you may have to upgrade your firmware to allow
your driver to support Enhanced CD.

Another prerequisite for Enhanced CD discs to be recognized by your
computer is:

Your CD-ROM device drivers must recognize Enhanced CD. This
last requirement means that your CD-ROM drive must be capable
of recognizing that a given disc conforms to the Enhanced CD standard. When an Enhanced CD disc is inserted into your CD-ROM
drive, your current device drivers must be able to differentiate between audio and data.

green book

The Green Book CD-ROM standard was introduced by Philips in 1986
and is the basis for a special format called CompactDisc Interactive,
or CD-I. Although CD-I using the Green Book standard is a general
CD-ROM format with the bonus of interleaved audio, all CD-I titles must
play on a CD-I player, because only this piece of equipment can decode the CD-I formatted discs with a special operating system known
as OS/9. A CD-I system consists of a stand alone player connected to
a TV set. Although your computer will eventually become your television and your television will eventually become your computer, this
is not yet the case. Consumers have been slow to embrace the CD-I
technology. The CD-I market is limited by the special CD-I development environment and the relatively small number of CD-I player
manufacturers.

A unique part of the Green Book standard is the specification for
interleaved data. "Interleaved data" means taking various forms of media,
such as pictures, sounds, and movies, and programming them into one
track on a disc. Interleaving is one way to make sure that all data on
the same track is synchronized, a problem that existed with Yellow Book
CD-ROM prior to the integration of the CD-ROM/XA.

orange book

The Orange Book standard is used to define the writeable CD format. Part 1 of the standard covers the new magneto-optical which is completely revisable. Part 2 covers the CD-R (compact disc recordable) for compact disc write-once media (which defines the Multi-Session format that allows for incremental updates to the media). Ordinary CD-ROM drives cannot write to CD-R media and can only play the first session on a Multi-Session disc.

access time

At the moment, there is no standardization of CD-ROM drives. However, there are a specific set of criteria which they require, and life would be easier if this criteria were standardized. Most existing CD-ROM drives operate with relatively slow access times and transfer rates compared to computer hard drives.

The access time is how long it takes to find and return data. The access time of an average CD-ROM is 300 milliseconds, while the access time for a hard drive is about ten to twenty milliseconds.

The transfer rate is the amount of data that is passed in a second. The transfer rate for CD-ROM is about 150 kilobytes per second, rooted in the technology designed to play a steady stream of digital CD music. (The transfer rate needed for noncompressed full-screen, full-motion video is approximately 30MB per second.) Dual speed drives help improve performance by providing up to 300KB per second transfer rates.

dvd

The next generation of CD-ROMs is called DVD, and contains up to 4.7GB of storage on a single layer and on a single side of a disc. The capacity can be increased to more than 17GB by making the discs double sided and double-layered, which means the CD drive now reads through two substrate levels, and thus the CD contains double the information in the same vertical space. The goal is to have a disc standard that will support a group of products for home entertainment to computers and eventually replace CD-ROM, Audio CD, video game, and video tape products of today.

DVD-Video, the first DVD standard to reach consumers, can store entire full-length movies on the space of a regularly-sized disc. Many of the Hollywood studios' top movies are now available on DVD-Video.

DVD-ROM is the next-generation computer disc format, similar to CD-ROMs we have come to know and love. DVD-ROMs hold much more data than current CD-ROM releases, allowing for advancements such as full-screen, full-motion video and high-quality audio.

Future formats are planned to include a specialized DVD-Audio system, DVD-Recordable disc and DVD-RAM disc (re-recordable). Beyond that, double-layered, double-sided discs are waiting on the horizon, which will be able to store twenty-six times the amount of data of a conventional CD-ROM disc—up to 17GB.

"DVD will have a very positive effect on the music industry," notes Sue Simone, vice president of Myriad Entertainment. "DVD is a logical extension of the compact disc format. It will finally allow all of the creative imagery, information, and music to be combined with all of the portability, programmability, and dynamic range quality that was started with the revolutionary CD audio format. No longer will music videos and art be simply viewed as advertising expenditures for the music industry. The consumer will be able to own all of the components that are created for any music title on a single, wonderful compact disc. The true beauty of this digital technology is that you can mix and match formerly incompatible recording formats like photos, music, video, and text together. DVD will be the medium that will allow full-frame video on CD to finally become a reality, and will allow CD-ROM to fully realize its hyped potential."

With so much space available, people are going to want to put more content on the discs. The content won't be music because that just wouldn't be cost efficient. You're just not going to have a disc with five hours of music on it selling for $24.95. This new generation of disc will add new types of content—video, liner notes, photographs, biographies, games, and higher quality audio. It's going to change what the recording scene is like. It's going to change what consumers expect when they go to purchase a title.

Enhanced CDs will find their niche and probably become mainstream, thanks to DVD. Movies will be the first product released on DVD disc, but there will be several versions of DVD, much as there are several versions of CD. DVD audio has the potential to be a tremendous increase in quality over conventional CDs if the authorities can agree to pinnacle standards. Instead of 44.1K audio (which is the sound quality for a CD), there's discussion of a 96 megabyte, 64-bit standard. DVD offers endless options. Suddenly, there will be plenty of space to create whatever the artist wants. Wait and see what happens.

Artists who belong to the interactive generation will create differently, adding interactivity to their works, or creating works that are interactive art. Listeners can have the band's whole story—a year in the life, a rock opera—on one disc. And of course, all DVD players will be backwards compatible, meaning a DVD player will play audio CDs that are currently available on the market, as well as new DVD releases. Imagine the possibilities. Music can be either interactive or passive. You could have a full album of music with just some videos on it that's not interactive at all.

"With DVD, you will undoubtedly have the ability to increase the resolution of the audio playback," offers Mark Waldrep of AIX. "Numbers that are being talked about are twice the sampling rate, and word lengths fill out to 20 and 24 bits wide. Basically it takes away any argument for analog. If there's ever been a death knell for the audiophile hanging onto his turntables, this is it."

Theoretically speaking, a DVD could contain hundreds of tracks. If you really, truly wanted to, you could put the entire Rolling Stones' catalogue on one disc. But that's probably never going to happen. Consumers generally prefer quantity for their money. You're still going to have albums within the seventy-five minute range . . . maybe it'll just come in six different languages. DVD will remove the space limitations, so that creative teams have no quality limitations. You'll be able to do the best high-quality, high-resolution audio, video, and graphics.

"Musician-artist-programmers look forward to being swamped with new interactive music titles to produce as we progress in this digital future," offers Sue Simone.

A potential danger of DVD is that the software industry may need to fill up a disc with as much programming and content as possible. That need to fill up the disc also causes an exponential increase in the cost of production and development, which companies such as Microsoft have found out, cannot be supported by the current installed base of consumer buying titles.

The good thing is DVD will help the Enhanced CD firmly take hold in the marketplace. Enhanced CDs have been looking for a home and have turned out to be a bastard child of the music and software industries. Neither channel knows what to do with this new hybrid format. If the standard moves to DVD, then the record stores may jump on the new standard format.

"Records have been around ever since 78 rpm shellac records," remarks music veteran, Paul Atkinson. "The carrier will change, the carrier will improve all the time. DVD is the next incarnation of the carrier. It will be the medium that's most available to the user and the most capable of carrying that information. DVD is the next one, but there will eventually be something beyond DVD."

the road ahead

Sound confusing? You're not the only one who is baffled by this muddle of technologies. Even bands like Bush, who have released Enhanced CD product are not clear on what's happening.

"It's quite a journey, isn't it really," observes Bush drummer Robin Goodridge. "We decided to do the *Little Things* CD-ROM because no one else had done one. In the future everyone will be doing them, so we wanted to get a grip about what we liked and didn't like about them. When we make the next record, we'll make a better one."

"As far as format standardization, I haven't got a fucking clue," Christopher Smith, president of the interactive label Om Records. "It's been back and forth for so long that we don't really care. We're going to use whatever works."

Mark Waldrep, the man responsible for the interactive part of the Rolling Stones' *Stripped* CD—the first Enhanced CD ever nominated for a Grammy—recalls the early days of Enhanced CD development.

"In 1989, I started doing work for Stan Cornin and the Warner New

Media Group. That's when we first got the idea for putting data on a music disc. It involved using a standard type of disc which puts data into track one, index one, with music starting at track two. We made a whole bunch of these discs using a Hypercard stack."

Mark continues. "There was a black and white designation at the front which would talk about the instrumentation, the composer's life, stuff like that. We created them for *The Magic Flute* and Bach's *Requiem*. That was the beginning. . . . It always stuck in the back of my head, this great idea of combining things. Those early products were primarily intended as computer products—as the data was under the control of the Hypercard playing the audio annotation and the piece on the Red Book track. Several years later, when QuickTime was developed, it dawned on me, as well as several others, that there is unused space on every CD that gets put out in the record business. I master records. We're always throwing away space because a normal commercial release is fifty to sixty minutes, leaving 150–200 megabytes unused. It doesn't cost any more to stamp them all around the edge. So why not put some multimedia on the outside?"

And they did.

Q&A: todd fearn

Todd Fearn has a background in the software business. His partner, Ed Roynesdal, knows the music industry. They formed Rev Entertainment in 1994 to concentrate on interactive music products and teamed up with Atlantic Records . . .

WHEN ENHANCED CDS WERE BEING DEVELOPED, WHY WAS MULTIMEDIA CONTENT PUT ON TRACK ONE?

Todd Fearn: It's speed. When they defined the standard, single spin drives were the popular drive at that time. You had to have quick access. You had quicker access on the inside.

The labels didn't want to put out CDs in those formats. Everybody was fishing around for months looking for new ideas. Philips and Sony started working on it in November 1994. They announced that they were going to come out with a new format that would do away with the whole track one problem. The thing that they came up with was Multi-Session.

Multi-Session was created so that people could use CD writers to burn to a disc more than one time. Before Multi-Session, you had one time to burn and that was it. The head drops, it burns, it lifts, you're done. Okay, that's a session.

What they did is create this Multi-Session concept, which is Orange Book. It offers the opportunity to keep burning more sessions. I could fill the entire disc up with data, or whatever I wanted.

Kodak started using this format for the Photo CD because you could keep burning more and more pictures to the CD. Then Philips said, "Well, why don't we do this? Why don't we put Red Book on the first session, and put Yellow Book (the computer data) on the second session." It's a perfect solution because the audio players don't know anything about Multi-Session; they only know about one session.

So if I take a disc that was burned with Red Book first, Yellow Book second, and put it in my audio player, the audio player only recognizes the first session. When the audio player gets to the lead-out area, it quits.

CAN YOU EXPLAIN TRACK ZERO?

Todd Fearn: Track Zero is another format that people started looking at. It's also based on a Philips and Sony patent. It's called the CD-I ready format—it's a mixed-mode disc.

Let me go back and explain a few things. Take a track. Every track has two indexes—zero and one. Most audio players start looking at index one—that's a definition in the spec. Index zero isn't really used other than for a positioning thing. But the computer can look at index zero.

So what they did was, they packed all the data between index zero and index one. That way the audio player doesn't know it's there, but the computer can read it. That's a hidden track, and that's based on the Philips CD-I ready format that was documented in 1992. You can use it anywhere you want.

IS THERE AS MUCH SPACE ON THE ZERO TRACK? IS THE SPACE PRE-DETERMINED BEFORE YOU LAY DOWN MATERIAL?

Todd Fearn: The space is always predetermined before you lay down the material. You have the same amount of space on the disc no matter what format you use. You can put as much data between zero and one as you could on the back end.

AND WHAT IS THIS TECHNOLOGY CALLED?

Todd Fearn: It's based on a Mixed Mode disc, and it has many names. It's called CD-I ready—that's the official format. It's also known as pre-gap or hidden track.

WHAT FORMAT IS REV CHOOSING TO DEVELOP ITS ENHANCED CDS?

Todd Fearn: We do whatever the labels want us to, and that depends on their licenses. Every label has their own license. Some labels don't have licenses right now for Multi-Session or CD-Plus. That license is from Philips and Sony and the other labels have licensed the right to create Multi-Session discs, same as they license the right to create audio CDs.

IS THERE A LICENSE FOR MIXED MODE?

Todd Fearn: There should be. What happened was with Yellow Book they didn't enforce the licenses so much. Mixed Mode is a Yellow Book offshoot. If it becomes popular, they'll come back and ask for licensing royalties.

THERE ARE SOME COMPANIES SAYING, "WE'RE NOT GOING TO BOTHER PAYING PHILIPS AND SONY TO DO MULTI-SESSION WHEN WE DON'T HAVE TO PAY ANYBODY TO DO THE MIXED MODE."

Todd Fearn: If Mixed Mode becomes popular they will have to pay.

HOW MUCH DOES IT COST TO LICENSE THE TECHNOLOGY?

Todd Fearn: They'll never give out that information, because it changes from vendor to vendor.

WHAT'S THE CHIEF DIFFERENCE BETWEEN ENHANCED CD AND CD-ROM?

Todd Fearn: There's no Red Book on CD-ROM. For Enhanced CD, you've got to be able to play it in your audio player.

chapter 2

enhanced cd:
building blocks

Technology has always affected my art in a very deep way, because I'm fascinated with gadgets and tools. I've often looked at a gadget askance and imagined a new way of using it which its makers never intended.

> —**Thomas Dolby**, recording artist, President and CEO of Headspace

audio specs

When you're creating Enhanced CDs, there are a couple of different ways to talk about audio. First, be aware of the fact that anybody who is making an album is extremely concerned about the process of merging multimedia and Red Book audio tracks into one product.

> *Primary Rule: The Enhanced part of the CD cannot in any way degrade or modify the sound quality of the Red Book audio tracks. You cannot, under any circumstances, modify those tracks.*

Herein lies the problem: on the Enhanced part of your disc, you have to make sure that all your other audio sources are up to a similar level of quality as the Red Book album tracks. The average album is audio mastered at 44.1 kilohertz with 16-bit resolution—meaning that the sound is being sampled 44,100 times a second with 65,536 possible levels. Though not the best possible quality, this does give you a fairly crisp sound with reasonable dynamic range. Anything less than this—say 22 kHz—and the quality can suffer immensely. Since the sample rate is half, it is much harder to achieve an acceptable sound quality using a medium that could potentially sound like a bad cassette.

"That's where you get into the voodoo of creative, artistic reality," notes audio expert Jimmy Hotz, vice president and chief technical officer for the Hotz Corporation. "Those who have the skills to deliver consistent quality can make a great deal of money as engineers and producers while many others may hardly make anything."

Of course, technology is evolving faster than you can say "badmotorfinger." There are ways to get 44.1 kHz sound out of Yellow Book technology. IMA audio is what they call it; it's the Interactive Multimedia Association sound format. The technology creates Yellow Book audio that sounds pretty close to Red Book, but uses a smaller data rate—one that's a quarter the size, so it saves space in a big way.

"IMA does a 4:1 compression, and I have my choice of doing it 16 bit/44 kHz, or 16 bit/22 kHz, or 8 bit/22 kHz or 8 bit/11 kHz," observes Ken Caillat of Highway One Media Entertainment, "with 16-bit being the highest quality."

sound quality

Most of your audio, particularly the stuff that's really rich and on video, you will have to create according to Yellow Book standards. Hope and pray that the majority of the sound you get has been equalized. If the bass and treble haven't been adjusted to the particular needs of what you're doing, you're just going to have to do the best you can. When you're planning your Enhanced project, just think about the sound. Ask for the DAT tape. Find out if they had the two tracks running during your session. Does the band have their demos? Maybe you want to mike any interviews and sessions you do from the same position so that the sound quality levels match.

access

You can program audio to play Red Book on your Enhanced CD, but Red Book audio will not work simultaneously while you're doing something cumbersome with Yellow Book data. If you combine Red and Yellow book, the head of your CD-ROM drive will be reading material from all over the CD, and it will get very confused. Inevitably you'll end up with way too much dead space during "scene changes."

"It's really hard to sync up video to Red Book, because one's going through a processor, and one's doing a play-through on a head," notes Highway One's Leo Rossi. "Anytime you're going to access anything Red Book in an interactive portion, your interactive data has to be on the hard drive. It can't run off the CD. If your CD is spinning, playing Red Book, and you're trying to access data, the computer's telling the CD to stop and go and find the data in Yellow Book, and that interrupts the Red Book."

If you have a computer with an external CD-ROM drive, you will have to have jumpers hooked up in order to play Red Book audio along with your Yellow Book data. Those jumpers must feed the Red Book packet into the Yellow Book section or there won't be any audio.

"I try to access Red Book audio as seldom as possible," advises Ken Caillat. "It presents all kinds of problems with the CD head having to get instructions from the Yellow Book section to play something off the Red Book. It makes the CD skip. I would only use Red Book when we had a complete album's worth of music and every inch of space was precious. We had to do that with Jackson Browne; rather than duplicating anything in Yellow Book, I just went and did it in Red Book."

audio options

An alternative to using Red Book is taking your sound loops and loading them onto your internal hard drive. Compare your hard drive to your ROM drive. Consider things like how many seconds it takes to load audio off of a double speed CD-ROM drive.

Let's say you want to have a healthy audio loop playing on your screen. If you've got a 900K loop, that takes three, maybe four seconds to load from your CD-ROM. Do you want the user to sit there for four seconds, or do you want to preload the audio onto your hard drive? If you've got a CD-ROM player and you've got an internal hard drive, most of the time the CD-ROM is working away, and the internal drive is not doing anything. If you're so inspired, you can move some sound files over to the internal hard drive, and it can be playing sounds while the CD-ROM is doing other things, leading to a more cohesive musical experience. If you choose this method, the question you must keep in mind is, "How much can you put on somebody's hard drive?"

go yellow

If space is not a consideration, the most consistent way to handle audio is to duplicate all of the necessary audio that's on the Red Book tracks. Usually that means a WAV file, or an AIF file, or a QuickTime audio-only movie at 22K sampling rate and a 16-bit word length. Going Yellow Book is obviously a compromise in terms of audio quality, but you don't buy a Stone Temple Pilots or Hootie and the Blowfish CD to listen to it on your computer over the whir of your hard drive. (Not to mention the fans blowing inside your machine.) You didn't buy an Enhanced CD to sit in your office chair and experience it through underpowered, tinny speakers. You bought the CD to listen to it through quality speakers in a quality listening environment.

The Yellow Book audio is sufficient for the short-term engagement that you're going to get from enjoying interactive liner notes and related goodies. Interacting with video or the Internet is a thing you do at your computer. Quality listening will be done off your stereo.

authoring audio

If you are using one of the standard audio environments that comes with the authoring software, you'll find that the program typically works as well with audio as it does with visuals. Authoring environments integrate all data types into a single mix, so Apple Media Tool, Director, mTropolis and the like should suit much of your audio needs—until you attempt to do stereo sound. Then you will find that there are going to be problems with mixing multiple track audio.

"When we made our Enhanced CD, not a lot of sound was done in the regular audio channel of Director," reveals Oded Noy. "This is because I usually have to load too much to the memory and I run over my 8MB limit for my end user. Most of the control I did from Lingo."

Director has seven levels of audio—you can stretch it and get a little bit more variation, but you may find that it's still not enough for an audio mix that meets your desires.

Then again, the sound off of your authoring program just might be good enough. Most sound programs have rudimentary mixers where you can mix microphone, line, and CD. You'd be amazed at how good some things play just off the sound card, if you're not really nitpicking. The user is playing the Yellow Book audio off of computer speakers as opposed to audio speakers, but it may just not be enough to suit your tastes.

audio note: ken caillat

Ken Caillat is a partner in Highway One Entertainment, one of the leading Enhanced CD and Internet design firms. Highway One has worked closely with groups such as No Doubt, Bush, Bonnie Raitt, and Jackson Browne. Prior to forming Highway One, Ken produced record albums for multi-platinum bands like Fleetwood Mac.

Ken Caillat: It's really important to have proper meters. Computers are not set to professionally record anything, not video, not audio; not if you're used to dealing with professional recorders. On a professional recorder for audio you've got a nice set of big meters; you know where your peak points are and where your distortion points are.

On a computer there are no meters. For a second, a little meter panel will come up, but it doesn't tell you all the information you need, so we use an external meter—like they use in the music industry.

In the recording business, they'll have a professional recorder sitting in the back room. They'll calibrate the meters on the mixing board to the meters in the back room—so they'll know that the board's meters are telling the exact truth to the recorder in the back room. We do the same thing when we record for Yellow Book.

To record music for an Enhanced CD, we use a program called Sound Effects. I like it because it has the best set of meters on it.

Once I'm in sync, I can shut the meter in the back room down because I now know my distortion point. The meters on the program are what I go by once they've been set. They sit right in front of me, and I've got knobs to control the volume.

Most computer users don't listen on hi-fi speakers. People will listen on little computer speakers or built-in speakers, which have less high frequency, less mid-range, less bottom end, less everything. So, after we record, we will use an equalizer to balance bass and treble so that it sounds the best on most people's computer systems. Then we'll put a little compressor on it. What we feed to the computer is perfect audio—perfectly compressed dynamically so it's not going to sit there.

When we're recording for an Enhanced product, we'll make sure all the audio comes in consistently at the maximum level, without distortion. You must take care not to change the intent of what the musician wanted to do when they made the music. At the same time you're acting like a mastering engineer, which is the final process of making a record. The mastering engineer adjusts all the volumes so that all the high frequencies are the same on all the songs. We'll go do the same thing, particularly paying attention to the playback medium of the end user's small computer speakers.

audio compression

When you compress audio, it adds a certain linearity to the words so they all come out at a good, consistent level. Beyond that, it can actually enhance how someone's voice sounds, make it sound richer and larger. Of course, audio compression is not a perfect medium. Every time you compress a sound, it brings up the noise flow around it. In the case of a spoken word, where you have a lot of ambient sound going on around the voice, you probably want to gate that off.

"For mixing in the digital domain, I use four of the Yamaha O2R professional consoles chained together for a total of 160 inputs with full four-band parametric equalization and dynamics on all of those inputs processed and mixed in the digital domain with 32-bit resolution," offers Jimmy Hotz. "The resolution at which you mix digital sounds together can make a great deal of difference! If you take something that was recorded with 16-bit resolution and send it through a

16-bit digital mixer, when you turn its level down to anything short of full volume, it will lose a certain amount of the clarity. This is because the detail of the sound that is finely distributed within all possible levels that change over time, based on the sample rate, must be represented by a smaller and smaller amount of numbers (less resolution as the level is turned down)."

Hotz continues, "On the other side of the spectrum, any level that is turned up to the point of clipping or distortion in the digital domain sounds very nasty because the waveforms actually square off more radically than they would on a more forgiving analog mixer. You cannot have too much headroom when it comes to digital mixing. Even if all your digital sources are 16-bit, when mixing several digital sources together it is necessary to have a much higher bit resolution (24-, or better yet 32-bit) in order to maintain a similar level of quality in the output."

As long as you've recorded properly, it doesn't much matter what the sample rate is; it can be 44/1 or 48/1, as long as it's pretty much maxed out and you didn't mix it down, there's no reason to be so concerned about how many other bits of processing were in the chain.

Every sound file goes through the process of leveling. You figure out what your output objectives are and work towards it. You have to figure out what kind of mix you want. Everybody in the music industry knows that the AM radio mix is a different mix than the video mix. A mix that's going to be compressed into a 22 kHz mono file needs a slightly different mix with slightly different post production. All of your audio should be mixed and reduced to sound good in that format.

"I really like the SAW digital editing software. For the price range of what it is, I recommend it," suggests Oded. "Except for synching, which goes in and out once in a while, I've been working it really big time and I'm happy with it."

balancing act

Here's the typical sound scenario and how you deal with it in Yellow Book audio format. Undoubtedly, you've got several different audio sources—interviews, some live audio, some songs, narration, and some ambient audio that goes along with the guys in the band making goofy videos. All the sounds are recorded with different mikes under different circumstances. Some is TV quality audio, other is audio that no one really cared about because it went along with the video they were shooting at the time. Wonder how do you get the balance to work properly? Mixing two 16-bit sound sections together can be a problem. You may have already maxed out here and there, so you'll have a tough time mixing those two things together because you'll peak out consistently and distort somewhere. Turn it down. In order to mix those things together and keep the articulation similar to what it was, you have to have a processor with a higher bit rate than the one where the sound was recorded.

"Make sure that all the audio is up on the editing station," instructs audio professional Mark Waldrep. "Take the QuickTime audio tracks, the interview audio, the music that's produced that will go on the Yellow tracks, and make sure that each one is dynamically optimized and bit-reduced or sample-rate converted at the highest possible standard. You need to run it through a fairly rigorous procedure, which at the other end results in individual, numbered, named sound files. The key is that they're consistent."

It's one thing to be looking at a product and understand that the guy was in a voice-over room with a microphone six inches from his mouth while he did the narration. But click twice and all of a sudden the voice is connected to a body in a QuickTime movie, and the microphone is three feet away because the character is now a visual with a frame around him. The sound quality jumps. Pay careful attention to those kinds of details when you're creating your product. Maybe when you're recording the voice-over, you want to set the microphone back a little bit to get more sound consistency.

sound quality

An Enhanced CD is an audio product, bought by an audio consumer, who is then going to listen to the audio on his stereo system. When he wants to enjoy the interactive liner notes, he'll put it on the computer, and the audio won't take precedence.

Perhaps you're hanging out with your computer, using your CD-ROM drive as a regular music player. Let's say you're listening to Primus' album, *Tales From the Punchbowl*, and since the tune "Southbound Pachyderm" is so cool, you decide that you want to find out more about the band, so you pull up some data. The great question lies before us—is the difference in sound between Yellow Book and Red Book that noticeable?

"Some of it is, other times you won't be able to tell," notes Leo Rossi. "It's an issue because bands don't want to sound like shit. They spend so much money making it sound right, why go backwards? If it was produced in stereo, it has to come back in stereo. I can't say, 'Here's your new song . . . and guess what . . . it's mono.' It's only 11 kHz and it sounds like it's coming out of a transistor radio at the beach. The band is not going to want to settle for anything less than perfection."

clean sound

Something you're going to encounter on PCs running Windows (You can hear all the developers out there going "Boo! . . . hissssss. . . .") is that Windows can't run two audio channels at the same time, whereas Macintosh can. (Loud cheering.) On Windows, if you have one audio file running, and you're not careful so it overlaps slightly with another audio file, the second audio will not come in. Think about this in environments which launch movies and songs. If you put an ambient sound loop in an environment while waiting for the user to press a button or watch an interview, be sure the ambient stops before anything else happens or you'll get zero audio. The downside to this is that the loop ends abruptly, which is not subtle at all.

In more established forms of media, like movies, you'll have one thing fade out as another one fades in. To date, most of the authoring tools don't do that extremely well, so you've got the *krcccch* boom as the driver head drops down and cuts off and the other one comes up. Avoid this aggravating noise as much as possible. Get your timing down.

get it right the first time

You've got to get your sound right the first time, otherwise it might come back to haunt you. Here's the nightmare scenario about how cutting corners can totally destroy a project.

Let's say you're working on a CD-5 (an Enhanced CD with five audio tracks—could be called an Enhanced EP). You're working with a young band who are totally excited about the project. Instead of doing stereo, you decide to save yourself the space and do 22kHz mono. Everybody in the production house thinks it sounds great, so it passes and no one ever thinks about it again.

Then the band members see the disc, and think "Oh, this is pretty cool," and they take the Enhanced disc to show their producer, tour manager, office, and everyone else in their circle. The producer checks out the Enhanced CD, and asks, "That's great, but why is it mono?" Then the band goes back to the developer and demands that the audio on the Enhanced CD be like it was created—in stereo.

Moving along on your production schedule, you've locked the disc up and you're ready to go to mastering. But the band members go to management and whine, "I don't care if they're finished, it needs to be right." The manager, seeking to make as much peace out of the chaos as possible, tells you that it has to be changed.

The developer has to hold up the presses and misses the release date.

All of the advertising and marketing around a record is based around one date to release. If you miss the date, all the marketing and promotion comes out, the consumer goes to the store, and the product is not there. You get cursed and you lose the sale, all because a developer chose 11 kHz mono.

That's why, if you're working with a band, get them involved. Keep them involved. Give them copies of the product as it's being developed. Tell them to play it for everybody and get as much feedback as you can. You'll get the weirdest requests back. Band member girlfriends and their brothers—people that the band draws their energy from—will ask enlightening questions like, "Why is the color not like the real video?"

experience helps

You can't learn everything on your first disc. You have to go through these scenarios to understand the things that could happen and head them off at the pass. This is where the experience serves as a big benefit.

the $64,000 question

If you're creating an Enhanced CD, and you're doing all of your audio tracks in Yellow Book, you may have two copies of a song on your Enhanced CD. It brings up legal issues such as who will pay for the separate copyright on the mechanical royalties associated with two copies of the same tune on one record. Suddenly instead of six-and-a-half cents per tune, it's now twice that in the eyes of the lawyers.

"If it's for private use, it would fall under statutory rates if it was audio only," observes Vincent Castellucci, administrator of licensing for The Harry Fox Agency, Inc. "If it's audio visual, everything in the contract is negotiable between the producer and copyright holder, including the territory, the term, and the use."

ambient sound

MIDI is good for sound effects, but if you think you're going to create a sound canvas for another group's Enhanced CD, ask first. Many musicians would consider the contribution of music from an outside source rather offensive. If there is a need for background material, or filler music, ask the band about it. You may end up getting some exclusive music for the Yellow Book—an added bonus that will keep your viewers coming back to absorb and admire the product. The audio is the glue that links a project together.

Generally speaking, it's better to have sound than silence. Sure, it can be the band's music, but if they give you the go ahead, have a party. Fill dead space with ambient sound, simple loops in either mono or stereo.

"I like to have stereo loops because it gives you that wider feel of sound, it gives you a bigger experience. So automatically, I'm giving myself trouble because I'm going to have double the audio size than if I had used mono," observes Caillat. "Using stereo means you've got to shorten your loops. The shorter the loop, the more easily you can identify it and it becomes repetitious. You've really got to pick good loops that work well and you can't tell that it's a two second loop. Or you can play your loop off the hard drive."

sound in sync

When it's all said and done—when you get your video compressed, your audio compressed, your movement through the folders, your executables all in, and you start the cross platform Beta testing process—you get to add in your ambient sound. It's almost like scoring a picture. You sit back and watch the Enhanced disc beginning. There's probably an opening logo followed by a sequence, maybe a fly-in of some sort. You have to synchronize music to all that with some kind of unifying sound effect that goes under that. Your sound will link it all together like in a movie.

All of the effects have to happen so that you're caught and drawn into the product. The sound is the hook; it gives you the whole picture of what's going on on this disc. Designing that sound is one of the most fun parts of the audio process.

Q&A: david traub

David Traub is one of the premiere music CD-ROM producers in the business. He has created products for artists as diverse as Queensryche and B.B. King. Traub's personal goal is producing mass media entertainment that teaches "human potential and helping people realize their brilliance and their dreams."

HOW DID YOU APPROACH THE AUDIO ASPECT OF THE QUEENSRYCHE
***THE PROMISED LAND* CD-ROM?**

David Traub: We gave the band a walk-around of the world, and they came up with a series of vibes. That's what we call them—ambient vibes. Then it would be the job of our audio company, C.S. Audio/Visual, to take those files—those vibes—edit them and thin them out, mix them together, mesh them, modify them, embellish them so they could be spread out across a world in such a way that there was variation within a world. You don't think you are listening to a loop all the time. Size requirements make you use a lot of loops and that gets very old, that was one challenge.

A second challenge was taking bits and pieces of their albums and integrating it in a seamless fashion into the vibes. We were always building this soundscape that was mildly narcotic, in the sense that people would grow used to this music and want to hear more and feel like, "Let's go out and buy the album again." We also got an added bonus. Queensryche actually created a song for the game as a payoff. It's a fantastic tune called "Two Miles High." They also scored the opening animation.

HOW DID YOU WEAVE THE BAND'S MUSICAL INPUT INTO THE REST OF THE AUDIO SOUNDSCAPE?

David Traub: Well, an authoring environment is as facile typically with audio as it is with visual. Authoring environments integrate all data types into a single mix. There were still problems with mixing . . . having multiple track audio, particularly on the Windows side. So we have an ambient vibe, and have an incidental sound effect on top of that. There were also problems with transitioning from one vibe to another one. The sound would stop. That problem hasn't been overcome yet, at least within the context of the authoring environment, which is a real bummer for us. But, you know, it's still in the early stages in terms of tools.

the objective

Now that you know the technical definition of an Enhanced CD and know a bit more about the technical aspects of sound, it's time to learn how to organize your content in a way that makes it easier to create one. Other than storage capacity and a few platform limitations, you can create anything that is technically and artistically feasible. Experiment and figure out what works best on the most platforms—that way you will reach the widest possible audience.

"You should always begin with what people already have created and make it better," states David Traub.

Your objective is simple. Create a magic space within the boundaries of the technology. This concept may best explain why the title *Myst* is currently the biggest selling CD-ROM game of all time. The creators, Robyn and Rand Miller, used existing technology and pushed it to its limit—building a product that was truly unique.

Creating an Enhanced CD is difficult enough to begin with. Don't make yourself crazy by trying to take the technology beyond where it's ready to go. Why push the envelope and make it work only on the Pentium? The technology totally determines what you can and cannot do. Sure, it's pretty harsh compared to what you imagine, but deal with it. Make sure it looks good.

"CD-ROM is really still a feeble reflection of what we already do anyway," observes Traub. "The video . . . you know, five frames a second, ten frames a second, it's very disturbing to people when they're used to regular video. But, technologies will only get better and better and better. The key is not to be technology-centric. You have to really focus on what it's going to take to engage an audience for their suspension of disbelief and their entertainment."

When you're working on an Enhanced CD, you know what works and what doesn't work. There are things that kind of work, there are things that really work and there are things that don't work. Concentrate on the elements that really work, they will tell you exactly what you need to do next.

Understanding the technology doesn't necessarily mean you're at one with it. You may have to do things you don't want to do. You may need to reduce the videos because they were too big or working with only 8-bit color. You may need to pin down more sprites before executing a certain movement because otherwise it will cost too much in the way of performance. When you create, you're constantly making movement and size tradeoffs. It's a grand balancing act.

"As a musician, I've learned that it's not about the technique of my playing, it's about this soundscape that you create when you play. Either it's magical or its not," offers Oded. "It doesn't have to be technical, and neither does the computer. It either creates the magic or it doesn't. If it breaks up, it won't create the magic for you no matter how nice it looks."

technical considerations

Technical considerations for creating Enhanced CDs and music CD-ROMs include:

- Authoring tools

- Delivery platforms

- Content: the amount, organization, and placement

- Playback capabilities

- Compression schemes

How do all of these considerations affect the multimedia producer? It forces the creative team to make design decisions before execution—which is why a project is typically storyboarded in advance of production. Getting your vision onto a CD is similar to creating a giant puzzle. Good puzzle builders have inquiring minds and calculate for variables such as:

- How much space will the music soundtrack take up?

- How much video footage can I incorporate into the project?

- If I use x amount of video footage, how much animation can I use?

- How much and where will other forms of audio be used in the project?

- What combination of text, illustrations, graphics, animation, audio, and video can be utilized to create the most compelling project?

- Does the project need to incorporate a customized search engine?

- How will the production team's choice of authoring engine and compression software impact creative decisions?

- How will my choice of genre, interface design, gameplay, and structure impact the programming aspects of the project?

- Can everything we want to do be done at a profit?

tools

Developers are using a plethora of application programs and authoring tools to create Enhanced CDs and music CD-ROMs. Some are choosing complex programming environments such C++, while others are choosing authoring tools such as Macromedia Director or Microsoft's Visual Basic. Another popular tool is the Apple Media Tool (an authoring tool no longer supported by Apple), which provides an environment both to author and program.

"Many developers use Director. Director's a pretty good tool, but it can be kind of clunky at times." observes Leo Rossi, corporate liaison for Highway One—the development company responsible for Enhanced titles like Jackson Browne's *Looking East*, and Bonnie Raitt's *Burning Down the House.*

"The reason so many people use Director is because it was the first mainstream tool kit," continues Rossi. "People learned to use it and they cataloged their Lingo library. Nobody wants to take the time to relearn. Some kid might come up and say, 'I'm using mTropolis and it's great,' and we say, 'come in and do it for us.' And we learn from them. You get to a point where you don't want to be in development anymore. I want to develop it, I want to make it look right, and I want you to code it and make it work. That's your job, do it and make sure it does."

The easy-to-use authoring tools basically do the hardcore programming for you. This drag-and-drop, object-oriented programming was designed for developers in need of a powerful construction kit to aid in their creation of a title. In other words, authoring tools are designed for the nonprogrammer. With most popular authoring tools, developers lose some flexibility in what they can design. However, the power of an authoring tool can be expanded via custom programming, whereby a programmer is hired to modify the authoring tool to perform a customized need of the developer.

When David Traub was producing the Queensryche CD-ROM called *The Promised Land* (one of the most expansive and best received music products to date), Apple Computer asked his team to work with their Media Tool program.

"We met with Apple and EMI (Queensryche's record company) and, on the condition that they would solve several problems for us, we agreed to author in AMT. It was more of a programming environment with authoring capacity.

"Apple Media Tool has a variety of components," offers Traub. "It has an authoring environment which allows for the production of relatively simple multimedia: slide shows and very simple CD-ROMs. But to do anything with any real complexity, and also to complete the product for shipping and cross-platform, you do have to understand programming to a degree. And the more complex the product you're creating, the more you have to know how to program. We are now experts in Apple Media Tool. Our expertise in that authoring system is certainly a proprietary advantage since there are relatively few people that understand it."

Apple Media Tool has been the authoring environment for several of the major music CD-ROM projects. Graphix Zone created both the Bob Dylan and Prince titles using Apple Media Tool. The band Squeeze also used Apple Media Tool for creating their *Some Fantastic Place* Enhanced CD.

"We are happy to be working with Apple and its music tools, especially because we've been using Macintosh computers for years," states Chris Difford, co-founder of Squeeze. "We find the Macintosh to be the most intuitive for creating our interactive music projects, and look forward to seeing further developments from Apple."

Macromedia Director is also a popular authoring environment, particularly among those developers that don't have major money behind them. Music products such as Yoko Ono's *Rising Mixes*, Zion Train's *Double Homegrown Fantasy* and No Doubt's *Just A Girl* were all made using Director.

Q&A: oded and galia noy

Oded Noy is a systems manager. Galia Noy has a background in architecture, and is an expert in 3-D rendering. Together they are two-thirds of the Hot Angels production team. Like many megabyte men, Oded is also a musician. He is the keyboardist in the group Onion. Currently, Onion is shopping for a record deal using an Enhanced CD Hot Angels created. The great benefit to this situation is that all content rights are in-house and the only limitations of the creative process were the team's imaginations.

WHAT'S YOUR BACKGROUND IN COMPUTERS?

Oded Noy: I've been with computers always. When I was a kid I had two visions of myself as an old man; I used to see myself sitting in front of a keyboard and playing, telling machines exactly what I want them to do. There is an art involved in taking a machine that can't think for itself and making it do something it wouldn't do. One of the elements I like about programming is doing things that nobody did before. I do my research, I look at other products. My basic operating premise is that whatever artistic idea comes up can be achieved in whatever technology. The magic of the idea is an overriding factor.

Galia Noy: I came here from Israel for the first time twelve years ago, and I got this feeling from America that everything is possible, you just have to be in touch with it. I returned to live in the states seven years ago and decided to get into computers. My background is in interior design. I've discovered that animation programs are very satisfying, because you can design it and see it right there as you're building it.

HOW LONG DID IT TAKE HOT ANGELS TO CREATE THE ENHANCED PART OF THE ONION DEMO?

Oded Noy: As a demo, it took us a month-and-a-half.

WHAT PROGRAM DID YOU USE TO MAKE YOUR ENHANCED CD?

Oded Noy: This is done in Macromedia Director.

WHY DID YOU CHOOSE DIRECTOR?

Oded Noy: It was the fastest road to get the best results in the time that we had. People are of two minds about Director: There are those who use a lot of Lingo and therefore like the software, and those that don't use Lingo at all and do not like the software. That's really the difference. In order to work Macromedia well, you need to get your hands in there and program it.

WAS DIRECTOR YOUR FIRST CHOICE, OR DID YOU GO THROUGH A PROCESS OF ELIMINATION?

*Oded Noy***:** I went through a process of elimination. There's only one way of creating an Enhanced CD. Your final product has to be done on a Mac. There's no way around that. But, in truth, I was considering either Director or C++ Write Everything. I'm happy with my decision.

WHAT MADE YOU CHOOSE DIRECTOR OVER C++?

Oded Noy: I didn't have time to develop that much code. Let's say that I wanted to make a wheel. In real life I know exactly what the characteristics are, I know how it behaves, I know what it should do, and then

I can just take one and roll it. Unfortunately in the computer world, it means I have to redescribe to the computer every element of that wheel; how that wheel behaves, what it does, what it does when it's on a flat surface and so on . . . describe all those different characteristics. It's like reinventing the wheel.

Ultimately C++ will give you a lot more control, but in our case there was no reason to do this. As a programmer, Director gave me enough. I can control a lot of different elements by controlling Director. So instead of needing to write all that code, I just wrote it in Lingo.

WHEN YOU'RE WORKING IN DIRECTOR, WHAT APPLICATION PROGRAMS WILL YOU USE?

Galia Noy: 3D Studio, Photoshop . . . I chose them because I'm used to them, and of all the programs I've seen out there, those are the best modeling programs. They give you a lot of freedom.

HOW DOES DIRECTOR INTEGRATE WITH DIFFERENT FORMS OF HARDWARE?

Oded Noy: It's not a fair question. There are so many different computer configurations . . . hardware requirements. If you have a double speed CD-ROM, that doesn't mean you're going to have the same transfer rate as another computer with a different interface for that CD-ROM. It doesn't. How big is your video card? How does your video card work on palette? How did you install your Windows system? All those issues affect playback.

WHAT WERE THE MAJOR OBSTACLES YOU HAD IN DEVELOPING YOUR ENHANCED CD?

Oded Noy: Trial and error and acceptance. That's what was hardest. Accepting the limitations of the common denominator: You have to work it in this way, but it looks much better some other way. I have a Pentium 120, a development machine, I can run a real time 24-bit AVI on half the screen and it will still look good. But obviously there's no way that a double speed CD-ROM will do anything like that. That's the limitation. The difficulty is to make sure that even the slowest machine will flow in your tempo rate.

alpha stage

The job is always easier when you have the right tools to work with. When you're developing Enhanced product, you should have access to both Mac and PC computers. Burn hybrid discs and test frequently so you can really see how what you're making works on the standard operating system.

Anyone who has created a multimedia project gives similar advice. Start testing early . . . all through Alpha stage. If there's a game element, how many different scenarios does the game have? If you develop down the x path, and it's supposed to branch off to y, z, a, b, does it? If it's an enhanced audio piece, if you push that button does it play? Have you optimized the placement of the content? Is the data streaming as efficiently as possible? Once you've found the problems, debug them . . . if you can. The most frustrating part of developing a CD-ROM disc is making it work properly. Do not underestimate the time it will take to properly test your product.

Q&A: christopher smith

Christopher Smith is the president of Om Records, an independent record label that has released several Enhanced CDs. Among the albums on Om's roster are a hip-hop jazz compilation called Groove Active. *Spiritual High* is a cosmopolitan ambient techno mélange.

WHAT ARE YOUR DEVELOPMENT TOOLS, AND WHY HAVE YOU CHOSEN THEM?

Christopher Smith: We've got a hammer. Screwdriver . . . wrench. A couple of wrenches, in fact. We develop primarily on the Mac. We use Director; we use all the Adobe tools. We use an Avid studio for all our video. We use Photoshop everyday. Everyone uses Photoshop and Illustrator. We'll do layouts in QuarkXpress and use Adobe Screen Ready to blenderize them into pics.

WHAT PLATFORMS DO YOU PRODUCE FOR?

Christopher Smith: Mac and PC. We do most of the development on the Mac, we have, actually, a Windows NT network in the office, which all the Macs are hooked up to, as well as all our Windows business machines, so we can import it back and forth between Mac and Windows very quickly and do testing on the platforms. It's sexy. Very sexy.

HOW DO YOU GET YOUR SOUND?

Christopher Smith: We have a music studio with a twenty-four-channel mixing board. We used it to design sound equipment with a sound designer and Studio Vision Pro, along with all kinds of other sound tools.

WHAT TECHNICAL HURDLES DO YOU COME ACROSS ON A REGULAR BASIS?

Christopher Smith: The actual programming, to get the functionality and make the thing work right. And, it's the limitations of the tools. I'd say the most limiting tool that we have is Director itself. And, unfortunately, it's probably the best tool out there. You have to work within the confines of what Director can accomplish. You could go out and just code the whole thing, but that would create a whole new set of problems for you. With Photoshop there are really no limitations at all.

timing

One of the major challenges faced when creating an Enhanced CD is timing. You have to be sure that the visuals and audio are in sync.

"If I play music from the CD, I constantly ask the CD, 'Where are you? Where are you?' And when it gets to what I want, I continue," notes Oded.

Undoubtedly, your Enhanced CD will work perfectly on the platform you've created it on, you'll sit there and watch it off of your hard drive and be completely thrilled. Then you'll burn your disc and play it, and you'll immediately notice the difference in access times. The access time for a hard drive is about 10–20 milliseconds, while the access time of an average CD-ROM is 300 milliseconds.

You also need to optimize your placement of information on the disc. You'll find that there are little problems because you told the head to play a video which is located in a certain spot. Meanwhile you programmed the disc to make a *chic-chic* sound when you click the mouse. There's a pause when you click on the video, because the head is going to get the *chic-chic* sound over on another part of the disc. Proper optimizing during the creative process is probably the last little thing you learn about making Enhanced CDs.

According to Ken Caillat of Highway One, "When you get good, you probably know what to do a little bit ahead of time. There are times when I've had a disc done and said, 'This is going to be perfect,' and then the CD hiccups. The head lifted up for a second because you had some rollover that was placed someplace else on the disc, and you didn't think that the head of the CD-ROM had to go travel to some other place."

Timing is everything because the first-time CD-ROM user should be able to have instant gratification, instant sensory candy. If the ROM driver takes too long to pull up what you programmed, you're going to lose the viewer.

last 15 percent

Completing a title without outside help is an extraordinary feat. Inevitably, the last 15 percent of a title is the hardest part, solely because of technology. Creativity has been put to bed, done. Your objective now is optimizing the disc to make all of the elements work most efficiently within the space allowed. You need to test it to see:

- Which videos work, which videos don't work?

- Do all the buttons work?

- Does the project fall within RAM parameters?

- What kind of color palettes are you drawing on?

- Will it work on a 486/66?

Alpha and Beta testing can be the most difficult part of creating any project. A strong Beta candidate is a product that works on all the platforms it's specified to work on; Mac, Windows, CD-I, whatever. You know it's at Beta stage when you can give it to your sales and marketing people and have them say, "This is a new product that's coming out."

configuration testing

After you have completed all of your test phases, and before you create your master, you should take your disc in for configuration testing. There are several places that can perform this function for you—places which are well-versed at testing programs against commonly used systems sold in the market; the Soundblaster boards, the Orchid Technology video cards, the Stealth cards. This way you find out exactly what's not working and how well the program performs in various "real world" situations. The report may come back and say the 486/66 with the Stealth card has a problem. Pentium 75 is great. NEC video architecture doesn't run with QuickTime for Windows.

When your bug report is returned, you have to decide what elements merit repair and what elements will not be fixed. Not all bugs send developers back to the drawing table. In fact, most programs that are released into the market have some type of bug. Your bugs should not impair the program on a very high percentage of systems on the market. Otherwise, you're asking for trouble.

the riaa

To help give some clarity to this burgeoning industry, the Recording Industry Association of America (RIAA) has issued some specifications for how they would like us to create an Enhanced CD. Any developer who produces a disc that conforms to these specifications and signs the RIAA "Enhanced CD" Certification Marks License Agreement can utilize the Enhanced CD mark on their product packaging. This seal of approval helps add to a product's credibility. The RIAA is also issuing certification to disc manufacturers. In a perfect world, all RIAA approved discs will be able to play on any RIAA approved drive.

The RIAA has issued a document called the "RIAA Enhanced CD Voluntary Specification" in an effort to create some guidelines within the industry (the document can be found in the Appendix of this book).

The Enhanced CD certification mark has been reprinted by permission from the Recording Industry Association of America (RIAA).

chapter 3

enhanced cd:
the blueprint

Music can measure how broad our horizons are. My mind wants to see infinity.

—Stevie Wonder

conceptualization

Now that your brain is awash with technical music issues, you will need to switch gears in order to develop the concept for your very own interactive music project. But before you begin to design anything, you must first develop a sense of your project's scope and content. To do so, you will have to flesh-out all of the creative elements that may become part of your finished title. Don't hold back. Now is your time to dream the big dreams—before you have to work within a budget or specific time constraints.

Start with a game of mental ring toss. Pitch ideas. Be objective. Study the merits of the good ideas and the not so good ones. Weigh each possibility. Before you know it, you'll tap into the motherload of creativity, discovering solutions for how to proceed with your project.

"Our creative process usually involves two or three people," notes Highway One's Ken Caillat. "When we first started, we would have eight or ten people and they would divvy up certain sections. We found, out of necessity, when we had many projects and were breaking them down into two man projects, that you could keep it more concise. You don't need more people unless there's a lot of research and a lot of animation going on. After we have the idea, we'll bring in the rest of the team. We'll have one person that will digitize the video. We have a graphic artist that will create the graphics. We have an outside pro-grammer that comes in and puts it all together based on the storyboard that we've done."

Keep in mind that the record label—you know, those people pay-ing your bills—will want some involvement. After producing Queensryche's *The Promised Land* CD-ROM, David Traub and his team launched into a multimedia project on Blues legend B.B. King.

"We began the project by brainstorming; myself and the producer at MediaX worked very closely with Alex Melnyk and Michael Shaun Conaway at MCA," claims Traub. "It was very much a partnership."

One of Highway One's early projects, *Virtual Graceland*, a virtual tour of Elvis Presley's Memphis mansion came about because of some environmental rendering software that Apple Computer had developed. Highway One saw a demo on the technology and thought, "Wow, wouldn't it be really cool to virtually walk around Graceland." They took the basic technology and added the cinematography and the ex-pertise of Hollywood to make the project really shine. In the case of *Virtual Graceland*, technology drove creativity, but the creativity was there to enhance the technology.

"We're in the business of selling emotions. We're not in the hard-ware business, not in the technical business," notes Kip Konwiser, presi-dent, KO Entertainment. "We don't care if the delivery system is on a potato chip—if that's the delivery system the audience has . . . and there is an opportunity to expand the emotional availability between them-selves and the artists . . . then it works for us. We pick our titles based on whether or not they strike us as emotionally veritable, useful, wor-thy, and applicable to this format. Do they belong on an interactive format, and do they ring emotionally true and fat enough to make enough juice out of the real estate that we are starting to occupy on a CD-ROM?"

recording your ideas

Here's your list of office supplies you might want to have handy to record the pearls of enlightenment which will spill forth during your brainstorming session:

yellow pad	tape recorder	white board
pencils	video camera	laptop

Be aware of the inherent problem of videotape; once you've taped everything, you've got to spend time weeding through the raw footage to find the ideas you liked. This process can take up a lot of extra time. Audio tape can be professionally transcribed for a reasonable charge. This may be a preferable option. White board and yellow pads are easy to use. Problem is, neither method produces electronic versions of your ideas. A laptop works great—especially if it's connected to a large monitor for group viewing. Last but not least—our friend the magic eight ball. It won't help you generate new ideas but it sure is a fun way to break the tension when all those "type A" personalities start locking horns.

During conceptualization, don't lose sight of your end goal. Your project should be fun and compelling. But you should also make sure your content is easy to access, clear, and accurate. Be sure it's the user and not the machine that controls all the actions.

If all goes as planned, your brainstorming/conceptualization session should produce answers to the following:

- Name of the project

- The project's objective

- The premise or goal of your project

- Your target audience

- Your limitations (budget, time, skill set)

- Existing projects you like and why

- Your competition and why your project is unique

- A rough timetable for each phase of production

organization

There are several traditional ways in which you can organize the content on your Enhanced product. Information can be cataloged by:

- Band members

- Songs

- Alphabetical order

- Chronological order

- Location

- Category

That doesn't mean you can't access information by using icons like dancing bears . . . just make sure the user understands what's going on.

"We have two kids here that are constantly involved with the development of the product," notes Hot Angels' Oded Noy. "I knew our Enhanced CD demo was ready when I said 'Go ahead,' to a five-year-old and I didn't have to tell him anything. He played on it and he wanted to play again a couple of days later."

Effective applications are consistent within themselves and consistent with one another. If a five-year-old can figure it out, you're definitely on the right track.

Secondary ways of accessing information for an Enhanced CD include links and indexes. Obviously you want to access information by subject, and you want to know about links to related areas. You might want to think about using an interactive linking software such as StoryVision to design where the links of your Enhanced CD will be placed.

band involvement

Most music artists today are hip to what's going on in new technology. They don't necessarily know the extent of what can be done, but they have an idea. Sometimes they'll come at you and say they saw some of the early technology. They'll comment, "I saw this disc and it wasn't that good."

As a content developer, it's up to you to come right back at them. Tell them about the latest technology. Inform and impress them and you'll find that most musicians will be very happy to learn about new ways to express their "art." A lot of times they'll say, "This is great!"

An Enhanced CD is a band's extended expression. It's another way for them to really explain what they mean. Bush had tremendous input into their *Little Things* and *Glycerine* Enhanced CDs.

"They were the best," notes Ken Caillat. "They were an up and coming band, they really didn't have time to worry about this, they wanted to get their music on the road. We handed them a camera and a box full of empty tapes and said, 'Send us stuff.' That was their creative input. There they are in some bookstore in the Midwest and one guy's shooting the other guy while they're clowning around. We were able to take that creative fun, cut the most interesting parts, and put it in the disc."

The Enhanced portion of an audio CD can be as much fun for the band as it is for the rest of the creative team. Tax their memories, make them remember the whys and wherefores—the details of making an album. They're more than willing to share it with their true fans, the ones that are dedicated enough to buy their albums.

As Enhanced CDs become more popular, the bands are seeing this as a projection of themselves. Some groups are making a real effort to create content, and work closely with the producer. Highway One filmed Duran Duran doing a live acoustic show on the beach in front of their offices. "Who knows if the CD will ever come out, but we have it logged, it's here," laughs Leo Rossi.

Older, more established musicians like Todd Rundgren and Yes are going, "Wow! I wish I had this twenty years ago." With all the new media staring them in the face, the younger musicians like Sarah McLaughlin, Primus, or Dogstar are used to creating extra content.

"We tell bands now, don't throw anything away," notes Rossi. "When we did Bush, the *Little Things* Enhanced CD, we said, 'Bring cameras on the road, bring footage back—8mm movie . . . any stuff that's interesting to you.' We gave the band the tools to extend their vibe."

If at all possible, it should be the band's "look and feel." They created the music. It's their vision, their vibe. They probably have a good idea of what they like and don't like. An Enhanced CD is an extension of them. To make the end product as compelling as possible, the artist that wrote the music should really be involved in it from the get-go.

If you can't get a band to be involved (which is often the case) do the next best thing. You can pick out a look and feel graphic from the album art. You can do a reference type title if there's existing footage. Put great graphics around it. Use a snazzy interface to it and try to make it as compelling and exciting as possible.

"Always connect the graphics—the look and feel, the style—with the artist for that particular project," suggests Mark Waldrep. "While the Rolling Stones' Enhanced is very much a graphic creation of ours, all those pictures came from Anton Corbin and the cover art came from Virgin Records. So what if I zoom in on Keith Richards' feet and lay some other images over the top of it? You still recognize this clearly as the Rolling Stones' *Stripped* record."

"As soon as the band gets creative control over the project, it obviously multiplies many times in difficulty," notes Steve Gray, vice president of Om Records. "It really does. They might think it's great, but what about this typeface? Can we put this typeface? Everyone has some comment with creativity. It's always great to have people in the creative process, but it can make your time frame much longer."

"One thing I run into is the question, 'How involved in the Cranberries disc were the Cranberries?' They were as involved as they wanted to be," asserts Ted Cohen, vice president of interactive music for Philips Interactive Media. "It's like saying, put some paint on the wall and I'll tell you if I like the color or not. Well, what color do you want? I don't know, just put a color up there and I'll tell you if I don't like it. That's a lot of what happened on the Cranberries project. We kept showing the band things, everybody involved was throwing ideas at them. People say that the Cranberries disc isn't hi-tech. It's not supposed to be hi-tech. It's supposed to feel like the Cranberries. The Cranberries aren't big metal buttons and wire mesh grids. It's overstuffed couches, they never get off the couch, that's the joke. Wherever they go, the couch takes them."

"Band involvement has been minimal because the groups that we've been working with don't know what we're making," suggests Mark Waldrep. "They're busy touring, they're not computer-type people. And inevitably, having the band involved slows down the process and costs more money. I certainly would not preclude somebody from wanting to look over my shoulder. I have been paid compliments from the Rolling Stones on down. The *Voodoo Lounge* disc that we did has a lot of animation, a lot of sound effects, and it creates a dark, alien kind of world. Stephen Ship of Mausoleum Records saw the disc and he called me and said, 'You know, every single time I deal with somebody, there's always something. . . . I can honestly tell you that I opened this thing up, viewed it, and I wouldn't change a thing.' So, people come to trust our design sense, our graphics."

"Jackson Browne was very involved in his disc," reflects music marketing specialist, Tom McGrew. "Bonnie Raitt signed off on everything. Bush did the same thing. In the case of the Beastie Boys, they made a CD-ROM on their own. It depends on the development group, what the development group is doing, and whose doing it. If the development group really understands the music industry, then they're going to work closely with the artist and get the artist all jazzed up."

Having the band involved in the creative process will definitely add time and possibly add headaches to your endeavor, but undoubtedly the outcome will far better represent the artist than if you're just shoving a bunch of content into the interface.

An Enhanced CD is a band's extended expression. It's another way for them to really explain what they mean. And a band doesn't always have to be there in the studio looking over your shoulder changing the typeface. Bush had huge input into their *Little Things* and *Glycerine* Enhanced CDs. Their involvement was done in such a way that it only aided the production process.

As Enhanced CDs become more popular, the bands are seeing this as a projection of themselves. Some groups are making a real effort to create content, and work closely with the producer.

Q&A: ken caillat and leo rossi

Ken Caillat and Leo Rossi comment on the collaborative process behind the making of Jackson Browne: Looking East.

HOW DID YOU GET THE JACKSON BROWNE ENHANCED CD PROJECT? DID YOU SUBMIT A DEMO OR A STORYBOARD?

Ken Caillat: With Jackson, we submitted a storyboard and we were able to say, "Here's some of the other stuff that we did." We showed him some other work we had done, and his imagination just went wild. His manager, the record company, they were all going, "Yeah, you can do this . . . you can do that . . . you can do this . . ." and they sold it themselves.

HOW WAS IT WORKING WITH JACKSON BROWNE ON THE *LOOKING EAST* ENHANCED CD PROJECT?

Leo Rossi: It was a pleasure working with Jackson Browne. He really got into it. He wanted every little thing changed. It was aggravating, but that's why the product's so good, it's his involvement, it's him. We felt the average hacker or computer company that would have gotten involved with Jackson Browne would have quit. There were guys here working twenty-four hours a day, day and night.

Ken Caillat: Jackson Browne was very critical of himself, and he wanted to scrutinize every piece of footage that we were going to use to make sure he was saying the right thing, giving off the right kind of vibe. We digitized 800 megabytes of information, and we had to cut down stuff that had already been computerized, so we had to get him on the computer. We ended up having three or four guys cutting different pieces down and he'd wander from machine to machine. It made us realize that we needed to get him out of our computer room. We needed to get him into an edit suite, where we could get him in and service him properly in a short amount of time.

HOW LONG DID IT TAKE TO PUT THE JACKSON BROWNE PROJECT TOGETHER?

Leo Rossi: We can say it took six weeks to put it together, but that's six weeks in time. In hours it probably took eighteen weeks because everybody worked really hard on it.

WHAT INNOVATIVE IDEAS DID YOU COME UP WITH?

Leo Rossi: We came up with a section showing how he writes a song, and portraying that in an interactive format. The first time you heard a song, you track it all the way through. Then you give samples of what it sounds like during development. From what it first sounded like to when it's done is such a difference. Jackson happened to have all the assets for that. So here was the sound check in February 1994, and it sounded like this, and the rehearsal date in '95, and this is when they rehearsed it for the record. Then you go to the tracking date and you hear what it sounded like when they were just finishing it. Then you hear the mix, the polished version. You've got the band talking about their parts and why they played this part, and why they played these parts. That's why the product is so good, because it's him—it's Jackson Browne—it's not Highway One.

Q&A: david traub

The Queensryche Promised Land *CD-ROM is one of the most acclaimed music CD-ROM projects to date. Two years in the making, it's a game as well as an expression of the band. It's appeal is both to gamers and fans.*

HOW DID YOU GET INVOLVED WITH THE QUEENSRYCHE *THE PROMISED LAND* CD-ROM?

David Traub: EMI has a band called Queensryche that was really bustling to do something in multimedia. So I flew up to meet with the band, along with Matt Macorin, CEO of MediaX, which is the production company that was the principal partner on the project. We brought up *Myst* and we brought up the Residents and we brought up Peter Gabriel's *Xplora 1* and a few critical music discs that showed them where the state-of-the-art was. We wanted something that was very psychologically derived, as nobody had done that yet.

We wanted something that was very dynamic—that was living and breathing and undulating and had a lot of beauty. We wanted something that was socially responsible. We came up with a concept on the spot that was very new and had never been done before. I describe it as *Myst* meets the movies *Being There* and *It's a Hard Days Night.*

HOW CLOSELY DID THE BAND WORK WITH YOU ON THE DEVELOP-MENT OF THIS PROJECT?

David Traub: Queensryche worked particularly close with us, as compared to, for example, Dylan—who was probably not involved at all—or Prince who was minimally involved and didn't show himself. Queensryche was involved in a key way throughout the process. They had some approvals, they'd brainstorm with us. We would periodically send them the materials and they would approve the look and feel, and they would have ideas. It was very much a new model—there was a partnership with the production company as a creative entity and the band as a creative entity. It was very much a new media synergy where we worked closely together.

storyboarding

Most Enhanced projects start off with a storyboard—a plan or outline of a program set forth in sketches or other images, and viewed in sequence to demonstrate flow, camera angles, props, etc. For the Jackson Browne disc, Highway One had to show Elektra Records a storyboard.

"Jackson loved it," observes Highway One's Ken Caillat. "He said it was brilliant, and we got half the money."

Even if you're not submitting your storyboard, it serves as your design outline, and is a very necessary part of the Enhanced CD production process.

"You do a storyboard and then start designing the environment, and you decide what kind of animation you'd use in designing it," notes Hot Angels' Galia Noy. "Basically, you work according to the storyboard: you're working off the storyboard for your entire project."

Not that your storyboard is a stagnant item. It bends, folds, and mutates throughout the creative process as your ideas evolve.

"It's not that it changes constantly. What changes is the actualization of the idea," elaborates Galia. "When you developed the storyboard that's when you develop the concept. Then you start designing, you render it once and you say, 'You know, the movement is not quite right, the lightening is not quite right, the colors are not quite right.' You bring it into 8-bit color and say, 'How do we render this?' It's constantly evolving."

As Highway One's *Virtual Graceland* was being brought to life, the team realized that trivial objects in Graceland contained stories unique into themselves. A trinket sitting on the counter with a good story behind it became a hot spot. Click on it and the rich story behind it unfolds.

"When you define the user experience, you define the interface design," declares Rossi.

submitting ideas

Record companies often ask developers to produce a working demo of their idea in addition to a written proposal. But demos are a double-edged sword. What you consider to be a rough demo might appear to be a finished product to the artist or record executive. Often times, artists can't see past this roughshod demo that you've created. If you give somebody a demo and they don't like it, there's a good chance you will lose the gig.

"For Bonnie Raitt, they asked us to put a demo together," states Caillat. "They showed it to Bonnie, and she said, 'Wow, I didn't want you to use that video, I look terrible there. Why did you use this?'"

It's not always that way. Highway One also did an Enhanced demo for Ravi Shankar. "We didn't know anything about Indian culture," continues Ken. "We didn't know if blues are good hues or if they're sacreligious. To make a demo for Ravi, you have to really go out on a limb. It took some work to do, but it turns out they loved it. But they didn't give me a choice, I sort of had to do it."

An alternative to creating a demo is showing them something else you've done, something totally different, a different artist, a different whatever. That way the record company can say, "Wow! That really looks great!" Also show them a storyboard. If they liked the story and they liked the idea, they can be Steven Spielberg in their own head. They'll picture the project, and think about a certain kind of graphics and these specific images, and that this will be great. The record company will do all the work for you, they'll make the sale.

"Usually it's a verbal description of what we want to do, sometimes there's a storyboard of what's going to be done," notes Caillat. "The best thing to do, because the record companies will ask you to do everything for nothing, is give them a basic proposal and a basic price, they'll like that. If they want more, we'll say you have to pay us something now. We break it down. If you pay us $50,000, we want $5,000 up front. We want another $5,000 on approval of the storyboard, and then we want another $15,000 on the capture of video and first Alpha. This breaks payment down into sections."

Make sure your storyboard looks good. If you submit a rough storyboard without getting your graphic artist to put together a proper presentation, you may scare the record company because it doesn't look professional enough. They want to see something that resembles the final product, even if it's just a demo.

Remember: the record business is a business. It's your job as a developer to transform your wacky, creative ideas into solid business propositions.

Kip Konwiser of KO Entertainment had this to say about his days working as an interactive writer/producer for Mickey Hart, legendary drummer for The Grateful Dead. "A lot of his (Mickey's) ideas were pretty out there. My role was to take all of that and put it into a bite-sized, consumable format that people could actually purchase; in other words, take the art and make it a business."

Great ideas are one thing. Making them fit into a budget is another. Once you've dreamed up your great, elaborate idea, you have to budget it out and ask yourself if you can do it for what you're getting paid.

As you get further along in this business, after the euphoria of actually creating product and getting it out there wears off, budgets become a significantly greater part of calculating projects.

"The way I'm starting to look at it is, say, you want to do something? Okay, what's your recoup on it? Ten thousand units? If it's 10,000 units and this is our wholesale price, then X is what we have to spend on production, and Y is what we have to spend on marketing," states Leo Rossi. "Then you have to find the right developer who thinks he can do it on that budget. If you can't find the right developer, then don't do it. If somebody comes up with a great idea for the price, then do it. Storyboard it out and try it. Then it's my job to make sure we stay on budget."

proposals

Now that you've got your idea thought out, the thing to do is put the proposal down on paper. This is not only for the record people and the band (like they'll actually bother to read it), but it will also clearly outline the objectives for your team. It clarifies deadlines, budgets, and goals. Plus, the document should serve as a clear-cut blueprint for the project. Your Enhanced CD or music CD-ROM proposal should cover topics such as:

concept	project budget
project time line	payment schedule
project summary	the project team
design	format
content	market
system requirements	packaging
advertising/promotion	resources
legal issues	production tools

CONCEPT

The concept briefly summarizes the project and objective of the program. Sometimes referred to as a "summary" or "premise," this is perhaps the most important element since it is commonly used to generate reader interest.

DESIGN

This is where you explain the look and feel of your product. You'll need to describe your interface and the environments you will use, your key icons, if there are game elements involved, what the product will actually look like. You should describe how you see the user interacting with the program. Is it a written set of instructions, QuickTime icons, graphic buttons? This is a good place to introduce a screen shot, photo, or sketch of what the graphical interface might look like.

FORMAT

Are you making an Enhanced CD, CD-ROM adventure game, Internet Web site? You need to clarify the format you're creating in and why this format is best suited for the project.

CONTENT

Where is the content coming from? What are the costs involved? Does new material need to be shot? Is there a secret source for archival material? This is the area where you specify the details of the media that goes on the disc.

THE MARKET

Who are you creating for? Why is this project necessary? This is the area where you talk about the potential audience for the item you wish to create. To demonstrate how confident you are that your idea will be a runaway commercial success, this is where you put your money where your mouth is. In short, you will explain why this project will sell, who will be buying it, how much money it could make, and why.

SYSTEM REQUIREMENTS

Here's where you wow the byte boys with your knowledge of the technological "feel" of your project. Is it a hybrid product? Are there any special technical considerations for this creation? Let your client know the technical specifications of what they'll be getting.

PACKAGING

Is your product going to be packaged in a jewelbox and sold in the audio section? Are you creating a CD-ROM which will be in a box that's sold with software products? Is there something in the packaging that will make it unique and more desirable?

ADVERTISING/PROMOTION

Gotta get the word out there. This is where you elaborate on how you're going to tell people about the product you're creating.

RESOURCES

Do you already have movie footage or music? Do you have the rights cleared on all your photos? In your resources section, you let your client know what assets are already available to them, especially if they're potential cost-cutting measures.

LEGAL ISSUES

Is there a possibility of defaming former band members because of a nasty quote? Are they suing their old manager? Are there potential rights problems, or should this be a breeze for the clearing house to handle? Projects become very expensive very fast when you have to bring in the $200-an-hour guys. Let your clients know what they're getting into.

PRODUCTION TOOLS

Photoshop? Adobe Acrobat? Macromedia Director? QuarkXPress? What programs will you use to create this product?

BUDGET

$$$$$$!! How much is it going to cost? And how is that money to be divided up among the members of the production team.

PRODUCTION TIMETABLE

The record company is going to want this disc yesterday. How long will it take you to create this project?

PAYMENT SCHEDULE

When do you expect to get paid? Will all the money be paid on the completion of the project, or will it be a process of pay as you go?

PROJECT SUMMARY

Drive home your sale. Tell them why they need this CD product and why you're the team to do it.

PROJECT TEAM

Here's where you include resumes or brief biographies of the principle players who will execute or add value to your project. Tell them who is involved in the project and what attributes they bring to the creation. It's a great place to promote your team and your company.

team think

Your production team will vary with the size of your project. If you're doing a massive CD-ROM project, like Queensryche's *The Promised Land*, it can be dozens of people. If you're doing a small, low budget project, it can be a single individual. Depending on the breadth and depth of your project, you may have layers and layers of team members. It's like everything else in this business, it all depends. "The way Highway One is structured is that I really drive the technology and keep us aligned with new technology," explains Rossi. "Ken Caillat's the real creative one, he comes up with great creative ideas by listening to the content. Then on the business end, there's Jim Martone, who does a lot of rights acquisitions and contracts and stuff that I don't want to know about anymore.

"All totaled, there are five of us, and everybody else is contracted out. There's no need to have people on staff unless you're doing fifty projects, and I don't think anybody's going to gear up to do that right now."

Assembling a project team is an important step in preparing your music project. There are a number of combinations of people you can put together. Here are the key players.

PROJECT MANAGER

A highly organized individual with good management skills is ideal for this role. A project manager has the responsibility of taking care of business. He coordinates the budget, schedules, and resources. He also deals with the clients. He supervises the project and makes sure all the elements come together as planned. He's not necessarily techy, but he understands all of the elements that go into making an Enhanced CD or CD-ROM. He acts as the project troubleshooter, and main motivator.

CREATIVE DIRECTOR

The creative director has the responsibility of making sure the disc looks marvelous. She may oversee several other players on the project, including designers, editors, artists, the band, animators, and programmers. The creative director has to coordinate input from all contributors and be sure the theme and design of the project stays consistent. An ideal creative director brings all of the aesthetic aspects into a unified whole without stifling the creative processes.

CONTENT COORDINATOR

Your content coordinator is the person who collects and manages all your assets. It will be his responsibility to procure the text, video, audio, and fast food wrappers needed for your project. He's also the person who should confirm that each piece of content has rights free and cleared for usage. Doesn't matter how great your look and feel is, if your content coordinator doesn't come through, you don't have the material to put in the project.

GRAPHIC DESIGNER

The graphic designer creates the layout and visual design of the electronic product. She lays out the screens, designs icons and symbols, chooses type faces and color schemes, and concocts the overall visual appeal of the project.

AUDIO DESIGNER

You're creating a product that compliments an audio CD, so be sure the sound is good. The audio person's key purpose is to make sure there is a continuous soundscape flowing through the project linking all of the separate audio segments into a unified whole.

INTERFACE DESIGNER

It doesn't matter how good your content is unless it's effective and easy to access via a clear, usable, and attractive interface. If it's not easily accessible, no one is going to bother with it. The interface designer is skilled in both visual presentation and electronic programming. He engineers the way you access the information. This includes menus, submenus, and links. It is up to the interface designer to organize the presentation of the information in such a way that meets the goals of the project. Keep in mind that the best interface designs are transparent to the user.

PROGRAMMER

Your programmer builds the engine that makes your CD-ROM product run. She takes the analog concept and puts it all together in digital format; getting her hands dirty in Director or Visual Basic. It is the programmer who has to sweat over access times and video/audio sync. This is also the dude who is responsible for making sure that the project runs on all designated platforms.

LEGAL COUNSEL

Someone has to draw up contracts and clear all the content rights. It may be a clearing house, lawyer, or paralegal, but this person is key to the finished project. Your content coordinator brings in all kinds of cool media to use on a project, your legal person is the one that gets permission to use the material.

team mentality

You don't necessarily need one person for each of these aspects of development. These are just the responsibilities that need to be delegated. When Hot Angels did their *Onion* Enhanced CD, their band director came up with the look and feel. They had two designers to render all the 2-D and 3-D animation work and a programmer. This was their core team, but everybody worked on it.

"When we work on the design, we go back and forth. It's a group project, totally," explains Hot Angels' Galia Noy.

"The drummer went crazy when it came to sound effects," adds Oded Noy. "He walked in here, and he had all these ideas, he knew exactly what everything needed to sound like."

Each production house is different, so you're going to have to decide what works best with your team and budget. AIX Entertainment works on a larger scale.

"We have eight people here," notes Mark Waldrep. "I do all the design, Bob does all the audio, Doug does all the video and editing of Premiere files. Cathy is the graphic artist, she does a lot of the stuff that relates to packaging, the cover art, and that kind of stuff. And then the other people are basically support personnel. Office support, general manager of the studio, and that sort of thing."

Many production houses are finding that smaller groups are more efficient. Figure the fewer people you have involved in the decision making process, the easier it goes.

That way, having a button made doesn't call for a board meeting. To add even more simplicity to the creative process, you'll find that if you can run Photoshop, Visual Basic, and Illustrator all on the same screen at the same time, it gives you the ability to integrate stuff quickly and efficiently. You can also minimize group input by using temporary video files and temporary audio files throughout the development cycle. Add the finished rendering or the finished movies at the last stage, after it's been approved through all the proper channels.

landing a gig

The record companies tend to have production houses they like to work with, but they're always into something new. Contacting the new media department to show them a disc you've created is not all that difficult. Aligning a proper production group with an artist on a project is really about trust and pairing people off. The trick is to match the band's creative vision with the production house that's best suited for the task. Some labels will have the band meet with several production teams, and then decide.

"A lot more bands have come with teams than people realize," notes Capitol Records' Liz Heller. "When an artist or manager comes in and they've got somebody, I try to work with that person first."

Thing is, the band buddy may not have the technology for the execution of the project. Gibby Haynes from the Butthole Surfers might have a very specific idea of what he wants to do, which requires a certain kind of technology. He knows what he wants, but perhaps he doesn't know computers well enough to see past the top level the graphic design, or the interface. A band isn't going to know who might be better at making certain technology work.

"Every situation has been different," reveals Heller. "The artist is generally most trusting of someone that they feel understands their creative vision in terms of graphics. If they could work with the guy who did their cover, or with the person who did their videos, they would be much more comfortable. Sometimes it's, 'Well, our road manager always buys me my Macs, and I want him to be involved.' I look for people that have the necessary technology background—those who can create, write that code, whatever is necessary in order for an artist to be able to do what he wants to do."

team size

Production team size is purely dependent upon the depth and scope of any given project. The smallest team size imaginable would be about six people: producer, designer, or creative director, art director, programmer, and part-time audio and video engineers. Teams can get as large as twenty people, however, management becomes a significant issue with teams this large.

"I've found it to be more efficient to use a smaller team over a longer period of time," observes Alex Melnyk, president of StoryWorks Interactive and former VP of Interactive Music at MCA. "Instead of using twenty people, I would use twelve team members and add three months to the production cycle. This of course is in an ideal world. A world which seldom exists in multimedia."

The ideal team size for most music CD-ROMs seems to be a team of eight to ten full-time individuals. This allows for a wide range of skill sets and an easily manageable size.

Q&A: david traub

David Traub's two music CD-ROM projects, Queensryche's The Promised Land *and B.B. King's* On the Road with B.B. King, *are good examples as to how the size of a team can vary.*

TELL US ABOUT YOUR PRODUCTION TEAM ON *THE PROMISED LAND* PROJECT. HOW MANY PEOPLE DID YOU WORK WITH? WHAT DID THEY DO?

David Traub: Wow, the credits are quite extensive. We had seven worlds to create. The Forest World, the five artist's worlds, and the Big Log environment. There are probably fifty or sixty people that have credits in the movie. But you have to understand that some of that was people working on the documentary itself. There was a crew on the blue screen. We probably had a total of fifteen artists. In some cases, one artist would be responsible for an entire world. In other cases, three or four artists would be supporting an artist.

We assigned an artist to be responsible for each of those worlds. They were responsible for the look and feel. We didn't have a creative director with a very strong control that dominated everything. We really wanted to operate on this continuum between the control of the creative director and the volition of the individual artist. We were very lucky working in Santa Cruz because there are many fine painters there. We actually went out and found fine artists and trained them how to use the 3-D tools and the paint tools, as compared to going out and hiring 3-D artists.

So you'll notice, not only is there a very painterly quality in many cases, and very different looks and feels. In creating the worlds themselves, there's a museum of artwork.

HOW MANY KEY PEOPLE DID YOU HAVE INVOLVED IN THE PRODUCTION PROCESS?

David Traub: There were probably three key people on the production team on the programming side. There were about maybe five key artists, with an additional key artist doing the opening animation. We had myself as producer. We had two principals of MediaX, which is the production company. Matt Macorin and Gabin Chancellor are the co-producers. Matt was responsible for programming, but was also very much an artist and a key artist, he was responsible for one of the worlds. Gabin was the creative director, he was responsible for Scott's World. So we had individual accountability on each of the worlds.

WHO WORKED ON THE AUDIO?

David Traub: We had an audio team—C.S. Audio/Visual. Reed Ridgeway and his associates were responsible for the soundscape. They worked closely with the band. The band would create vibes—the soundscape that plays over an area in the 3-D domain. It was C.S. Audio/Visual's job to take those vibes, to modify them, enrich them so that they could be spread around the world with some diversity. They were responsible for the soundscape. C.S. Audio/Visual also was a partner on some of the authoring as well.

HOW BIG WAS THE TEAM ON THE B.B. KING TITLE?

David Traub: We hired six artists to produce ethnocentric art in support of B.B.'s experience. The metaphor is his bus, Big Red. And he traveled to five different locations in his life: where he grew up, Minola, Beale Street—where he became famous, his blues club. There's an airport metaphor where you can go flying and go and see some of the other experiences, such as when he visited with President Bush. There's also a virtual museum to Lucille where all of the artists, such as U2, pay homage to B.B. King. And, en route to each of these worlds on this bus you can see a painted picture, a story picture that describes that world. Again, an experience. We use experiential metaphors as compared to just having an interface. We don't believe in interactive liner notes.

HOW BIG WAS THAT TEAM?

David Traub: The B.B. team was maybe three artists. We had one programmer on B.B., one producer and then we had the audio team of C.S. Audio/Video. They were the producing team in partnership with MediaX. Really, that was about it . . . and we had the designer Michael Shaun Conaway, and Alex Melnyk, the executive producer.

The Real McCoy Enhanced CD

Minds Eye Media
1256 3rd Ave.
San Francisco, CA 94122
(415) 665-9577
www.mindseyemedia.com
shockme@mindseyemedia.com

David Greene
Creative Spark
2108 Hayes St. #1
San Francisco, CA 94117
(415) 387-3925

Real McCoy's *One More Time* Enhanced CD design proposal courtesy of Minds Eye Media, San Francisco, and David Greene, president of Creative Spark. Copyright 1997. All Rights Reserved.

I) Main Interface

The program starts with a 3D animation of the Real McCoy logo spinning across a field of molten lava. As the logo spins into the center of the screen (A) the product interface (B,C,D 1, 2,3) appears around it. The band's logo remains in motion while the user is at this screen.

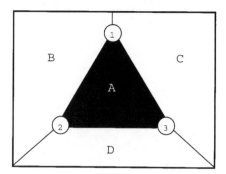

Interface Elements

a) Logo View Window

This part of the screen is where the cool stuff happens . The band's logo is in constant motion while the background changes, shimmers and morphs as the user moves the mouse over the other elements of the screen.

The next three elements are the hotspots for entering the primary areas of the product. When the user moves the cursor over these areas they will trigger both audio and visual events.

b) The Video Button

Click to enter the video viewing portion of the product.

c) The Party Ball Button

Click to play with the Interactive Party Ball Dance Mix.

d) Band Biography Button

Click to enter the 3D world of the Real McCoy's History.

The next three buttons provide basic product functions. These elements will also react to mouseovers in a similar fashion to the buttons outlined above.

1) Help

Click to bring the user to the help screen.

2) Credits

Click to activate the credits for the album and enhanced CD production teams.

3) Quit

Click to bring up a screen which enables the user to either quit or check out Real McCoy merchandise.

2

Real McCoy's *One More Time* Enhanced CD design proposal courtesy of Minds Eye Media, San Francisco, and David Greene, president of Creative Spark. Copyright 1997. All Rights Reserved.

II) Video

In this section the user may choose one of three videos for viewing. The videos are digitized to play at a size of 320 x240 pixels and can be expanded to play at larger size if desired. They are presented inside a 3D interface in which the user has controls over the choice of video and the standard video controls of play, rewind or stop.

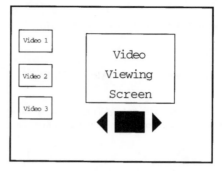

We would like to use one video from the new album, one from the old album, and one live clip. Due to disc space considerations these videos need to be edited to roughly three minutes each in length for a total of nine minutes.

3

Real McCoy's *One More Time* Enhanced CD design proposal courtesy of Minds Eye Media, San Francisco, and David Greene, president of Creative Spark. Copyright 1997. All Rights Reserved.

III) Interactive Party Ball Dance Mix

This section is designed to allow the user a dynamic interactive experience in which the user can create an audio/visual dance mix.

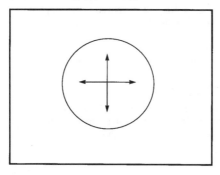

In the center of the screen the video ball appears accompanied by a looped soundtrack. The user has the ability to rotate the ball right/left and up/down. When the ball rotates, the music and the background start to change. The music becomes more intense, the ball turns and the background shifts to various colors and patterns in time with the beat of the music. Once the ball stops turning, the music reverts to the original soundtrack and a small window opens on the ball. Inside the window is a short video clip of one of the band members. These video clips are short sound bites which will both entertain and amuse the user. (Examples: OJ saying "In the house." or one of the girls singing, or blowing a kiss as the screen fills with lipstick traces.) In this section the users can get a "feel" for the individual band members and enjoy an interactive dance mix of their own creation.

We hope to include between 16 and 24 video clips which are to be produced by The Real Mc Coy. These video clips will be recorded on Super 8 tape and will be played in a window sized 160x120 pixels.

4

Real McCoy's *One More Time* Enhanced CD design proposal courtesy of Minds Eye Media, San Francisco, and David Greene, president of Creative Spark. Copyright 1997. All Rights Reserved.

IV) Biography Section

In the biography section the user enters a three dimensional environment which they can turn 360 degrees. Scattered through this environment are various glowing items which float in mid air. These items range from video screens for band interviews to objects such as concert tickets or photographs. When the user clicks on an item a short presentation which covers a section of the bands history will appear.

The floating objects fall into four primary groups.

1) Video screens

If the user clicks on one of these they will see a short video of one of the Real McCoy members speaking. There can be up to 4 of these clips, lasting 30 seconds each, for a total of 2 minutes of video.

2) Pictures of Band Members.

Click on a band member to find out their personal information.

3) Memorabilia

These items could be virtually anything, ranging from concert tickets to cocktail napkins. When the user clicks on an object, a voiceover describing a story which accompanies the item, or description of a certain period in the history of the band is heard. While the voiceover plays the user will see other photographs which correspond to the content of the voiceover.

4) Discography

Also floating among the objects in this section are pictures of the band's albums. If the user clicks on an album a list of songs on the albums and their lyric sheets appears. We would like to include a small snippet of each track (10-20 seconds) but may need to conserve disc space and only features selections from hits or personal favorites of the band.

5

Real McCoy's *One More Time* Enhanced CD design proposal courtesy of Minds Eye Media, San Francisco, and David Greene, president of Creative Spark. Copyright 1997. All Rights Reserved.

Materials Needed From Band

A) Audio

1) Product Soundtrack and Party Ball
Tracks from the new album. If possible, we would like to be able to receive isolated tracks. i.e. vocal only or drums and bass only for both albums.

2)Biography
There will be between eight and ten history movies in the Biography section. Each of these movies will have a short audio voiceover lasting between 20-30 seconds in length.

B) Photographs

1) Main Interface
One for each of the band members, preferably with one of OJ with head tilted to the right, one of the girls with her head tilted towards the left and the other in a horizontal position.

2) Biography

a) For this section we need promo photos with accompanying personal information on each of the band members.

b) Memorabilia
These are the items which will be used to trigger the short history movies. These objects can be anything from a Club flyer to a matchbook cover. There will be between 8 and 10 of these objects.

In addition to the object which triggers the voiceover, we would like to include other photos which correspond to the event or situation being described. The photos which accompany the history voiceovers should be limited to no more than 5 pictures each.

6

3) Merchandise

Before exiting, the user has the option of viewing any Real McCoy merchandise that is available for sale. We need to include photos of this merchandise as well as instructions as to how it may be purchased.

C) Videos

1) Video Section
Three videos each edited to three minutes in length. We would like to feature one live video and one video from the last album and the current album.

2) Biography Section
These videos should be of individual bandmembers making statements regarding their personal beliefs about the music, the history of the band or whatever subject they desire to include. The total time allocated for these videos is 2 minutes, so the statements need to be succinct and to the point.

3) Party Ball
Brent had mentioned the possibility of shooting some footage for this project with a Super 8 Video cam. This footage can be used for the Party Ball section of the project. When shooting this footage please try to shoot in front of a solid color which is different than what you are wearing. Ideally the footage should be shot in front of a solid blue background. One easy way to do this is to purchase some large sheets of blue paper, which can be found at almost any art supply store.

Since these video clips are for the party ball dance mix, they should be of the band members having fun and acting funky. Between 16 and 24 clips can be included in the party ball section.

7

The following are a few basic ideas for Party Ball video clips.

1) OJ saying "In the House"

2) One of the girls blowing a kiss

3) One of the girls singing

4) OJ doing a short rap

5) OJ dancing

As the project develops, we can work together to find clips which showcase the personality of the band members and their music. When making these clips just remember two things: 1) have fun 2) keep it short.

D) Easter Eggs

In computer terminology an Easter Egg is a feature of the product which is hidden from the user. In order to find these "eggs" the user must experiment with the product to find out where they are hidden.

An example of an Easter Egg is a hidden video message from the band which only plays when the user holds the "option" key down while clicking on the Party Ball. Instead of spinning the Party Ball, the hidden video is played.

We would like to include some Easter Eggs in this product and need some feedback from the band as to what they would like to hide in the product. These Easter eggs will be included after we have determined the exact amount of disc space and production time needed for the main body of the product.

8

Real McCoy's *One More Time* Enhanced CD design proposal courtesy of Minds Eye Media, San Francisco, and David Greene, president of Creative Spark. Copyright 1997. All Rights Reserved.

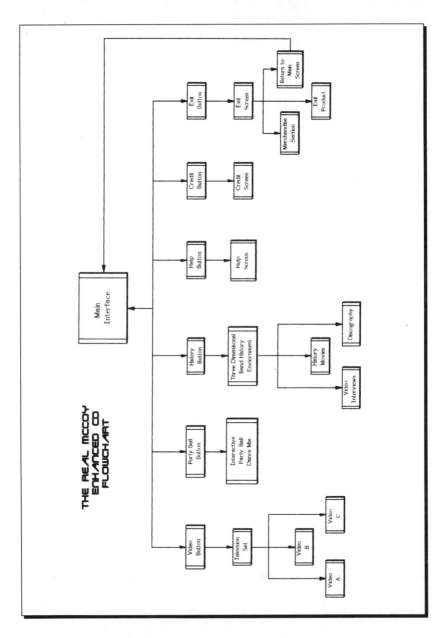

Real McCoy's *One More Time* Enhanced CD design proposal courtesy of Minds Eye Media, San Francisco, and David Greene, president of Creative Spark. Copyright 1997. All Rights Reserved.

In Search of The Lost Chord

Executive Summary: In Search of The Lost Chord is a journey into the human psyche where chivalry and compassion are the keys to winning the game. This interactive adventure game on CD-ROM transforms the player into the hero within the classical hero's journey. It features a challenging gaming structure embedded within an interactive story-line, stunning computer graphic environments and a dramatic soundscape by the Moody Blues. We intend to create a truly compelling 3D immersive experience that has, at its core, a desire to uplift humanity.

Design Philosophy: The underlying philosophy to the structure of the game lies in creating a symbiotic balance between, the game, the story, the landscape, and the soundscape. Each gaming element will depend upon the landscape and soundscape for solution as well as serve to forward the overall story. By integrating the above into a cogent design, these components both inform and depend on each other.

Audience: As it enraptures and entertains, In Search of the Lost Chord will provide many hours of game play and exploration for:

- Gamers appreciating story based titles such as "Full Throttle".
- Adventure gamers playing titles like "Zork Nemesis".
- The intellectual and spiritual minded.
- Inner explorers who love personality profiles and are searching for a deeper meaning in life.
- The "Counter-Culture" including the Cyberset, Generation X'ers and the "Hip" Baby Boomers.
- The fans of the Moody Blues.

Competitive Advantage: In Search of The Lost Chord is unlike any other game ever produced for the following reasons:

In Search of the Lost Chord CD-ROM proposal courtesy of Michael Shaun Conaway, MediaX and Phillips Interactive Media. Reprinted by permission. All right reserved.

2

- It features a series of 38 intensely beautiful, 360 degree navigable 3D panoramas inspired by 14 inter-linked, story-based puzzles. This artwork will reveal the power of state-of-the art computer graphics based upon artists like Bosch, Parish and Dali.

- It is a surreal, interactive, hero's journey which creates a robust story-line featuring an intricately designed game of time travel, discovery and values-based problem-solving.

- It is a psychic mirror for the player based upon Jungian typology. Game play will enable our expert system to score a Jungian behavioral evaluation. As one of the pay-offs, this feature will identify the user as one of 16 archetypes.

- It features a lush and haunting soundscape derived from 30 years of the music of the Moody Blues. The soundscape has been carefully crafted as a subtle means of facilitating the evolution of both gaming and storytelling.

The Game: In Search of The Lost Chord invites the user to solve the ultimate challenge, to discover the Lost Chord. This chord is found inside and outside all of us. It is known as the primordial sound of the universe. Once the eight melodic phrases of the Lost Chord have been discovered, our hero can save the Lost World, transforming it into the Free World.

The goal of the game is to solve challenges that allow our hero to travel deeper and deeper within the increasingly fantastical levels of a Mandala structure and collect the missing notes of the Lost Chord. At the center of the Mandala, our hero will face the ultimate challenge. If this final challenge is solved and the Lost Chord is played, the Mandala will shatter, releasing magic back into the Lost World, thereby transforming it into the Free World.

The more implicit and subtle goal of the game is to outsmart the shadow forces, which have consumed all the universe's beauty. The hero can do this by exhibiting honorable behavior at each decision point in the game.

In Search of the Lost Chord CD-ROM proposal courtesy of Michael Shaun Conaway, MediaX and Phillips Interactive Media. Reprinted by permission. All right reserved.

3

Heuristic Structure, Jungian Typology: Over the span of the game, a profile of our users will be collected by an expert system integrated within our authoring. Our hero will be identified as one of Jung's sixteen archetypes. Once the hero completes all three levels of gaming, they will be rewarded with their personality profile before facing the final challenge.

The Story: As the dehumanizing Cold Hearted Orb of The Lost World continued to suck the magic of hope from the universe, the Mentors, as visionaries foresaw the coming age of darkness. In defense, they created a series of magical worlds integrated within the ancient form of a mandala in which the final remnants of humanness are hidden.

Known as the Land of Make-Believe, this universe of mystical worlds awaits a hero who might be able to defeat the shadow of the Cold Hearted Orb. Success within this magical reality is the only hope for returning humanity to its true condition. However, that success can only be won by a hero of true character and compassion.

Thus begins the adventure, stuck within the lifeless Lost World, humanity works day in and day out before their computer screens, enslaved by the establishment. As our hero interacts with their computer a face appears on the screen: "X105019 are you working or did I just detect a series of personal inquiries? You had better watch your performance index today. No overachieving, no underachieving."

On the desk top of our hero's computer, he or she will find two icons. One is labeled "work". If our hero clicks on "work", page after page of numbers flash by on the screen. The other icon is labeled "Kingdom". If he or she clicks on Kingdom, the normal conventions of the computer begin to break down. A voice takes over the computer. "Are you the one we've been looking for?" it asks.

After answering a series of questions from the voice, our hero is sucked into the Land of Make-Believe where they will be given the chance to Search for the Lost Chord and transform the Lost World into the Free World.

Mythological Structure: In Search of The Lost Chord takes the player on an enchanting odyssey of the mind, a modern hero's journey crafted according to Joseph

In Search of the Lost Chord CD-ROM proposal courtesy of Michael Shaun Conaway, MediaX and Phillips Interactive Media. Reprinted by permission. All right reserved.

4

Campbell's classic structure of storytelling to facilitate heroic transformation. This structure was first detailed by Campbell in his book "The Hero with a Thousand Faces". The intended effect of using this structure will be to give our hero the experience -- and eventual resolution -- of the mythical adventure.

The Game by the Hero's Journey:

- *The Ordinary World:* The game Begins in the Lost World, an Orwellian world of suffering. Our hero is different from the rest, resisting the command to be efficient and unremarkable.

- *The Call to Adventure:* Our hero is called when a heuristic mentor hacks into the hero's computer and offers them the challenge of freeing magic and creativity, thus saving humanity that is trapped in the Lost World.

- *Mentors and Guardians:* Our mentors will each give the hero a talisman; The Book of Spells, The Key-Ring (for the Keys to the Kingdom), The Flute (to record the notes), and the Mandala Map. This will take place in the outermost realm of the mandala, the first four worlds.

- *Threshold Crossing:* Our hero must finally make the leap and cross from the first to the second realm, a world which according to Campbell is "a dream landscape of curiously fluid, ambiguous forms, where the hero must survive a succession of trials".

- *The Tests:* In the eight inner-worlds our hero will face eight challenges, each reflecting a specific moral/psychological dilemma; Compassion vs. Cruelty; Joy vs. Sorrow, Tao vs. Control, Peace vs. War, Other vs. Self Love vs. Hate, Rebirth vs. Death and Wisdom vs. Ignorance.

- *The Supreme Ordeal:* The simple secret of the Supreme Ordeal is that hero's must die so that they can be reborn. This is the main test of the hero that takes place at the center of the mandala. Here the hero faces their own shadow.

In Search of the Lost Chord CD-ROM proposal courtesy of Michael Shaun Conaway, MediaX and Phillips Interactive Media. Reprinted by permission. All right reserved.

5

- *Apotheosis:* Once having faced the supreme ordeal the hero is then catapulted to the level of the divine. This is the section of the game where the player experiences the first pay-offs; the Jungian Typology and the music video.

- *Resurrection; Back Across the Threshold:* This is the climax of the story when the original conditions of the story are resolved. Our hero will witness the transformation of the Lost World into the Free World. This final payoff includes the animation of the transformation of the Lost World and the return of the hero to the Free World.

Soundscape: In Search of the Lost Chord features a robust and haunting soundscape derived from the music of Moody Blues. The soundscape has been carefully crafted as a subtle means of facilitating the evolution of both storytelling and gaming.

The Moody Blues are the masters at immersing their listeners in the realm of magical, mystical and profound experiences. In Search of The Lost Chord uses this same underlying, experiential structure that has been so successful in their music. We believe that drawing upon the essence of the music to creating rich gaming, storytelling and explorational environments will redefine the genre of interactive adventure games.

Disc Architecture: In Search of the Lost Chord will be comprised of:

- 38 thematic navigable digital sets made of 38 panoramic nodes and approx. 160 ray-traced stills.
- 12 major puzzle and story based problems.
- 1 to 4 new Moody Blues tracks.
- 1 music video designed as one of the payoffs to the game.
- 20 minutes of live action video and character animation.
- A Moody Blues ambient soundscape comprised of over 40 songs.

Conclusion: In Search of The Lost Chord uses an underlying, experiential structure that has been so successful in popular games and films. It takes the player in hand and leads them through a unique and magical journey with discoveries of tremendous beauty, and often, unique insights into the human condition.

In Search of the Lost Chord CD-ROM proposal courtesy of Michael Shaun Conaway, MediaX and Phillips Interactive Media. Reprinted by permission. All right reserved.

things to think about

Before you dive into production on your interactive music project, remember to keep these pointers in mind:

- *Simplicity:* The interface and interaction should not only be clear, they should be simple. Todd Rundgren, one of the first musicians to get involved in multimedia proclaims, "The more clicks you have to go through to get the thing to work, the worse it's working."

- *Consistency:* Strive for a consistent design.

- *Participation:* Multimedia should entice the user to participate and go further into the multimedia piece.

Good multimedia is like having a quality conversation. The topic of conversation can be as basic as making a selection and receiving a reply or as complex as a debate on nuclear arms. It is the interaction between two "intelligent" elements, the user and the program.

chapter 4

enhanced cd:
production phase

In a beginner's mind, there are many possibilities, but in the expert's mind, there are few.

—**Zen saying**

EDITOR'S NOTE

This chapter provides an overview of the Enhanced CD production process, including an insightful case study of the making of an original Enhanced CD title. Despite what you may think, there is no "right" way to produce an enhanced property. And there may never be. Producing such a title is a collaborative effort between professionals in both the music and multimedia industries, working together to produce the finest possible end result. If you'd like to follow up this book with an in-depth look into the production process of multimedia, music and/or sound, some fine resources to consider are: Multimedia Sound and Music Studio, *by Jeff Essex, published by Random House New Media;* Enhanced CD Factbook, *by Josh Warner, published by Apple Computer;* Multimedia: Making it Work, *by Tay Vaughan, published by Osborne McGraw-Hill;* Multimedia Demystified, *by Vivid Publishing, published by Apple Computer and Random House New Media. You can also find in-depth articles on interactive music issues in* Music & Computers *magazine published by Miller Freeman.*

mission statement

The production process for an Enhanced CD project can proceed more smoothly if a mission statement is developed before any work begins and is referred to when the project veers off course (it most likely will). A mission statement should clearly state the project's objective. Your design team should be reminded to refer to the mission statement often, reflecting on the "goal" of the production. Issues such as money, scheduling problems, and unforeseen delays can destroy the morale of your team. Your mission statement can act as the project's "moral compass," helping to keep everyone focused on the true objective of the piece.

"We set out to make *The Promised Land* as the world's first non-violent, cross-gender, values-based eco game starring a heavy metal band," expounded David Traub. "Our goal was to propagate their music, speak to their audience, and more importantly, expand beyond their audience and introduce whole new populations to who they are. So very early on, we knew what we were creating."

The mission was to take a branded asset—in this case, the band Queensryche—and explore its values, issues, perceptions, etc. It was accomplished through intense psychological interviews, translating that information into visual metaphors and gaming structures that were parallel to the personalities of the individual band members.

When creating the project, MediaX had a mission. They knew what they wanted the project to say, and they accomplished their objectives.

The objective of Jackson Browne's Enhanced CD, however, was to provide insight into the artist's songwriting.

David Greene's objective with Real McCoy's Enhanced CD was to remove the unnatural barrier between the band and its legion of fans. To do this, David worked closely with the band's leader, O-Jay. He turned O-Jay's playful, inquisitive personality into real gaming elements within the disc. That way, Real McCoy's fans could get inside O-Jay's head, and glimpse O-Jay's true personality simply by exploring the title.

scheduling

No matter how much time you are allotted to produce a project, most likely, it will not be enough time. Record companies (your publisher) will give you under eight weeks to develop a project from concept to final gold master, seldom more. So, you will have to make all the pieces come together within the time allotted. The following tips may help keep you on track:

- Preproduction will allow you to specify what's to come as best as possible.

- Prototyping will yield the first working representation of the product. It should come complete with concepts.

- There will be art milestones, where your artwork is completed. You may create production milestones for graphics, interface, etc.

- Once production schedules are set, the next milestone is Alpha testing. Alpha is typically 80 percent of all artwork done, 80 percent of functionality and, ideally, no crash and bugs.

- Then on to Beta. When you're setting your schedules, expect the unexpected and leave time to correct it. You know once you hit Beta stage there are going to be bugs. Leave plenty of time for testing and getting the bugs out.

tracking assets

When you are creating your project, it is essential to implement a co-ordinated system for tracking all of the elements that will make up your title. Why? Imagine having to open twenty-five files to find the one file you're looking for. For a designer under deadline, this scenario would be a complete nightmare. Yet it's a scene repeated all too often among novice developers. Organizing your media files for an enhanced project is essential. You'll want to be sure you have an efficient system for tracking your assets, such as a production bible which serves as a detailed roadmap containing all your production notes should any questions or problems arise during development.

"It's good practice, but generally, we've just been so hectic that we haven't had much time to do much else than back up," offers Ken Caillat. "We back up everything and put all of the graphic files onto a tape (DAT back-up tape) or we'll burn it on a master CD that contains the program files and master files, and then we place that someplace with our storyboards. That's more of a clean up task, like putting away the dishes after a barbecue."

"When new ideas are coming into a project, there must be some extremely well-organized method of keeping track of all the new stuff. Otherwise, material will get lost or confused or jumbled or misconstrued," claims interactive writer/producer Larry Kay. "As soon as the production gun fires, I believe it is time for everyone to bring new ideas into the production very judiciously. Otherwise, budgets and deadlines disappear."

A numerical system has been found to work effectively in many production camps. Interactive writer/director Douglas Gayeton breaks down his projects into sequences.

"Each sequence is assigned a 'name' or 'address.' In a sense, it's a code which relates to what the location is or what action is happening," claims Gayeton. "On one production, it got to the point where I could say JA-3A-M-2 and everybody knew what that was."

Writer/designer, Terry Borst and his writing partner, Frank DePalma, organize their projects using traditional three-by-five index cards.

"The great thing about index cards is that you can lay them on the floor and walk around the structure of your project. The cards can double as your flow chart. We have a couple of photographs of the two of us standing amid some pretty wild structures."

Since there are no proven methods for successful project organization, the choice is yours. Just make sure the method you choose works for the entire production team.

development stages

We asked Highway One's Ken Caillat to outline the typical steps involved in the development process of an Enhanced CD title. Here's what he said:

- Meet the artist; banter around some ideas.

- Draw up a basic storyboard with flow charts. Sketch the screen interface with all the buttons . . . everything that will have to be created.

- Review and critique the storyboard.

- Sit down with the graphic artist and programmer. "I'll usually pull them both into the same room and I'll say 'here's the deal,'" enlightens Caillat. "'We're going to go from here to here. This is where we're going to play three videos on a 320 screen. We're going to need a stop, we're going to need a pause, we're going to need a fast forward button. We're going to need a volume control. I want to have touch lyrics."

  "The programmer will ask me things that I can't write down, 'Is that going to go into autoplay when you go into that screen. Is it a random set of buttons?'"

  The graphics person will take a week or two and come back with some rough sketches. By that time the programmer should have a running program.

- Secure your content. After meeting with the graphic designer and programmer, send out a list to the record company requesting content. This might consist of final footage on Beta SP, the B roles from various video shoots, interviews, album art press kits, things like that. Review it all and capture what you need.

- Tie your graphics into the graphics used to create the record package. If they're using blues and greens, do the same. If you can, get the person who did the graphics from the album to send over their album art and all the components of it so you can take some of those elements and tie it into one package.

- Process the video. Remember to color balance the video before you start digitizing.

- Do the same thing with audio. Run it through a set of external meters, external equalizers, external limiter compressor to balance the audio and optimize it.

- Compress these elements using standard compression techniques. To convert the movie, Highway One uses Movie Cleaner, and then compress with Cinepack because that seems to cross platform pretty well. After the movie is compressed it has to be flattened, sometimes resized or mapped. If it's green screen, do green screen processing.

- Name all the files with a uniform coding system. All files need to be cross platform (reduced to an eight letter-dot-three letter format, capitalized so the PC will recognize it). You should name each segment of video, the artist regarding songwriting, the artist regarding guitar; specify that so you know what each interview is called when you're placing it in the Enhanced project. Put these files in the right folders, organize them. Use one folder, keep a backup somewhere, keep updating, throw away the other stuff, you don't need fifty copies of the same movie, particularly if you've got the beta handy—you can keep redigitizing if worse comes to worse.

- Finalize the interface. The graphic artist comes back with the screens, now you must figure out the placement of the other content. Where is the text going to be? Is the text going to move? Can I link to the CD from the lyrics?

- Agree on the "button" thing. You can have a whole company just on 'Buttons are Us.' It takes a while before the graphic artist gets it and then it's great. Then it's a question of do I want the button to give me some acknowledgment? Is it going to be a button and you push on it and you see it get depressed and the shadow changes, and then come back out again? Do you want it to glow when you push on it? Do you want it to make a sound? What kind of acknowledgment do you want? If it's loading something, do you want to put a little clock up, meaning that you've got to wait?

■ Create a final folder and test everything. You'll put the movies into the folder. You'll get your executable program that will talk to those movies. Work out a process where you can easily move the drive with all of your content back and forth from a Mac to a PC. Highway One uses a thing called Formatter 5. We format a drive, half of it as Mac and half as PC, both halves will appear right on your desktop, you've got your Mac side and the PC side clearly sitting there on the Mac. Work on the Mac side and make sure the program runs really well. Then you make sure that all the exact same movies are in the PC side. Take executables that you just perfected on your Mac side and drag them over to your PC folder. Turn off your computer and take that hard drive over to the PC, and you run it on the PC. There will be palette issues. Watch the transitions, watch the dissolves. The audio may come in different. The screen may pixilate different. Adjust anything that is weird, tweak that stuff. Shut down your PC and take your drive back to the Mac. Take the executable that you just had on the PC, drag it back over the Mac and launch it back on the Mac to make sure that the changes you made on the PC didn't screw something up on the Mac. Go back and forth and back and forth and back and forth until it's all working right.

it is alive!

Once you start developing your project, you're going to find that it takes on a life of its own. Usually what is born is a brother of the original idea. There may be technical limitations or the available assets may change. It could be that your team changes and that alters things.

Changes to your original plan do not spell imminent disaster for your project. It's not a good or bad thing. It just means your project becomes different. Evolution pulls the project in a new direction. If you're creating an Enhanced CD for a record label and you have a flexible client that will allow the project to evolve, you will be alright. Just make sure you stay within your budget.

play time

Gaming CD-ROMs are designed to provide hours of enjoyment. Forty hours tends to be a good target for most full-scale, retail titles. Enhanced CDs are designed to engage the user for a three-to-eight hour period. Demos, such as the *Onion* Enhanced CD demo, have twenty minutes of play, merely a taste of the possibilities.

The amount of play time for your title depends upon the available space left on your disc (after accounting for the music) multiplied by the depth of user-content interactivity.

deep purpose

Are you merely enhancing an album, or is there some deeper meaning or purpose to your project? Record companies may want to maximize the benefits of the Enhanced CD format, and such strategies are not always artist based. Ask your publisher if the disc is to double as a merchandising vehicle. Perhaps the record label's catalog will be included on the disc. Should an electronic ordering component be built into the disc? How about software to link directly to a Web site?

so little space, so much stuff

Be wary. Everyone from the design team to the lead singer's mother is going to give you input and tell you what they would like to see included on the disc. The good part (and bad part) is that there are space limitations. When you get down to it, there's not a whole lot you can do with 150–200 megabytes of space on a disc. A lot of developers will initially create enhanced material that takes up too much space. In such instances, the material will need to be edited down. A developer may have to sacrifice the quality on the video so the data rate gets smaller. You may need to substitute stills in place of motion video. In some places, you may need to 'go mono' instead of stereo, saving half the data rate of the audio. You've got to weigh everything and keep only the most crucial components essential to the enhanced experience.

The Jackson Browne enhanced disc started with 800 megabytes of digitized video and had to be cut down to 150 megabyes. It was just cut and cut and cut. Once you've hit your bottom line and you think there's nothing more you can do to make your material fit in the allotted space, ask your publisher or artist for his or her input.

testing, testing

When you're building an interactive project, you're testing all the time. Whenever you create something new, you test it to see how it works. Your first true test of your ability, however, is when you demo your first prototype. Try it on a PC and see how it "plays" compared to your Mac version. You need to test navigation elements, color specifications, sound clips, and system conflicts, among other things.

Testing is crucial since it provides instant feedback on what works and what doesn't. You'll have time to fix program "bugs" before you turn in your completed master. If you fine tune your project as you go, you should sidestep major surprises later on.

Even if you've been testing all along, the Alpha testing phase is the first formal testing period for a multimedia product. It starts at the end of the production stage and is generally completed in-house. The objective of Alpha testing is to make sure that the system does not crash, that screens do not freeze up, that all navigation components perform as they were designed. Generally, there are three areas to address during Alpha testing:

- *User Testing.* Sometimes performed before production begins, yet always improved upon during production. User testing involves making sure the interface is intuitive, consistent, and effective to actual human testers.

- *Functional Testing.* This is also known as "testing to spec." Does the project fulfill the requirements outlined in the proposal? Functional testing will reveal minor errors such as buttons which lead to no action, or a link to the wrong content passage. Larger problems might be items such as system crashes. Functional testing will allow you to locate these problems and correct them.

- *Content testing.* Make sure the materials of the multimedia product are accurate. You want to check for everything from misspelled words to inaccurate subject matter. Facts need to be checked, text needs to be proofread.

beta testing

Beta testing starts once your production appears to be complete. The objective is to lock down a gold master so that the title can be readied for distribution. Key areas of Beta testing are user testing, compatibility testing, and bug testing.

During Beta testing, the project is taken out of house and given to various focus groups to try. It's user testing, which also means testing the effectiveness of the interface to see whether or not your design really works, and people actually enjoy the design. The second kind of testing is compatibility testing, to see if the product will work across all of the platforms specified in your contract. Bug testing, which results from both user testing and compatibility testing, looks for crashes and fix-its.

Beta testing starts when the artwork is 95 percent finished and there are no discernable crashes and bugs. At this point, you'll want to give the project to potential clients so they can test the disc and report back to you with problems or comments. In exchange for this service, Beta testers should be offered free or discounted copies of the product. Your Beta test audience can range from a half dozen people to tens of thousands (Microsoft and IBM, for example, do large scale testing on their products).

The number of Beta testers that you use should depend upon the complexity of your project. Be advised that from 20 percent to more than half of the people you give the disc to for Beta testing will never respond or offer feedback. Most likely you'll have many Beta phases and many Beta masters before you arrive at the finished product—the elusive gold master.

gold master

The holy grail of software production . . . the pot of gold at the end of the rainbow is submitting the gold master. Simply stated, your gold master is the final project you submit to the publisher. Your gold master should be free of bugs (hopefully) and ready to go to press, package, and hit the store shelves.

completion is bittersweet

When you're creating an Enhanced CD, you may find that your principal challenge is to finish the disc. Undoubtedly you'll run into problems with the authoring environment, especially if you haven't used aspects of it before. Additionally, you'll encounter problems if you do not follow your storyboard to a "T" and stick to your initial specifications.

"In the end, the greatest challenge is to reconcile two things; the desire to have the greatest product ever produced and the need to finish it in a timely manner within the context of the commitments to marketing channels," states David Traub. "And to finish in a manner that doesn't have bugs, so you can actually make money. That is the greatest challenge."

It doesn't matter how great your CD project is. It's like a band recording an album. No one is ever quite satisfied. You know you could have done more or made things much better with a little more time and cash. But now you know better for the next project.

"Completion is always bittersweet," notes Traub. "If you step back and look at how much content, how much media, how much richness there is and then you compare it to anything else out there, you are in touch again with the overwhelming sense of exhaustion associated with all the thousands and thousands of hours that everybody spent creating the work."

case study: real mccoy

Real McCoy's One More Time *Enhanced CD was a joint production between Creative Spark and Minds Eye Media, San Francisco. The project was produced by David Greene, president of Creative Spark (davidg@creative-spark.com) and Nathan Vogel and Sherri Sheridan of Minds Eye Media (shockme@mindseyemedia.com). What follows is David's case study detailing the development of the project.*

In the summer of 1995, the Real McCoy exploded on the music scene selling over three million copies of their debut album *Another Night*. The lead single, "Another Night," topped the charts in the U.S. and in other countries around the world.

For their follow-up album, *One More Time*, Real McCoy decided they wanted to provide their fans with a deeper experience, which led to my relationship with the band and the Enhanced CD project described in the following case study.

GETTING THE GIG

Prior to the Real McCoy gig I had been working as an interactive music consultant. I had worked with Aerosmith and Geffen, Giant and Sony Music to help define their interactive media strategies and create interactive products.

I met Real McCoy's music director, Brent Arqovitz, through a mutual friend, and we began discussing adding an interactive component to their next album. My dialogue began with Brent and O-Jay, Real McCoy's band leader, around December of 1995. By March, 1996, I was asked to send a basic proposal, which included an outline for an Enhanced CD with an accompanying Web site and all the associated costs. In response, I sent the letter dated March 5 which you'll find included in this case study.

After that, we had a number of discussions and then waited for approval from the record label to start the project. In early April, I was informed that the label had approved a budget which was somewhere in between the two prices that I'd quoted. What they had decided was that they wanted an interactive element for the album which included the interactive dance mix but no Web site. The next steps were to develop a design specification for the product and assemble the production team.

PRODUCTION PARTNERS

I chose Minds Eye Media as a production partner. I had known the company's founders, Nathan Vogel and Sherri Sheridan, for a few years and had always been impressed by their work. One of the things that inspired me to work with them was their knowledge of Shockwave for Director. In fact, Sherri was a member of the original Shockwave development team at Macromedia and was the first person to post a Shockwave movie on the Web.

For those who don't already know, Shockwave is a technology that allows small Director movies to play across the Web. Shockwave movies need to be smaller than 300K, which includes the sound, graphics, text—everything that you need to create a compelling interactive piece. This 300K file is used to create a projector which is roughly about 100K and can quickly be downloaded from the Web. While perfecting their skills with Shockwave, Nathan and Sherri had developed new production techniques which significantly decreased the file sizes. With only 170 Megabytes available on the Real McCoy disc for the entire interactive portion, I knew that we would need all of the space-saving tricks they had up their sleeves.

When I first approached them, I had already started on the design spec you'll see later in this case study. We then sat down and discussed the realities of the proposal—the technical issues, how to produce the project within the allotted budget, how to work together as a team, pounding out a realistic production schedule, what materials we would need from the band and when would we need them, how the credits would be shared, and all the other issues you need to get straight before production can truly begin.

After we had thoroughly discussed the issues and reached an agreement, I forwarded the proposal to Real McCoy's management. About a week later the band approved the script and we entered the next phase of the production process.

LEGALITIES

This is where I've seen a lot of interactive music projects get bogged down. The legal issues when dealing with music and video can be pretty complicated, and I cannot stress how important it is to have contracts that everyone agrees to and signs. Contracts are for everyone's protection: the multimedia producer, his/her partners, and the band. Everyone involved in the process must have a clear understanding of what is expected from them, and when. Without adequately addressing all of the issues pertaining to media rights, content deliverables, product milestones, and payment structure, you will create major headaches which may jeopardize the success of the project.

For the Real McCoy project, I choose the firm of Jacobs and Conklin as my representation. I did not make this choice lightly. I had researched their past clients and had found them to be exceptionally skilled in the area of Interactive Law. It is important that your legal counsel truly understand the intricacies of interactive law. This is a new field and not many attorneys are fully familiar with all its ins and outs. When selecting an attorney, make sure the firm has experience in the field. If it doesn't, you run the risk of signing a contract that is not in your best interests. There is only one thing worse than not having a solid contract, and that's having a bad contract which binds you to unrealistic expectations or unreasonable rates of pay.

Prior to having the contracts written up, Robert Wieger, Real McCoy's manager, and I discussed all of the details in depth. We decided to have the contracts bind us to the original design proposal under the following terms:

- *Final Delivery.* In exchange for the compensation package, I was responsible for delivering Real McCoy a finished cross platform Enhanced CD based upon the design proposal.

- *Compensation.*
  Flat Rate. Fifty percent of the production fee paid at the start

of production, 25 percent upon receipt of the first milestone, and 25 percent upon delivery of the completed project.

Other Compensation. This was for reimbursement of reasonable expenses, i.e. phone, fax, overnight deliveries, and twenty copies of the finished CD.

Standard Rate. We negotiated this fee in case there were modifications to the product beyond the scope of the flat rate. This fee would be applied for modifications made to items that had already been approved or if the interactive portion needed to be edited to be smaller than the agreed size of 170 megabytes after it had been completed.

- *Track One Issues.* Real McCoy and its label are responsible for choosing the method and securing the technology for incorporating the multimedia into the final product (AIX, pre-gap, Blue Book, etc.)

- *Credits.*
  Jewel Case. The production company logo will appear on both the back cover and inside the liner notes.

  Interactive Credits. Inside the multimedia production there will be a button which leads the user to the credits for the interactive production team.

- *Content Approval.* Upon receiving materials, Real McCoy has three days to approve or disapprove. If it does not respond within the three days the materials are considered approved.
  This is a very important item. Remember to be very specific about who has approval and how it can be tracked, i.e., e-mail or certified mail, return receipt requested. In this case, all materials were to be delivered to the band's manager and approval made in writing from either O-Jay or Robert Wieger.

- *Materials.* Materials for the project—music, video, and photographs—were to be provided by Real McCoy. These materials were to be provided royalty free with all rights issues cleared.

This section was the most complicated. After much discussion we finally worked out the details for the deliverables, which I will discuss later in this case study.

MORE LEGAL STUFF

In addition to the contract with Real McCoy, I had another contract drawn up which formalized my relationship with Minds Eye Media. This contract specified our roles and responsibilities. Once again this contract used the design document as the benchmark for our activities. Going into this project, we all understood that there would be a great deal of overlap in our jobs and that together we were all jointly responsible for the delivery of the final product.

The important thing to remember about contracts is that besides being legal obligations, they are guidelines for people's behaviors, and you need to give people a little room to move. If the approval comes back a day late and it does not interfere with the production schedule, let it go. Remember you are working with these people—not against them. Contracts can provide protection in the worst case scenario—where the project is going wildly off schedule and over budget; in the best case scenario a contract is rarely referred to because the parties involved are all living up to their agreements and are willing to communicate and compromise.

LIQUID PRODUCTION SCHEDULES

One of the hardest lessons to learn about producing Enhanced CDs is how to create a product that is both creatively satisfying and produceable within your time and money constraints. Typically budgets aren't very large, the amount of disc space is limited and, most importantly, most of the materials needed to create the Enhanced CD are not available when you begin production.

In an ideal world, Enhanced CD production would be sequential with the album production, meaning that the enhanced portion of the disc would be produced after the album, its packaging and accompanying videos were completed. In the real world, that scenario only happens if you are working on catalog material for a box set or greatest hits package; otherwise you will be working on projects where a significant percentage of your source material simply has not been created yet.

We refer to our solution to this problem as "liquid production scheduling." This means if certain materials are not available you work around them, like water moving around obstacles which have been placed in its path. If the logo is not ready, use place holders. If the final mixes for the album are not completed, use rough mixes. The idea is not to let lack of finished content delay the production schedule.

A word of caution: You need to be very clear with the artist and his management regarding the final deliverable dates for the materials. If you do not, you may find yourself in the position where the project goes over budget or you miss your deadline because you have not been provided with the final content in a timely manner; your contract must protect you against this possibility.

On the Real McCoy project we used a variety of production scheduling techniques to ensure that neither one of those options would happen. In the design document, we created a variety of screens and activities where we could use a significant amount of place holder art. Through discussions with the band and its management, we worked out specific deliverable dates for content, and how the approval process would work in the absence of the final artwork.

THE REALITIES OF CONTENT DELIVERABLES

The project started on June 1 and the final product was to be completed by August 1. Initially, we had asked for all materials from the band by June 15 in order to make the due date. After we discussed the situation it became apparent that June 15 was not going to happen: the album was still in production, the video shoot for the first single hadn't even been scheduled, the artwork and new logo were going to start production sometime in July, the band had recently had a change of personnel, and no new photo shoots were scheduled until July. Quite simply, we were trying to work with materials which did not exist.

In the end, we had to sit down with the band and determine a deliverable schedule that would allow us to create the product they wanted without creating undue stress in its or our organization. The first thing we needed to do was reschedule the final due date from August 1st to

August 23 with the milestone date for the band's first look at the product moved back to July 15.

This "first look" milestone was important because we needed Real McCoy's approval that the project was proceeding to its satisfaction and we needed the milestone payment. This first milestone assumed the band would be able to approve the progress of the project even though we still did not have the final content.

To accomplish these goals, the band agreed to send us all the new photographs by July 15, with some flexibility on our part to fit in some photos that were taken later. They were very cool about the music and actually provided us with rough mixes of the new album on DAT in June. They also agreed to send the final mixes as soon as they became available, and allowed us the opportunity to request special mixes (i.e., drums and bass only) as needed. We used the old logo as a place holder until they delivered the new logo (no later than August 1). The final due date for the videos to be delivered to us was August 9. For the party ball and history sections, O-Jay agreed to personally shoot some footage using a Hi-8 camera, and promised delivery within two weeks of any written request.

The most important understanding we came to was that delays in delivering materials would most likely cause delays in the completion of the project. They understood that it would be impossible to keep an August 23 deadline if we didn't receive the new videos on August 22. We found the band to be sympathetic to our production needs, so working out an equitable and realistic delivery schedule was relatively easy.

As you can see there was a lot of give-and-take in these negotiations. Remember, when you schedule your content deliverables you need to work with the band and tailor the project to meet both their needs and yours. The way to avoid hassles is through communication. If that means that you need to reschedule the milestone dates or completion date due to the nonavailability of content deliverables, bring it up at the start of the project.

Work together with the band and management and you'll find that they usually are genuinely willing to understand your needs and will respond positively to honesty and professionalism. It's better to be realistic and address issues which may not be entirely comfortable than to miss a project completion date.

THE FIRST LOOK

On July 15 we gave Real McCoy its first look at the project. This was a completely functional prototype which included:

The Main Interface Screen

For this screen we used a large variety of "place keeper" art work, a series of old photographs and a variety of frame grabs from the band's videos. We designed the screen using several layers in Photoshop, understanding full well that a large number of the photographs would need to be replaced for the final project.

The Video Section

For this section we digitized a portion of three different videos and placed them inside the 3-D television set we had modeled. This way the band could see how its videos would look inside the final product. We did not digitize the full videos for this section since we were not sure if these were the videos which would be included in the final product. That determination would be made after reviewing the rights issues for the existing videos and determining the number of new videos which could be produced before the release of the new album.

Moonscape

In the spec document this area was described as an exploration zone where the user could rotate a full 360 degrees and trigger information about the band by clicking on various items which were located in the environment.

We had given O-Jay a variety of choices for this environment; an underwater playground, the desert at night, a blue lagoon, or a fantasy moonscape. O-Jay selected the moonscape and for the first look at the product we included a fully rotational 360 degree turn through the moonscape with one item to click on, a heart-shaped locket containing a video of O-Jay.

The Interactive Party Ball Dance Mix

This section of the product had not been designed as a game nor was it intended to be an informational item. The party ball was designed to be, well . . . a party ball. Nothing more, nothing less. It's simply a fun multimedia interaction with the band where the user can get a feeling for the personalities of the band.

An "Interactive Party Ball Dance Mix" is basically a mirrored disco ball located on the center of the screen. Behind the ball is a funky background. The user can click on the top/bottom or left/right side of the ball. When the ball is clicked the music and background changes while the ball turns in the direction the user clicked. When it stops, a small video (usually about five to ten seconds) plays and then the user can click the ball to turn it again.

For the final version of the product we intended to include between sixteen to twenty-four videos, but for the first look demo, we included only five very rough video examples.

All of this content was burned to a CD 1-off and FedEx'd to the band members. The response came the next morning; they loved it, and we all breathed a sigh of relief. Even though you know you have created something of great beauty, it helps if the people paying you like it. In this case, we were very fortunate that what we had been thinking and building was nearly identical to what the band was looking for.

The response was so positive that Real McCoy agreed to expand the project. You see, during the course of building the prototype we realized that it would be a much stronger product if it had an overview which tied the various elements of the product together. We were lucky to have someone on our team who was very experienced at 3-D modeling and special effects creation. Previously, Nathan had won a variety of awards for his modeling skills and was anxious to create a 3-D club to house the various elements of the product.

So after sending a prototype, I contacted Robert and discussed the feasibility of expanding the project to include a 3-D environment. He and O-Jay were very receptive to the idea and after getting approval from the label, they agreed to increase the budget by 25 percent, and we started to build Club McCoy.

The inclusion of the club also had ramifications regarding the production time line. By this point we were getting close to August and a variety of elements needed for the production had been pushed back. This was neither good or bad, it simply was reality. One thing you learn when working with artists and labels is that release dates are fairly flexible and subject to change. In this case the album release date had been moved back, so the video and photo shoots were moved to late August; consequently, there was no way the product could be completed by August 23.

Once again Robert and I discussed the realities of deliverables for the project. The photo shoots were not going to take place until the second week of August and the video shoot was probably not taking place until mid-September. Therefore we agreed that the project was not due until after the final video edit was delivered towards the end of September. This would give us enough time to complete the club, party ball, moonscape, and video shell and simply wait for the new video to be the last element incorporated into the project. We told Robert that after having the final video we could deliver the completed project within a week to two weeks. This was acceptable to him and we all got back to work.

GETTING THE BAND INVOLVED

In my opinion this is one of the most important aspects of creating an interactive music title. When I worked with Aerosmith I actually got to sit down with the band members to help them design their rooms and incorporate their input into the overall project. It's this type of personal interaction with the band that is necessary to create a title that will resonate with its fans.

Here are a few things you should try to remember when working with the musicians.

Don't Get Intimidated

Granted these people may be some of your favorite musicians, but they are human and are usually as interested in your work as you are in theirs. After all, your project is an extension of them. Sure they may be rock stars, but it's not every day that someone offers them the opportunity to be creatively involved in designing an interactive experience about themselves.

Do Your Homework

It sounds incredibly simple, but I've seen people who didn't do this and consequently had a much more difficult time relating to the musicians and the project itself than was necessary. Watch the band's videos, listen to their albums, know their lyrics; this not only will help you understand the band's body of work, it will give you insight into their mindsets and personal characters.

Be Prepared
Interactive product design is outside the realm of experience of most musicians. Be prepared to provide the musicians with a general framework within which they can express themselves.

This is what we did with the Real McCoy design document. As you may have noticed, everything in the document is in stick figures. This was on purpose. We could have sent a design document filled with lots of flashy graphics, but that would have been limiting for the band. At that stage in the design process, I wanted the musicians to have the room to use their imaginations. In essence, we provided them with basic concepts for housing their content that we knew could be built within the boundaries of the budget.

We knew that we could build an interactive "Party Ball" as outlined in the document, but we wanted the band's input to breathe life into it. Our goal was to turn it into an interactive showcase piece which reflects the style and aesthetic of Real McCoy. We were very fortunate that O-Jay was an accomplished photographer and was willing to shoot the new video footage needed for this project himself.

The first thing O-Jay agreed to shoot was a "behind the scenes" piece of the video shoot for their next single. Adding this to the video viewing section offered the user a rare insight into the creative process behind a music video shoot. In addition to shooting the "behind the scenes" video, O-Jay agreed to shoot the footage needed for the moonscape and party ball sections.

It is interesting to note that the moonscape has changed direction and is now a "fan utility" instead of "history" section. This change occurred after having several conversations within the production team. One of the things that I had mentioned to Nathan and Sherri was that Robert had stated that the band's primary audience was twelve-to-sixteen-year-old girls. Sherri, our art director, had a very different take on the history section. She felt that teenage girls could care less about the band's first gig. Sixteen-year-old girls want to know if O-Jay has any pets or what his favorite color is. For me, this was a radical change in thinking. I'd never been a teenage girl, and quite frankly, I didn't feel anyone would care about a band member's favorite color. Guess what? I learned a powerful lesson.

When I discussed Sherri's concerns with the band, it turned out her instincts were right on. The band knew its target market and instead of creating a "history" section, decided that the focus should be a "fan utility" section. In this section, the user could now find out information about individual band members, rather than tracking the chronological history of the band. The band told me that the history information would be included on its Web site, and it wanted the Enhanced CD to give its fans something a little more fun. So for this section, we wrote up a list of questions to be posed to band members, and sent them to O-Jay to shoot.

For the party ball section, we discussed a variety of options ranging from graphic interpretations of the band's songs to showcasing the band members. For both technical and artistic reasons, we decided to go with the band members. We felt that this section provided the users the opportunity to get some face-to-face time with the band members in a fun and inviting format. When talking with O-Jay, we asked him to take his video camera with him backstage, in the studio, to parties, and whatever else he felt would showcase the band and its personalities.

In essence, we asked him to just have a good time and take his video camera along. We would be responsible for finding clips we needed from the raw footage. Before shooting, we gave him a couple of basic technical instructions, such as, when possible, shoot in front of a solid background which contrasts your subject's clothing, so we could add our own background graphics. What we really wanted was for O-Jay to go for it. We figured if he was having a good time shooting the footage it would come through in the final product.

TIPS

Music First
As much as we might wish it were different, people are currently not buying music-based multimedia products in large numbers. They are, however, buying CDs that happen to contain an interactive experience

but, as it has been in the past, the primary selling point is still the music. Therefore the resources of the artists and their labels are focused on the business of making and selling music. This means that the needs of an interactive production are often low priority items. They fall behind the music and video production scheduling, the tour planning, press releases, merchandise design, and a variety of other functions that happen for both the label and the bands.

As an interactive music producer, you must learn to work within the framework that is provided and try not to get frustrated. The best way to address this issue is to be very clear up front about content deliverables and the approval process. Emphasize that delays on the band's deliverables will cause production delays on your end. Enhanced CD production is a difficult business which is in a very early stage of development. Understanding, patience, and professionalism will go a long way toward helping you to achieve success.

Pre-Production

This is where I have seen many multimedia projects fall short. For Enhanced CDs, this step is even more critical since the budgets are not very large and the turnaround time for these projects is usually fairly short. With adequate preparations (i.e., storyboarding and scheduling) you can prevent your dream project from turning into a nightmare.

Don't Reinvent the Wheel

As I stated above, the budgets and time frames for these projects are usually not large enough to cover grandiose ideas. Unless you have adequate time and budget parameters, stay with concepts that you are confident can be completed.

To do this, you need to figure out new and interesting ways to present information which play to your development tool's strengths. The best example in the Real McCoy project is the party ball. On-screen, it's fun and different. But in reality, the programming is very simple and easily created with off-the-shelf development tools like Director without any special coding needed. Try to avoid the need to build your own production tools and code library because it is very expensive and time consuming.

You Are a Tool

This is sometimes a hard one to swallow, but it is the truth. People do not buy an Enhanced CD because of your technical skill in production. They buy it because they like the band and its music. Your job is to help the band create the best possible presentation of its music in an interactive format. So keep your eye on the prize and try to avoid gratuitous forays into the area of interactive wankdom.

Have Fun

Remember, you're building rock 'n' roll products. It's okay to be silly, strong, perverse, do the unexpected, or whatever you feel is necessary to get the band's message across. So have fun . . . crank it up and go for it.

—David Greene

chapter 5

enhanced cd:
marketing &
distribution

My philosophy about creating on the computer is that what you create has to bring you to its "world." In the scheme of things, the computer screen is not very big. I want to be able to capture you and bring you inside this world . . . make the screen become larger than life, just like a good movie.

—**Oded Noy** of Hot Angels

golden age to digital era

Citizens of the world are spending more time behind their computers than ever before. And youths—fourteen to thirty years of age—make up the majority of the core users. The fast-paced revolution in computer technology is often paralleled to the overly-optimistic Googie culture of the late fifties to early sixties—a time when far too many John Q. Citizens began spending more time in front of the television set than was thought to be wise. A lot of modern innovations spawned from the golden age of the boob tube—TV dinners, game shows, Pong, remote control devices—technogadgets which now play essential roles in our everyday lives.

There's a similar phenomenon taking place in the digital age. Lots of ordinary, intelligent people are spending hours and hours basking in the glow of their computer monitors. And, it's a phenomenon that's growing. Just think, a lot of the junk that is developed and broadcast to your televisions—sitcoms, quiz shows, soap operas—are being developed and broadcast to a computer screen near you.

For a long time now, the record companies have been struggling with the meaning of the interactive music experience. They are learning to listen and trust the younger generation of executives. The technology savvy ones have been burning senior executives' ears off about the magic of the Enhanced CDs. Through determination and the slow process of tentative trial and error, the record companies are getting a handle on how to produce and market Enhanced CDs.

"Enhanced CDs can be paralleled to the peace movement of the sixties," observes MCA's technical evangelist, Albhy Galuten. "Do they accomplish the objective at hand? That's your call."

The long-term objective of Enhanced CDs is to enlighten the populace about the integration of music and new technology. By the time people become aware, the war may be over. Will technology have evolved above and beyond? Doesn't matter. Enhanced CDs are an important interim step in the evolution between here and there.

When you went to buy an album in the sixties, you expected to buy a record with a cool album cover. After you bought an LP and put it on your turntable, you expected good production from the album and a record that didn't scratch too much. Back then, you listened to a twenty-minute side, flipped the record over and listened to the other side.

Today you expect to buy a CD that lasts anywhere between fifty and sixty minutes. If it's placed in a multiple-disc tray with other CDs, you can play music all day with one touch of the play button.

The biggest impact the Enhanced CD seems to have had to date is that it's breathing new life into the single. The CD-Single is a simple, low budget (often under $10,000) Enhanced CD that is created from a pre-designed template. Check out Hootie and the Blowfish's disc *Old Man & Me*, Natalie Merchant's *Wonder* or Junior Brown's *My Wife Thinks You're Dead*. You have the song, you have the video, bio, some photos, some interviews, some merchandising and *voila*, there you are. Simple, easy, effective.

"We think CD-Singles are a good way to get into this technology," notes Nikke Slight, the new media point person at Atlantic Records. "Inexpensive products that are done in a template design are a cost-efficient way to venture into this new area."

The Enhanced CD audience is a lot bigger than people think . . . and growing every moment. First, let's talk computers. Half of the U.S. population—110 million Americans—have access to a computer. More than half of those computers have CD-ROM drives. That's a potential market of 60 million people.

"How many people that used to open that album cover own computers? Maybe a lot," proffers Highway One's Leo Rossi. "How many people see the computer, not as a computer in their office, but as an entertainment piece in their house? The adult of tomorrow definitely does. The computer and the TV are one unit. But there's still this void of people who grew up with vinyl and CDs that see the computer as a work thing. They have to be urged to try it, and they have to have a good experience."

Let's look at the what's going to happen to the Enhanced CD market in the coming years. In the autumn of 1996, a half-dozen companies began marketing set top boxes, some of which will play CD-ROMs and offer Internet access—*bam*—a new market.

The customer base for Enhanced CD will soon be as large as the record buying public. The market is there, consumer awareness is not.

The major drawback to the mass acceptance of Enhanced CDs and CD-ROM is that music is a total social experience in both its creation and its enjoyment. Even when you listen to music by yourself, you feel like you're sharing it with a lot of other people. When you work on a computer, even if there's a room full of people looking at your monitor, you're alone. It's a singular experience. Making the lines cross between these two disciplines is the main issue as to whether music CD-ROMs are going to become a big financial thing or not. It's not a technological issue.

So, what is it going to take to establish Enhanced CDs as a viable business? Visionaries who can see the profit margins down the line. The record companies are not going to be able to cost justify an increase in spending just to make the consumer happy. Bottom line is profit. When Enhanced CD sales (combined with ancillary sales from merchandising and related products) become a profitable venture, the music business will embrace it with open arms. Until then, music entrepreneurs struggle and persevere.

a viable experience

Music delivered via a computer is a completely unique experience. Music is normally a very social experience—you listen with your friends at a club or while crashed out on a beanbag chair with a room full of so-cial outcasts like yourself—soaking in the latest MTV video.

A computer is different because it is a much more enclosed and personal environment. The screen is usually a lot smaller and the sound quality is not as good as television. You're sitting closer to the screen. The lighting is different. Social circumstances are different. It is a dif-ferent world of experience.

If you can create a CD-ROM that—from the first click of the mouse—transports the user into a world that enhances her understanding of music, you've accomplished the ultimate goal of an Enhanced CD producer.

"The goal or objective should be to give the consumer a one skew item that encompasses the things that they would be interested in, on one piece, for one price that's below the average CD-ROM price, and, allows the purchaser the option to view or not to view the additional content as well as get more information on an artist for very little more from her pocket," observes Deborah Anderson, New Media Market-ing manager for Island Records. "This product piece then serves three purposes: most importantly, selling the respective release. Secondly, providing direct additional promotional information that in some cases may never get the same viewership by traditional mediums. Third, it can assist in or may contribute to the result of an increase in ticket sales. But, it will take the cooperation and involvement of all the par-ticipating entities to make the Enhanced CD a simple, less-confusing, recognizable, and viable purchase for the consumer."

target buyers

This market is so young that no one really knows for sure who the tar-get audience is for Enhanced CDs.

"We have to identify who these people are and how they're look-ing at entertainment," states Tom McGrew. "How do they want to be entertained today? What turns them on? What turns them off? What motivates them?"

Those are all questions that are still to be answered. Titles are cur-rently being released with several demographic groups in mind. Projects by artists like the Rolling Stones, Yoko Ono, Bonnie Raitt, and Jackson Browne obviously appeal to the over twenty-five crowd, while discs from younger bands like Monster Magnet, Blues Traveller, and Soundgarden are targeted for a more teen-oriented market.

"There's a multiplicity of target markets, and that's the problem," confirms McGrew. "You have two markets—under twenty-five and over twenty-five—each looking for something completely different."

It will most probably be another year before it will really be defined. "There are no experts," confirms musician Todd Rundgren, who is redefining himself as an interactive artist. "There's still a lot of confusion, a lot of room left for definition. No one has made the killer app that defines the way artists will work in this particular medium in the future."

Trial and error, that's how the art form of Enhanced CD is being created. There is no forum or general agreed-upon consensus of what Enhanced CDs should be. There are only developer's concepts of what the form should be and where it is going.

old habits die hard

The major record labels have been hesitant to produce many Enhanced CD titles because there's a risk involved. Let's face it, the corporate world is full of lemmings. And, according to McGrew, "In the record industry, no one ever wants to be first. They're going to wait until the force is on, when they are being forced to do it."

Many of the standard ways the labels promote music don't work any more. For instance, take the singles model. First, labels released vinyl singles. Then it was the cassette single. Now it's the $3.49 CD single. The labels are using the same model that they used in 1952 to sell music. What is the justification in that? Market the way they did it twenty-five years ago? Forty years ago? Labels are using the model that they've always used because that's the model that they are used to—and nobody's forced them to change. Perhaps the Enhanced CD will change all that.

enhanced product sold as software

Software retailers have taken a somewhat different approach to the Enhanced CD product line. Since music titles are new for them, they've taken extra steps to ensure that Enhanced CD products are displayed in a way that will stand out from the rest of the products in the stores.

Software stores are finding that selling Enhanced CDs creates a window of opportunity for them to expand their product range. They've had buyers coming in for years who have mainly been buying productivity, entertainment, or business CD-ROMs and floppy discs. By setting up an Enhanced CD section within their entertainment department, software dealers can now cross over and capture a music buyer at the same time.

"When we distributed the Kitaro disc, we figured about 10 percent of the people actually bought it because it was an Enhanced CD," calculates Mike Gaffney, vice president and general manager of music for Navarre Corporation. Navarre is the leading wholesale distributor for Enhanced CDs in both the music and computer software retail worlds. "We figured that because we distributed the Kitaro disc not only into music stores (through our subsidiary, Digital Entertainment), but through computer software stores, we captured a lot more sales than we would have."

"Keep in mind that the Enhanced CD industry—actually the entire interactive title publishing business—is at an important and critical juncture," states Paul Palumbo, an author and consultant to the entertainment business. "The industry is—and will continue to be—volatile and subject to the same market forces as any other 'hits' driven business. Everybody agrees the 'hits' nature of the business is a clear driver behind the strong consolidation trend working through the market. An estimated 4 percent to 10 percent of the CD-ROM products are actually making a profit in any one year. Given that reality, creating a hit is important because, simply put, that's where the money is. Not only is this where the money is, but a successful title will go a long way toward guaranteeing a publisher a crack at locking up shelve space for the next title release. But it's also a catch-22 because the industry is not mature enough to predict with any degree of certainty which titles are going to be hits."

software store packaging

Software retailers didn't take to Enhanced CDs initially because many Enhanced CDs were packed in standard jewel boxes like their cousins, the audio CD. Software vendors were used to CD-ROMs and diskettes packaged in the spacious airbox. The benefits of the airbox are so people can pick up the package and marvel at the screenshots and examine the system requirements. A few years back, the music consumer rejected the extra cardboard that used to come wrapped around an audio CD. So there was definitely a difference of opinion going on between music and software CD consumers.

Packaging Enhanced CDs in two different types of packaging was rejected—too damn expensive. Enhanced CD products went into software stores with jewel box packages, but placed in their own special display. So, if you walk into your local software store, you'll find anything from the Rolling Stones to Dogstar to Kitaro in a self-contained display.

"It was pretty interesting because during the first major test that we did during the 1995 Christmas season in the Software Etc. and Babbages stores, the number one seller was Kitaro. The number two seller was Soundgarden," notes Gaffney.

The Prince Interactive CD-ROM, which was exclusively distributed by Compton's NewMedia, was sold in record stores, software chains, and all related retail outlets. The chain that sold the most per store was Office Depot. No record company has an account with Office Depot because the chain doesn't carry records. But that's an example of how Enhanced CDs need to be sold. You have to make the product available in a variety of non-conventional music outlets.

"We believe that you have to market these kinds of titles in many more kinds of outlets than record stores. They need to be marketed in software stores and online, in all kinds of outlets," notes new music evangelist Paul Atkinson. "One of the great potentials of this medium is the fact that it is software as well as being music, and therefore should be available in software stores, rather than sold exclusively via record stores."

What makes Enhanced CDs even more attractive to software distributors is that traditional CD-ROM titles have a short shelf life. Music product, on the other hand, has a far longer shelf life. The Beatles product has been on record shelves for more than thirty years, and Capitol Records is still selling more than $100 million worth of Beatles albums a year. The nice thing about the audio industry is that you can always reissue albums in the latest format—vinyl, 8-track, cassette, CD. Enhanced CDs will inevitably follow the music model.

enhanced product sold as music

Enhanced CDs are a bright and shiny new product—which means the consumer is clueless as to what it is. Music retailers don't necessarily know how to demonstrate a Hootie and the Blowfish Enhanced CD either. In many record stores, you'll find enhanced products buried in the bin under the artist's name. Unless it's specially marked, or you know the Enhanced CD title by name, you would hardly recognize that the product held in your hand was something quite unique and revolutionary.

For the time being, most record stores are treating Enhanced CDs like music titles. After all, they are audio CDs at their core. But when will the record industry and music retailers start treating Enhanced CD products as something different?

Five years ago, the trend in record stores was toward increased floor space. Superstores and megastores sprang up everywhere.

At the same time, the tastes of young consumers have changed. In the seventies and eighties, kids lived and died for music. They're not really into music like when we were younger. We listened to MTV and radio a lot more. Now, there are other things that will take a kid's attention away. If you play a game, you're not going to listen to music because you're concentrating on the game. Or if you're watching one of 157 channels, you're not going to listen to music. The consumer does what he wants to do, and the consumer's desire for music has shifted. Where is it shifting to? Nobody really knows yet . . . it's not the same as it was.

"I always look at the consumer, because the consumer holds the key," offers Tom McGrew. "Everything else is bullshit. Everyone thinks, 'We'll tell the consumer how to buy. We'll tell the consumer how to do this.' How many times have you ever been able to tell the consumer anything?"

People shop differently now. Today, the number one retailer in software/CD-ROM and in music is the same store. Two years ago, everybody would have said, "oh no, you're wrong," because the number one music company was Musicland and the number one in software was Software Etc. Well, Best Buy—the K-mart of the nineties—was number one in 1996. This is because it's offered more selection, and it's focused on music and promoting music. Plus it has the lowest prices on CDs at retail.

This paradigm shift came about because Best Buy's strategic marketing person noticed that everybody in the music business had increased floor space between 10 and 35 percent, and figured that music must be a rapidly growing industry. Best Buy immediately decided to carry music and to use it as the primary way to get customers into the store. It made its music sections look very good, and offered a lot of selection.

This has caused a crisis in record stores—and allowed for an industry shift. As there was a need to fill space, record stores started looking at independent distributors. Suddenly independent labels such as Trauma, Interscope, Epitaph, and Death Row were able to break into the major record stores. Now, independent releases account for 20 percent of record sales. It should also leave an open slot for enhanced product—as enhanced discs are selling better as music product.

"The Cranberries' *Doors and Windows* is available both ways. It's available in jewel box, it's available in software box. It sells better as a jewel box in a record store," reveals Ted Cohen of Philips Media. "It sells as a record product. It sells as a Cranberries product, it's a cool Enhanced CD. It's not selling as a computer product featuring the Cranberries. It's artist driven. It's music driven."

Q&A: mike gaffney

The leading distributor of Enhanced CD products into the consumer channel is the Navarre Corporation. The New Hope, Minnesota-based company is a wholesale distributor in both the music and computer software retail worlds. Mike Gaffney is vice president and general manager.

HOW DOES NAVARRE DECIDE WHAT TO DISTRIBUTE?

Mike Gaffney: We look at Enhanced CDs the same way we look at a straight-ahead music piece. If the label, and the artist, and the management of the band have created a compelling enough music piece, and the artist is available to be promoted and marketed—which would create a demand for that piece—then the enhancement is just adding extra quality for the consumers.

HOW FAR ALONG IN A DEVELOPMENT PROCESS DOES SOMETHING HAVE TO BE BEFORE YOU'LL SEE IT?

Mike Gaffney: It's very early on. Beta is fine. Beta stage is just like getting a test pressing of a music piece.

WHAT PROCESS WOULD INDEPENDENT DEVELOPERS GO THROUGH TO GET DISTRIBUTION THROUGH NAVARRE?

Mike Gaffney: They would have to make presentations to us. There's a difference to me between a developer and a publisher or a label. Developers, at that point, are strictly that, they're kind of like producers in a music studio. They aren't necessarily the ones who would want to become the record label or the software publisher.

HOW MANY LABELS DO YOU WORK WITH?

Mike Gaffney: We have a very limited line-up of labels. We're only working with forty to fifty labels at any given time. A lot of other music distributors who work with independent labels are working with 300, 400, 500 of them. Because of our elite clientele, I take the presentations based upon what type of personnel they have at their labels, and what they know about this industry. What kind of access they have into publicity and marketing and touring and radio and video? I want to know about all the different things that create a demand for a music entertainer. And so I look at them one by one in that way.

WOULD YOU BE LIKELY TO GET MORE EXCITED ABOUT ENHANCED DISC OR AN AUDIO DISC ON AN UNKNOWN BAND?

Mike Gaffney: It would excite me more if I saw something that was coming to me enhanced because it just means to me that those people have put that much more into that artist. Enhancements are something that they feel are going to make the artist more recognizable or more accessible to the consumers, to the fans. But, that's not the only thing that's important. If the label has the ability to market that artist and create a demand for them, that's what I look at first. Plenty of great music comes across my desk, enhanced and not enhanced, but if I don't feel like the personnel at the label have done enough work, or gained enough knowledge as to how to really create that demand for those artists, then I either send them in another direction for distribution, or I nurture them along with what they need to learn.

I like projects that are well thought-out in the front end. If they understand what kind of distribution system we are compared to WEA or Priority Records, if they've done that kind of background work, that means to me that they're really in touch with their project and what they're doing. That excites me.

pricing

Another of the big glitches in the rise of the Enhanced CD market is: What are these things going to cost? Nobody quite knows. Right now they're experimenting with Enhanced singles, CD-5s and two-sku album products, but no market leader has emerged.

"They should be the same price, there shouldn't be two-sku," states REV Entertainment's Todd Fearn. "It costs more to produce this than it does an audio disc, but not that much more. You just have to keep the budgets down."

Enhanced CDs should be on full-length albums, space permitting.

After all, you've got a captive audience—fans of the band who purchased the CD in the first place. If you've sold them one thing, you can probably sell them more. What is this captive audience worth? Do you charge them more? How much more will they pay? Do you have to release it simultaneously?

"If you don't charge more for the enhanced part, it has no perceived value," notes Bruce Hartley, senior director of new media for Mercury Records.

"My real feel on this business right now is from talking with some of the retailers," observes Highway One's Leo Rossi. "I don't think people accept an enhanced product that is $19.95, it has to sort of be transparent. If you're going to go buy an enhanced record, it should be maybe fifty cents, a dollar increase."

"CDs are already expensive enough," counters Hartley. There in a nutshell is the glitch in the Enhanced CD market. What is the answer? CD-5?

"Bonnie Raitt could have established the market if her enhanced disc took off. Here you have a major star and the price point is $5.99," observes McGrew. "Price points on enhanced products need to be between $5.99 and a regular record price."

McGrew's model of this industry has record companies making money in the long term, if Enhanced CDs sell units.

"It's another reason for someone to buy it if there's something really cool on it, or if there's a built-in hook into a Web site, or if there's another way of making money," McGrew offers.

new marketing opportunities

There's one particular scenario that has captured the music industry's attention: a CD-ROM owner buys an Enhanced CD version of a previously released album because of the addition of an unseen video, a special backstage glimpse of the artist, or a new creative treatment only available on the interactive music disc. This attraction will help stimulate back catalog sales. Many of the labels' marketing elements, like music videos, will get a second life. Sounds beautiful, doesn't it?

For an industry getting its legs, you'll need a mixture of patience and perseverance. Rereleases of popular albums by bands such as the The Doors and Elvis Presley and "best of" compilations in the Enhanced CD format are soon to come. If you're looking for clients, you'll get your best results from categories of artists likely to get funding for Enhanced CD.

Established artists who release albums over a long period of time are sometimes referred to as catalog or "career" artists. These artists have existing assets, such as concert footage, photographs, lyric sheets, and a catalog of albums that continue to sell to a group of dedicated fans. Pink Floyd, Kiss, Fleetwood Mac, and Metallica are members of this eclectic group.

Let's not forget that the video game audience and the new music audience are closely linked. Younger music fans are computer savvy and see the computer as a toy as opposed to a work tool. These younger fans have multimedia capable computers and want to learn more about their favorite artists. So keep an eye on the breaking bands getting a push from their labels. Know what bands are on schedule, what's up for release. If their last record was on MTV's Buzz Bin and on the radio, pay attention.

Enhanced CDs are currently an underground movement, and the record companies are looking for some guidance and direction. Early enhanced titles by groups like Monster Magnet and Two Minute Hate were not necessarily stickered as enhanced product. You had to hear that the CD was enhanced and then check it out. Now, as product hits Alpha phase, companies are starting to think about marketing ideas for these products. Ways of getting the word out on Enhanced CDs include demos for magazines and giveaways for retail. As the disc goes through Alpha testing, a marketable version can be developed, so by the time the development company is Beta ready, you can hit the magazines—particularly the interactive ones—and the stores and the giveaways.

The key to establishing Enhanced CDs as a viable industry is all cross-promotion and marketing. As with all music, you need to build interest in the artists. Enhanced CDs, in conjunction with an Internet setup, are a relatively inexpensive way to target the core audience and expand their perception of the artist.

This expanded perception could be exposing the fan to new music.

For example, if you like Elton John, you'll probably enjoy Joshua Kadison. If they were on the same label, you could offer a Kadison song sample on the Elton enhanced, and maybe the Elton John enhanced product will sell units for Joshua Kadison. Cover the cost of Elton John new tech marketing campaign by having a Web site tie in and selling links to products Elton endorses like Diet Coke, Gianni Versace. Sell back catalog and merchandising to benefit The Elton John AIDS foundation.

Like album costs, with a little creativity new tech marketing costs are recoupable, even profit-making. The hurdle is to get the bureaucratic dinosaur record companies to expand their corporate philosophies and make the commitment to making this new industry work.

part two

internet music

chapter 6

internet music:
it's the content, stupid

Music produces a kind of pleasure which human nature cannot do without.

—Confucius

wiring the planet

Once upon a time, a couple of highly competent technophiles at the European Particle Physics Laboratory (CERN), saw the need for a tool that would help interconnect teams of international physicists. A primitive form of what we now call the World Wide Web hatched from a simple hypertext program, which was later expanded and posted for the Internet community to test, deconstruct, and improve.

Hypertext and hyperlink are terms used to describe the ability of the user to explore and create his own path through an environment. Buttons, text links, and graphic icons are common hypermedia which appear on Web pages. Organizational characteristics of most media we are familiar with—books, feature films, plays—are meant to be experienced linearly. From page one of your favorite novel to its last page, from the opening screen of a blockbuster movie to its closing credits, linear organization has a definite beginning, middle, and end. Its stories and messages are designed specifically to play off of its linear structure. Hypermedia, on the other hand, is different. It's the secret ether which fuels our addiction to the Web because it's a dynamic approach to organization—functioning simultaneously as a touch screen table of contents, footnote finder, information microscope, research tool, electronic encyclopedia, twenty-four-hour storefront, broadcast network, and a worldwide distribution system—all at the touch of a finger.

"There have been a lot of artists, writers in particular, who over the past two generations have been trying to figure out how to break the confines of a book—a book starts on page one and goes to the end," explains writer/designer Douglas Gayeton. "If those people were starting now, they would be doing interactive. Because, interactivity is all based upon the principle of non-linear thought. And that is the way we think. I could talk to you and never finish a sentence—or finish an idea—because our minds are like that. And I think that's why people have gravitated toward interactivity. Not because it's a fad, but because it really captures the dimensionality of thought. Thought is not a linear process. It's a multi-plane, multi-dimensional process. And an experience that allows you to assimilate and capture the essence of how our thinking processes work is a tremendously fascinating and exciting thing."

Hyperlinks are really HTML (Hypertext Markup Language) codes whose job it is to find things for you. When you click a hyperlink, you're really telling your browser (Netscape Navigator, Microsoft Internet Explorer) to go find a resource, Web site, or run an application. The browser knows exactly where to go by following a hyperlink's URL (Uniform Resource Locator) which functions like a telephone number, then interpreting your request using a protocol called HTTP (Hypertext Transfer Protocol). When you type "*http://*" into your Web browser's locator, it's as if you were dialing a worldwide area code.

How does the Web work? In simple terms, the Web is made up of several components, all working together in global harmony (well, most of the time). They are:

- Web Servers

- Content

- Hyperlinks between Content

- Web Browsers

Web servers are basically the individual computer systems interconnected to the Internet. Content is better known as the text, images, music, and other resources you place on your server. Hyperlinks connect one piece of content to another, and Web browsers interpret and display the content on your computer screen. Simple, right?

content in context

Now that you are wired to the rest of the world, it's time to talk about the kind of content that people are creating. Everywhere you turn, everybody is talking about this great Web site or that lousy site. Music artists, developers, writers, record execs, music fans, teachers, school kids—you name it—are all creating Web experiences to showcase their creativity or business savvy.

"A Web site should be fun, inviting, something you want go back to again and again. But not too commercial," states Charles Como, who has a virtual monopoly on the entertainment promotion Web site market. Como and his company, underground.net, have created sites for artists such as Megadeth, Van Halen, The Beatles, Duran Duran, White Zombie, Monster Magnet, the Lollapalooza festival, Seal, Adam Ant, Lenny Kravitz, Andrew Lloyd Webber, and Steely Dan—among others.

A few years back, underground.net's Megadeth site for Capitol Records (*www.bazaar.com*) walked away with the gold medal from *New Media* magazine's InVision Awards for best site on the Internet. The unique feature of the now-defunct Megadeth site was an electronic postcard service. "I found three or four programs that were freely distributed," Como explains, "and put them all together in such a way that when a user typed something, we merged it with a graphic image then mailed the custom postcard to a friend."

Web experiences vary dramatically in theme, presentation, material, graphic design, and functionality. Some sites are created by amateurs in their free time—loyal music fans paying homage to their favorite artists. These content creators are not "in it for the money." Rather, it's a way for them to express their feelings toward a musician or band while communicating with others who share a common interest. In a best case scenario, the site is endorsed by the artist or record label (either officially or unofficially) and is well promoted—resulting in thousands of home page impressions. Such a site is now much more than one fan's form of expression. It's a marketing and research tool as well.

"Most of the record labels realized early on that this was going to have a major effect on their business," explains new media evangelist John Bates, "I think it's smart for people like Susan Mainzer to encourage the development of hundreds of 'fan' sites on the Internet. As a PR person from a major label like Island Records, that is a very cool strategy for her."

Perhaps more important than marketing, such "fanzines" provide a rare glimpse into the mindset of the music fan—their likes, dislikes, concerns, and desires. It provides valuable customer feedback and research at a primal level.

Other Web sites are created by experienced designers, business entrepreneurs and record labels—mixing music, commerce, or a bit of both. Of course, the amount of energy, time, and money that will be pumped into a Web site depends heavily on what the site is being designed for. Is it a personal Web site, corporate image site, broadcast center, or content distribution site?

points of interest

There are literally thousands of music-themed Web sites available over the Internet. Each site has its good points and bad. But they are all free to explore. Here are a few "must see" sites you should visit as soon as you get the chance. You'll notice that each location has its own unique approach to "interactive music."

IUMA

The Internet Underground Music Archive (*www.iuma.com*) is a platform for independent bands and artists to share their music with the world. One of the oldest music-oriented Web sites still in operation, IUMA sidesteps the traditional channels of distribution and goes directly to the end user.

IUMA has established a formidable online presence; there are now approximately 350 thousand people visiting the IUMA site per day. A pretty amazing feat considering the site grew out of one band's need to be heard.

"IUMA President Jeff Patterson and I had a band called The Ugly Mugs and we had a hard time getting our music heard," claims Danny Johnson, creative director for IUMA. "Like other up-and-coming bands, we had trouble booking shows. The IUMA Web site was our way of showcasing our band. Over time, it grew into the wonderful monster it is today."

The IUMA site now has major corporate sponsors such as Levi's, Honda, and Intel, and strategic alliances with service firms such as the compact disc production house Discmakers.

The IUMA site helps create a buzz about a band's music. Bands like Tabula and Creed write testimonial letters about how having an online presence has given them valuable exposure.

"IUMA was fairly small when we joined in," shares Oded Noy of Hot Angels Multimedia. "I sent them a picture, I sent them a thing that I wanted for a button, I sent them all the text, and I sent them a DAT and they converted all the stuff. They did all the layout and put three of our songs up. We decided we were going to go with their maximum rate with everything. It was like $125 and we said that's worth it."

Today, it costs $240 to put one song up on the IUMA site. It's a simple process. Just call (800) 850-4862 and they'll give you all the details. You can have your own personal band promotion up and running within minutes.

Though not everyone gets signed with a record label after appearing on the site, you do get feedback from all over the world.

"IUMA is the kind of place you get exposure. Even today, I still get responses," confirms Oded. "There was this guy, Massimo, from Italian radio . . . he had his own show about American music. He downloaded a song and he really liked it. We went back and forth like six or seven times. In the end, he asked for a tape and he put the song on the radio a couple of times. He wrote back that people liked it. That was a very satisfying experience."

iMUSIC

Taking a completely different approach, iMusic (*www.imusic.com*) is a news, information, and sampling site for music lovers. The site offers various sections of interest: *Music News*—this section links visitors to hundreds of music news sites available on the Internet; *Artist Showcase*—used to profile cutting-edge bands; *Chat Rooms*—a meeting place for music enthusiasts; *iMusic Features*—a module aimed at club music and concert fans into bands like Chemical Brothers, No Doubt, Leftfield, and Prodigy—users can sample live musical performances and archived events broadcast from around the globe; *Radio Stations*—this is a music sampling area broken down by music category—users can listen to and vote on their all-time favorite songs; *CD Reviews*—this section does exactly what is says—it reviews CDs; *Bulletin Boards*—this area of the site links users to a huge list of categorized bulletin boards available online; and finally, *iMusic Store*—this is where users sample and purchase their favorite CDs.

BILLBOARDLIVE

Billboardlive (*www.billboardlive.com*) takes another approach. The site is a virtual environment which mimics the look and flavor of an actual Billboard live entertainment complex. If you're a fan of author Neal Stephenson, imagine Billboardlive as the music version of the avatar nightclub, The Black Sun, a key location in Stephenson's novel, *Snow Crash*. Billboardlive is an online destination—a virtual music club where visitors can sample an electronic restaurant menu or grab front row seats to an online performance of their favorite band at the click of a mouse.

EMUSIC

Emusic (*www.emusic.com*) is an online music catalog (similar in look and feel to CDNow). When the site first opened a few years ago, it proudly proclaimed that it was "the fastest, easiest, and most enjoyable way to browse the world of music today."

Site explorers of today qualify for discount prices on over 100 thousand music titles which can be purchased via secure electronic transactions with quick delivery. Many of the albums profiled on the site contain cover graphics and audio clips. There is even a chat room for visitors to meet other like-minded music fans.

CDNOW

CDNow (*www.cdnow.com*) is a music emporium designed as a convenient way for music lovers to search for, sample, and order music titles online.

REALNETWORKS

RealNetworks, Inc. (*www.real.com*) develops and markets software products and services designed to enable users of personal computers and other digital devices to send and receive real-time media using today's online infrastructure. RealNetworks' RealAudio system is a client-server based streaming media delivery system for the Internet. With the RealAudio Encoder and Server, providers of news, entertainment, sports, and business content can create and deliver audio-based streaming multimedia content through the Internet.

With the RealPlayer, users equipped with conventional multimedia personal computers, voice-grade telephone lines, and higher bandwidths can browse, select, and play back streaming multimedia on-demand, in real-time without download delays, as quickly and easily as using a standard cassette player/recorder. The RealPlayer, RealPlayer Plus, and RealAudio Encoder are available for download from the RealAudio Web site (*www.real.com*).

Since the introduction of the RealAudio system in April of 1995, over 10 million Players have been distributed including 8 million from the RealAudio Web site (which averages over 40 thousand downloads daily).

THE DJ

TheDJ web site is a new type of Internet "radio station" streaming over sixty continuous uninterrupted channels of music over the World Wide Web. Licensed by both BMI and ASCAP, our goal is to make TheDJ the most popular source of music on the Internet.

TheDJ (www.thdj.com) is a subsidiary of Terraflex Data Systems, Inc. Since its inception in March 1996, TheDJ provides an exciting alternative to traditional radio broadcasting, effectively revolutionizing the radio experience through the quality and diversity of musical content.

For instance, TheDJ Web Radio allows users to listen to music through their Web browsers. The Radio has ten customizable pre-sets, a "Rate This Song" feature, and a "Buy This CD!" link, allowing listeners to purchase the music currently being broadcast. To listen via TheDJ Web Radio, users must have Netscape 3.0 or Internet Explorer 3.0. Additionally, listeners must have RealAudio 3.0, a 28.8k Internet connection or better, and a multimedia computer.

ADDICTED TO NOISE

The online "zine" Addicted to Noise (*www.addict.com*) is one of the most popular contemporary music news and information sites on the Web today. Addicted to Noise editor Michael Goldberg is a former *Rolling Stone* editor. The site looks and feels like an online magazine but functions like an interactive resource center.

TUNES NETWORK

Tunes Network (*www.tunes.com*) is building what it hopes will be the Web's most comprehensive music backbone that allows users to intelligently discover, preview, and purchase music. The company has developed the music discovery technology, extensive content partnerships and cutting-edge infrastructure to make available more than one million song clips, personal recommendations, music communities, and online purchasing to the thousands of Web sites visited by millions of users.

Through its award-winning Web site and its network of affiliates, the company offers consumers free access to the world's largest body of rich, interactive music content, a large selection of music products (currently over 250 thousand), convenient online shopping, and the most advanced set of features, including an artist notification service, personal recommendations, intelligent music communities, and personalized music programming.

Existing Web sites can become a Tunes Network Affiliate and can gain access to the world's largest library of licensed music content and technology. Affiliates are thus able to focus on enriching and differentiating their sites instead of investing in technology and managing audio encoding and database projects. Furthermore, they can immediately generate incremental revenues by offering on-site purchases of music and highly-targeted advertising.

SONICNET

Under the Paradigm Entertainment Group banner, SonicNet (*www.sonicnet.com*), the ultra-hip music "event site" that specializes in live online music events, recently teamed up with sister news site Addicted to Noise to form a powerful new music community.

AUDIONET

AudioNet (*www.audionet.com*) is a network and distributor of audio content over the Internet. In a distributor role, AudioNet contracts with content providers on a "fee" basis, starting at $5,000 per event. Events often include alternative music concerts, but also shows by established artists and institutions interested in the medium (i.e., jazz artist Winton Marsallis, and organizations such as the 4th Annual Country Music Radio Awards). Event programming, music concerts, shows or other audio programming are the network's broadcast specialties. Recent AudioNet sites such as *Policescanner.com* (police chatter) and *deadradio.com* (music of The Grateful Dead) are both scheduled to be twenty-four-hours-per-day programming areas.

AudioNet has an impressive list of entertainment partners which include multiple independent record labels, independent artists, 100+ radio stations, E! Online, VDONet, @Home Network, WebTV, Vxtreme, RealNetworks, Lifetime Television, independent celebrity chat show hosts, Microsoft, Intel, NFL, NCAA, NHL, MLB, etc.

AudioNet pays fees to BMI and ASCAP for the right to broadcast music programming, and all SonicNet's affiliate radio stations are available on a 24/7 basis.

@HOME NETWORK

@Home Network (*www.home.net*) is a broadband distribution network with music-enabled programming as its areas of emphasis. TCI, Cox Cable Communications, Intermedia, and Comcast are currently @Home residential market affiliates. Combined, these Multiple System Operators

(MSO) pass about 40 percent of U.S. TV households, but the service is only available in eight markets and has a relatively low installed base. The network has been architected to accommodate about 10 million customers.

There is an opportunity for digital music producers to syndicate Web-based programming with @Home Network according to Charles Moldow, director of media development. @Home is a discrete platform adjoining, but separate from, the Internet. Similar to WebTV, the uniqueness of the platform appears to open the door for incremental distribution and program syndication. Beyond an introductory package containing management bios, a working demo, development plan, and budget, @Home is looking for producers who understand how to leverage the "value" of its network (i.e., speed) into a more multimedia-rich experience.

Current @Home entertainment partners include 3DO, AudioNet, Digital Planet, Discovery Channel Online, E! Online, Film.com, Inc., Gamepen, Hollywood Online, Net Noir, Riddler.com, SegaSoft, Spot Media Communications, and Women's Wire.

JAMTV

JAMTV (*www.jamtv.com*) founded by midwestern concert promoter Jam Productions, is essentially a network of radio affiliates that offer exclusive concert webcasts. The site offers daily news, discographies, and video clips.

The company's strategic partners include Microsoft, BackWeb, RealNetworks, Intel, Ticketmaster, iChat, Pollstar, and CDNow.

According to JAMTV CEO Howard Tullman, print magazine giant *Rolling Stone* has acquired a stake in its online music venture and the new affiliation will jointly create *rollingstone.com*, which they hope will eventually blossom into the ultimate online source for music lovers.

MUSIC BOULEVARD

Music Boulevard (*www.musicblvd.com*) claims that it is the ultimate online music experience. Owned by New York's N2K, Inc., Music Boulevard is stocked with over 200 thousand CDs and cassettes spanning every music genre: rock, country, jazz, hip-hop, folk, classical, dance, and more. Music fans can quickly and easily browse through the site's massive online catalog by music type, or search for their favorite recordings by album name, artist, or even song title. To help consumers make educated purchasing decisions, Music Boulevard contains artist biographies and discographies, album reviews, magazine articles, cover artwork, as well as the Internet's largest selection of audio sound samples.

Site visitors can also check out who's topping the Billboard Magazine charts as well as Music Boulevard's own proprietary charts. Reviews from publications such as *SPIN*, *Fanfare*, *Dirty Linen*, and *Puncture* are also available through the site. Music Boulevard is also the exclusive music store for MTV and VH-1.

RITCHIEBLACKMORE.COM

Ritchie Blackmore is one of the seminal heavy metal guitar players of our time. He was a founding member of Deep Purple and Rainbow, two of the most influential music groups of the 1970s. As a musical artist, Ritchie has written such classic songs as "Smoke on the Water" and "Highway Star."

In 1996, one of Ritchie's fans created a Web site devoted to the artist, his fans, and his music. His unofficial shrine to Ritchie became so popular with music fans that the original webmaster could no longer find the time to properly manage the site. In early 1997, Ritchie Blackmore's management company contacted new media producer David Greene of Creative Spark and asked him to revamp and manage the site (which has now become *www.ritchie blackmore.com*). The all new Ritchie

Blackmore site now averages over 250 thousand hits per month. Pretty impressive for something that started out as someone's hobby.

You might be asking yourself why a rock 'n' roll guitarist feels the need to promote and maintain an official Web site.

"Ritchie's site serves many purposes," claims the site's producer David Greene. "It's a great way to maintain contact will the fans, disseminate information on upcoming events, and it allows the fans to get a little closer to the artist."

The success of *www.ritchieblackmore.com* is no accident. Many hours of hard work and dedication to the "fan experience" is perhaps the secret to the site's growing popularity in cyberspace. The sites strong look and feel, its functionality, as well as underlying structure, makes the surfing experience simple to navigate.

"There are several areas on the Web site that have become quite popular," asserts Greene. "One section promotes 'Blackmore's Night,' Ritchie's new medieval acoustic band that he formed with his long-time partner Candice. Ritchie and Candice have opened up their personal photo album and posted never-before-seen photographs online, with personal commentary from Ritchie. Another area of the Web site that has grown really popular is the 'Post Cards from the Road' section. The band is currently on tour in Europe, having just wrapped their Japanese tour. They have been sending me postcards from all the locations of their tour which I then scan and place on the site. We've found it to be an inexpensive way for the band members to add their personal touch to their Web site without having to spend a lot of time on it. After all they are in the middle of a world tour. This way fans can sort of vicariously live life on the road with the band through the Web site. Another key section of the site is an on-line fan club where we disseminate time-sensitive information to our core visitors. Right now, we have over one thousand fans signed up on our mailing list."

The great thing about a Web site such as *ritchieblackmore.com* is that the site itself serves as both an entertainment destination for fans and marketing and communication tool for the band.

"Recently, we announced a private concert through the Web site and fan club mailing list," tells Greene. "The free show was essentially an open rehearsal to showcase the bands new music in front of a live audience before they began the Japanese leg of the Blackmore's Night world tour. The show was booked solid within twelve hours. With only four days advance notice, loyal fans arrived for the exclusive Long Island show from as far away as Atlanta and Chicago. It was amazing. We even ended up posting photos and reviews of the show from fans who attended."

As part of a larger, more comprehensive strategic partnership, Ritchie's Web site is currently sponsored by ENGL, a German manufacturer of amplifiers. The band also uses its site for on-line commerce by selling a video companion to the new *Blackmore's Night* album directly from the site. At the present time, phase two of Web site's evolution is open to discussion.

"We are currently in discussions about adding a number of new media elements to enhance the site. Everything from on-line audio/video sampling to a complete merchandising section. The site may even evolve into two sister sites—one a low bandwidth experience and the other a fully functional Shockwave showcase with streaming audio, streaming video . . . the whole nine yards. But nothing has been decided on as yet."

testing the waters

Now that you have a basic understanding of the Web, how it functions, and what some Web sites are doing, it's time to ask yourself whether your great idea for an Internet project merits an interactive format. Not all ideas are original. You may think that your hot new Web site concept is a one-of-a-kind stroke of genius, but how do you know for sure you have something nobody else is doing already?

If you have what you believe to be an original premise for an interactive music project, the first thing you should do before you dive into production is research the market. Identify the genre, interface methodology, structure, and points of interest found on existing Web sites to identify how your idea compares. Read every Internet-related magazine, surf and search the Net, visit trade shows, talk to others working in the field—whatever guerrilla sleuth techniques are at your disposal. Keep in mind one important reality—no idea is truly original. Chances are, the seeds of your premise have been dreamed up before by someone else. Your goal, therefore, is simple. To create an original way to express and experience your idea.

What if you're designing an interactive music Web site for someone else—as in a work-for-hire for a client, for instance? Well, a writing and design skill set is an obvious must. Good organization skills, communications skills, and a background in HTML programming would be nice.

What key questions should be asked of prospective clients before you begin? We posed this question to John Bates. Here's his advice:

- Why do you want a Web site?

- What do you hope to accomplish?

- What is your budget and your commitment to ongoing maintenance?

- How far up the chain is this greenlighted? What departments still need to sign off and what departments are already gung ho?

- What is your position in terms of the legalities? What can you include on the site and do you have permission to use the content?

- Who are your strategic business partners?

Once you and your client understand the depth and focus of the project, you'll need to hammer out an agreement. Once you have a deal worked out, you may want to create a design proposal, a document outlining the details of the project (see chapter 3). Design proposals are used by content creators to ensure that the production team and the client are both speaking the same language. Sign offs are built into every milestone to streamline the design and development process.

"Each stage of the production process must be approved by the client before you move on the next stage," claims designer Dennis Archambault. "That way, the client knows exactly what they'll be getting. It's also insurance for the content creator. If a client isn't happy with something, you can always point to a signature and say, 'So-and-so approved this on such-and-such a date.'"

Even after your design proposal has been approved, you're not necessarily on the road to production. "It's in the nature of the client that once you think you have a final, the next level up says, 'Why don't you let me see it?' The next thing you know, you don't have a final anymore," adds Archambault.

site design tips

Here are some tips for designing a dynamic and compelling Web site. Obviously, there are no hard and fast rules to live by. They're simply guidelines to consider.

BEFORE YOU BEGIN

- Decide on major topics for the home page.

- Create a flow chart showing user movement through your site.

- Collect graphics, text, and music. Log all file names, file sizes, and formats for quick reference later.

DOES YOUR CONTENT MERIT AN INTERACTIVE FORMAT?

- Just because you can, that doesn't mean you should.

- Can your idea/message/story be better expressed in another medium?

- Does your content have a preexisting audience?

- What new features will be added to enhance your content?

- If your concept is so amazing, why isn't someone else already doing it?

IDENTIFY CLIENT NEEDS/YOUR NEEDS

- For a personal Web site, your content is limited only by your skill set and your tenacity.

- As a work-for-hire content creator, your writing and design skills must meet the needs of your client.

- There are several questions you may want to ask your client:
  - Do you prefer a specific style of interactivity?
  - Do you wish to implement specific tools / software?
  - Can I see examples of design styles you like?
  - What time frame do I have to work with?
  - What are your budget parameters?
  - Are you committed to maintaining your site?
  - What do you expect from me?
  - What do you expect from my work?

IDENTIFY YOUR GENRE AND AUDIENCE

- Genre will effect the look, style, and tone of your project.

- Investigate sites which target similar demographics. What's being created and why?

- What is the actual size of your market? What is its potential size? Why is this genre successful?

IDENTIFY YOUR COMPETITION

- Identify competitive sites that have won awards or get lots of traffic.

- Market research saves time and cash.

- Embrace your enemy . . . don't reinvent the wheel. What are the most compelling elements of your competitor's Web site? How can you improve on its model?

THE WEB'S COMPELLING DESIGN FEATURES

- The ability to view text in various styles.

- The ability to present graphics on the same page as text.

- The ability to embed within a flow module (Web page), connections to other flow modules, or connections to other parts of the same flow module.

OPTIMIZING YOUR SITE

- Your nameplate/banner should pull the visitor into your site.

- A strong, visually effective nameplate calls attention to your site (subtle or not).

- Your nameplate should trigger something emotional/visceral in the visitor that will inspire them to respond.

- It displays your "spark of imagination" that created that strong graphic.

- It contains that all important "hook" that turns your visitor into a regular, returning client.

- Research shows that approximately 90 percent of Web surfers only visit a Web site's home page, rarely venturing into the site.

- Icons or other content indicators should be easy to identify and point visitors directly to the information they may need.

- Placement of nameplates/logos is an important strategy . . . a visually stunning "first impression" or a practical, "search engine friendly" design incorporating a nameplate with text and other icons.

- Create a modal interface.

- Optimize download time. Large graphics or animations with slow download times may frustrate visitors and impede return visits.

- Provide localized versions when possible.

- Avoid language/symbols that could be deemed sexist or ethnically biased (unless that's the intent of your material).

UNDERSTAND WEB COPY

- Web site copy is different from copy used in traditional print media.

- As hypertext, Web site copy becomes interactive.

- Part of the reason for hypertext is to allow the user to bypass material they are not interested in and go directly to what they want.

- Good copy is dramatic copy.

- Compelling copy pulls your reader into the content.

- Commercial copy integrates a sense of marketing strategy.

- Textures may distract from the copy. Experiment with colors and textures before posting your content.

WEB IMAGES

- Web site images differ from images in traditional print media.

- Images are more memorable than text.

- Appropriate images can reduce cultural and language barriers.

■ Images communicate a great deal of information quickly.

■ Images can be ambiguous, communicating unintended meanings.

■ Poor images may distract from the message.

■ Professional image design requires specialized technical knowledge.

DOWNLOADABLE VERSUS STREAMED AUDIO

■ Decide whether you should use audio on your Web site. If you choose to use audio, decide what kind of audio experience you want your listeners to experience before you begin.

■ You'll need to acquire a sound source—create it yourself or license it from an authorized reseller. Then you'll need to prepare the sound source for Web delivery or Web broadcast. Finally, you'll need to integrate the sound into the code of your Web site.

■ Downloadable audio is the easiest to set up—the sound file is archived on your server and a listener must click an icon to have the audio file transferred to her system. Listeners cannot experience a "live" audio feed and must sometimes wait a while for the file to download.

■ Streamed audio refers to a stream of uninterrupted audio. Listeners experience a Web site's streamed audio much like a radio broadcast, using one of several audio players on the market (RealAudio, ToolVox, Shockwave, SoundStream, etc). The advantage of streamed audio is that listeners experience streamed audio instantly, making it ideal for background music.

chapter 7

internet music:
blending art and commerce

The music industry realizes how much new technology can help it because they've seen that help in the past. What compact discs did for the music industry was absoultely open it up; made it grow. The World Wide Web is doing the same.

—**John Bates**

the bleeding edge

Back before the compact disc hit the market in the early eighties, the digital master recording of any album would be converted to a vinyl disc and pressed like any other vinyl record. The record companies weren't that interested in moving into CDs, as they already had vinyl pressing plants and all the machinery necessary to make records. Finally, when the labels realized that music and technology converged, and there was no other way to go, they made the transition from vinyl to CD.

Now, the World Wide Web represents new renewal and growth for the music industry. The facts are all there, laid out clearly in numbers and statistics. The demographics for Web users are very close to those of the music buying public. In January 1996, it was estimated that there were 15 million Americans on the World Wide Web (6.4 million households) and perhaps 30 million people connected worldwide. That figure looks to grow to 40–50 million in 1997. The average Web browser is thirty-two years old, and there's a 75 percent chance that he's male . . . a very close skew to the average record buyer, and even closer to the average musician. How many technophiles do you know who play instruments? More than half, right? Studies indicate that there is a 70 percent crossover between music fans and megabyte men. (As an entertaining aside, Internet studies show that Web wenches persevere on sites longer than byte boys. Guys like to channel surf.)

Wascally Wabbits on the World Wide Web and music fans like to be on the cutting edge. (Or is that the bleeding edge?) Makes sense. Music people are early adapters. There may be as many music sites on the Web as there are sites in any other category.

"Look at the number of sites clustered around a particular topic on the Web; sex is number one, but nobody talks about that. Number two is music. Just in sheer numbers of sites, it makes you realize that music is playing a big part in what's going on in the Internet," confirms John Bates. "Music drives Internet technology. People are working on streaming audio and streaming video to deliver music across the Internet."

"There's this thought process where people think that the Internet has become the most important thing to the music business," observes Capitol Record's Liz Heller. "In actual fact, music is the most important thing on the Internet. The demographics of the Internet users are very close to music demographics, so that's part of the reason why it has received so much focus."

appeal of the web

At the moment, the Web is a lot more popular than CD-ROMs. The reason is money. Consumers have to buy CD-ROMs. The Web is (at the moment) free. Businesses find that ROM-based projects are expensive, and the big companies are getting tighter with their ROM budgets because profit margins are not guaranteed. On the Web, your audience growth is exponential, you can reach everybody whose interested as opposed to everybody who has purchased the disc.

"Music is a global product," notes Larry Rosen, CEO of N2K. "There are no language barriers, people all over the world are into music. And the idea of having a network to link these people together is very, very exciting."

Prior to the World Wide Web, music was broadcast via radio stations. You may have a radio station in France, another in China, another in Japan, and one in every city in the United States; but, there was limited opportunity to broadcast music around the world. The Internet is the infrastructure for a truly global village. It's a very exciting point in the evolution of humankind.

From a business standpoint, the Web represents:

- Freedom from distribution strangleholds;

- Freedom from being dependent on mass media for marketing and promotion;

- The ability to communicate directly to your constituency in a two-way fashion.

The Internet will not work effectively as a sole promotional formula. It needs to be synergistically incorporated with other forms of marketing and promotion. When marketing a band, stick your URL on your advertising, put it on your bios, stick it on the album itself. The Net is another part of the advertising process.

What's particularly cool and effective about having the URL on the album is that it's a good way to cultivate repeat buyers. After Billy Bob in Des Moines buys a Smashing Pumpkins record and plays it 900 times in nine months, one day, he's going to look at the CD cover and wow! There's a URL on there. Holy moly! A whole new world opens up. (You could have hooked him months earlier if the CD was Enhanced and linked up to the Web site, but hey, we do the best we can.) Billy Bob downloads the page and finds thirty seconds of a new song from the new album, and then it's the try-before-you-buy scenario. Suddenly, you've got something that you just don't get from traditional distribution; a repeat buyer. Try-it-then-buy-it is definitely where it's at, repeat buyers are where it's at, and that's part of the model for the online artist.

"If you look at the statistics on people visiting Web sites, the vast majority of people haven't visited more than fifty sites, and they haven't even visited more than ten in-depth," exerts Bates. "What that says is you're creating loyal followers to a Web site. Those people are getting the editorial slant from that Web site, finding more groups that they like through the Web site, and then they are able to go and follow the band, buy their CD-ROMs, find out more about their concerts. A Web site enables a music following to keep up with what's going on with the band. The Web's creating not only a more loyal following, but enabling the following to be more loyal."

net distribution

Currently, purchasing music and related merchandise follows an archaic model. If you want to buy a magazine, you go to a 7-11, liquor store, magazine shop, bookstore, supermarket—the options are endless. If you want to buy a record, you basically have to go to a record store or department store. If you want to buy a T-shirt from the artist you bought the record from, you can't buy it in a record store. You'll have to wait until the artist goes on tour and then purchase the shirt at the show. You may be able to send away for it via the mail. Chances are you can't even go to a retail store or a shirt shop and buy it. If you want to buy a video, you have to go to a video store. You can't go to the Beastie Boys shop, survey and buy everything that the Beastie Boys have to offer.

The Web represents a huge shift in how we communicate and how the music industry sells records. Consumers are still opting for record stores over purchasing material online, but if they can't find what they're looking for in a store, they'll look to the Internet.

Music veteran Todd Rundgren added his thoughts during a speaking engagement at MUSICOM, a conference of music professionals.

"It's no longer a question of selling a finite element: a disc or even a piece of sheet music," claims Todd. "It's selling a relationship to people and this is completely different than the model that the business is based on now. The biggest problem with the current record industry model is inventory. The reason people succeed or fail is mostly because of inventory management, making exactly the right number of discs to meet demand. With a subscription-based and direct delivery system like this, you know exactly what the demand is up front. The demand can only increase as time goes on. So I have come around to the realization that I'm not trying to sell product to people. I'm trying to form a relationship with people, one in which they are my patrons, rather than the record company underwriting what I do. The people who listen to the music directly underwrite what I do. That's the exciting new thing from my standpoint."

"I think that most labels are still a little wary of the Web," claims producer David Greene. "It has the potential to be both a boon and a detriment. The detriment is the Web's potential to circumvent their business by creating an entirely new distribution model. Labels have a lot of money tied up in their distribution networks and are simply not ready for the mass distribution of digital music across the Internet. It opens the door to a lot of messy situations ranging from digital piracy to individual bands developing their own distribution sites.

"On the other hand the Net is a fantastic promotional tool for the labels," Greene continues. "Most of the record label sites are good and functional but none have yet to create a truly amazing interactive experience. I think the majors need to start to take a long range view of their interactive media strategies to coordinate their online services with the interactive capabilities of Enhanced CDs and DVDs. What they would do if they were smart would be to create content on the Enhanced CDs and DVDs that eventually would become components of a larger on-line presence for the label."

A study by Jupiter Communications indicates that music grosses more money than any other non-computer business on the Web. Macey Lipman Marketing found that 41 percent of major music retailers have been affected by the Internet. Not necessarily sales-wise, as online sales currently account for merely one-tenth of one percent of total album sales, but in terms of marketing and promotion.

Analysts are expecting Web commerce to grow to $4 billion by 1998. According to Yahoo's Entertainment/Music directory, there are currently more than thirty-five thousand music-themed Web sites. Undoubtedly surfers buying habits will shift with time, resulting in more online sales and a major shift in the music distribution business.

Currently, there are numerous music retailers on the Web, including popular watering holes such as CDNow (*www.cdnow.com*) and Music Boulevard (*www.musicblvd.com*). Even conventional record stores like Tower Records have Web sites from which they sell records.

The Web makes music distribution easy. When you release a record by an artist, the goal is to have that record become available in every territory of the world, and to promote it and market it on a global basis. Prior to the World Wide Web, international promotion and marketing was difficult. People who were giant fans of a particular artist in Poland might not hear that the artist had a new record out until three months after its release. Now, you can put that information up on the Internet and instantaneously, fans around the world can get information on a new release. This is one of the most cost efficient ways of marketing and promotion. You can put something neat up on the Web that has a life of its own for cheap—basically the sweat off your brow. To put something on the Web, your biggest expense is time. The amount of money you need to produce something compelling on the Internet can be the cost of the hardware and software that you need to create it.

"The Net has sold a hell of a lot of back catalog because people have an easy way to access cataloged titles like never before. Isn't that a surprise," chuckles Tom McGrew. "If back catalog material was in a retail store, you'd probably sell it in a retail store."

A few enterprising artists such as Todd Rundgren are developing Web enterprises that may one day circumvent the traditional record labels by offering new methods for distributing music to the masses.

"It's nearly impossible for preexisting record labels to make a commitment to delivery through the Net because of their relationship to retailers, the brick and mortar stores who are the ones who have the most to lose in this whole process," asserts Rundgren. "There still will be record companies who underwrite the expenses of producing, promoting, and marketing music no matter in what form it comes. The problem is if record companies start to direct market to people, it pisses off Blockbuster and all these others. They say, 'Wait a minute, you're cutting out our customers and reducing our business by direct marketing to them.' The element that has to be replaced electronically is that brick and mortar record store before anybody like Atlantic or Warner can make a full commitment to direct or electronic delivery. This is the middleman component. There has to be a Web component that is Tower Records or Blockbuster on the Web to broker music. Those who buy expensive music here, cheap music here, put it together into a reasonably priced package that's appealing to consumers, and compete that way, but the economics of doing that is different."

Q&A: larry rosen

Larry Rosen is the chairman and CEO of N2K, Inc. and a veteran in the digital technology field. His record label, GRP Records, which he co-founded with partner Dave Grusin in 1982, was the first jazz label to adopt an all-digital recording philosophy by releasing all titles on compact disc. Rosen now positions N2K as a leading new media and music entertainment company. N2K's Web sites—Music Boulevard (www.musicblvd.com), Rocktropolis (www.rocktropolis.com), and Jazz Central Station (www.jazzcentralstation.com)—offer a complete range of online music entertainment, including CD sales and distribution. N2K's new record label, N2K Encoded Music, is a vision for what's to come in interactive music.

WHAT'S N2K STAND FOR?

Larry Rosen: Need to Know. The Internet is the future way people will communicate. Eventually, everybody's going to have a computer in his home and it will be part of people's function in their day-to-day lives, whether they make reservations for a plane, do banking, homework, use it as a library, or for music. They're going to be using a computer connected to the Internet and databases that reside on the Internet to do everything.

HOW WILL THE INTERNET AFFECT THE CURRENT SALES STRUCTURES THAT EXIST FOR MUSIC?

Larry Rosen: For certain products, it becomes potent. For something like a pair of shoes, well, you could see that there's a pair of shoes, but there's no way you could really touch and feel that pair of shoes. So it's always going to be compelling to go into a store where you can pick them up and touch them. Music is different. You can get more information about music online than you can going into a record store. In a record store, you can't even open up the package. The Internet can have all the liner notes inside of the booklet, could have all the pictures of the artist, you could have conversations with the artist through a chat directory. You'd know about this artist's touring schedule, you could get all the information about this artist as well as hear sound samples, see the cover, really touch and feel the record, and buy it right there at the same time.

HOW DO YOU SEE THE RECORD COMPANY MODEL SHIFTING THROUGH THE END OF THE MILLENNIUM?

Larry Rosen: The end of the millennium is not that far away, so nothing quite so radical is going to take place. You'll see the beginning of the shift. The model that works right now is that an artist is signed to a record company for five to seven years on an exclusive basis. The record company has the majority of the leverage in the negotiation of the deal. It's more or less preset that the artist would receive X amount of royalties. The record company in turn would advance to the artist the amount of money necessary to go make a record. Out of the sales of that record, the record company takes back all the cost of making the record before they pay the artist royalties. The artist needs the record company because of the infrastructure of the distribution systems. They need to have a company that will do the marketing, get the record into retail stores, and get it displayed.

The model that's eventually going to prevail is one where the artist is going to finance her own record, produce it, and divide the distribution rights up. She'll let Mr. Record Company distribute the record only into the record retail stores. Because the artist is paying for it, she's not signed to the label for five years, she's not obligated to the record company.

Then, she would go to a company like N2K and have us distribute the record electronically, or to all the people that you have online in these particular areas, and we're going to receive "X" percentage of these sales.

HOW DOES THIS BENEFIT THE ARTIST?

Larry Rosen: The artist, in reality, is the one who should receive the majority of the income from the record because she's the one who created the music in the first place. Without that . . . the distribution systems don't mean anything.

So, a greater percentage of the profit can end up going to the artist, a successful artist . . . and then the distribution systems would receive their percentage, and online aggregates like N2K would receive their percentage. That's how the music industry is going to change.

try before you buy

It used to be that if you liked what you heard on the radio, you'd go out and buy the record. Something that music fans can now do is actually listen to the music before they buy an album. Hey! The try-before-you-buy scenario has worked in supermarkets since the beginning of shopping history. Everybody samples that hors d'oeuvre of cheese sitting on the deli tray. After sticking that tasty morsel in his mouth, he's likely to realize that he wants more, and buy it.

The concept of "listen before you buy" was first presented by the Hear chain of music stores. Traditional music stores like Tower Records and the Virgin Megastore have gone in the direction of providing a try-it-then-buy-it situation by setting up listening kiosks or booths in their stores.

You can do the same thing on the Web, download thirty seconds of music and hear what a song off the Metallica album sounds like. It's a new form of marketing. And soon the audio will be better online.

"Eventually, the technology's going to exist where you could electronically transmit a particular record to the person," observes Larry Rosen. "You're going to say, 'I like what I hear, send it to me right now.' It would be electronically transmitted. You would take those sounds and convert them into bits and send them to somebody on the other end, on a global basis, and they would store it."

Soon enough (years? months?) you'll be able to download a disc's worth of album quality sound right into your home. There are pundits who feel that Electronic Commercial Music Distribution (ECMD) will be the preferred method for purchasing music in the next millennium. Pay for it, download it, and access it on a whim. Consumers will be able to pick and choose and customize the collection of songs they're going to purchase, and they'll either be able to access purchased music by computer whenever they like, or download tunes onto a recordable CD.

net marketing

The obvious, immediate benefit of the Internet is that it's an easy way to develop a better relationship with potential customers. Labels large and small have set up their own domains. One of the forerunners in this area is American Recordings. Not only does it have a great site, (*www.american.recordings.com*), but it's also behind the Web Wide World of music—a link library of music Web sites.

"Instead of putting records out there for five thousand people, three of which might buy our records, we can focus on the three people that might buy a record. We've turning our marketing method into a better service model," offers American Recordings' Marc Geiger.

If you're a fan of an artist, you generally learn about the new album through traditional mass media channels. You may pick up a *Rolling Stone* magazine and a see an ad, or hear a song on the radio. That media input might motivate you to buy the record, it might not. The Internet offers an economical way to increase consumer awareness, and allows those in charge of marketing and promotion to communicate directly to the artist's fan base.

"That personalized market has never taken place inside the music business before," observes Geiger. "It's way too big. The Web now enables us to do this. If I can get the e-mail address of 40 percent of the people who bought the last Black Crowes record, I can have Chris Robinson do a 50K video interview that I can download to everybody, or send them an e-mail that he personally signs. Those fans would be pretty psyched, and I think that will lead to more sales. If we can sell things that way instead of mass marketing, it will yield more profit."

The Web will let you win a signed record from the artist, receive a personal e-mail, or download a spoken interview. Suddenly you're feeling closer to the band, and a fan gets the impression that "this musician really cares about me." The result is that the fan is really going to support the musician.

If you've got great content, the World Wide Web is a godsend for you because it allows people to access it in many different ways and across many different platforms. You can log-in on your computer, talk to people about a concert that you're watching on your TV and listening to over your stereo. MTV has hooked up with America Online to let people talk about videos on TV over their computers while they watch the video. Suddenly everyone is Beavis and Butthead, able to publicly critique the material that's out there. The Web augments all the things that people like to do and offers a richer experience.

Bob Vogel, president of Softmail Direct, says the aim in taking messages and products to the Web is to "make sales and generate leads." The Web is at once a distribution medium and an environment to seal the deal. He says the action goals of promotion on the Web are no different than print: namely, to build image, create awareness, further the sales process, and even close the sale.

The good news for small developers is the Web offers them an opportunity to give potential customers much more content and information than through any other medium. It's also interactive, personal, and fast. The Web is a great way to educate because content can begin where traditional promotion and awareness building leave off. Vogel lists several strategic Web promotional concepts:

- Create a unique URL (home page address) for every single product.

- Link direct response Web content to ads promoting that specific product (don't send users to a generic home page with many other products).

- Provide product incentives to capture name/address.

- Test everything: price points, sources of inquires, content, etc.

- Always ask for the order.

If you look at the traditional ways artists communicated with their fans, they had their LP and they had an album sleeve. There were interviews in other forms of media, like magazines.

"Back in the late seventies, record labels were more or less dependent on print in order to let people learn about their new releases," states Andy Secher, editor of *Hit Parader* magazine. "This was even before MTV came along! That was revolution unto itself. But video was only the start of the technological revolution."

In the mid-eighties, a few years after videos became a standard form of promotion, the CD came along. You could put more music on the disc (albums generally can't hold more than an hour's worth of music without a loss of fidelity, CDs allow seventy-four minutes of music), but you had less space for art. The World Wide Web has the potential to be the best of all worlds, for musicians and music lovers.

"One of the major benefits the Web offers to music is that it's diversifying the audience and diversifying the type of music that's out there," remarks John Bates. "Because of the diversity, people's tastes are enabled in a much more eclectic manner."

Bandwidth, or the ability to use the existing bandwidth, will make a tremendous difference in the way we can view materials on the Web.

"It's going to be easier to find ways to compress and get around needing more bandwidth than it is to install new infrastructure," remarks Bates.

As developers tackle the bandwidth challenge, the Web could feasibly evolve into a perfect substitute for radio. (Not that the big media giants in this country would allow it.) You could listen to music on your computer, and assuming that the Internet will become the ultimate music archives, you'd be able to pick what music you wanted to listen to. Of course, your car radio will still feature FM and AM frequencies.

As this book goes to press, the purchasing model of the Web is already in transition. Online commerce today is mostly supplying services for people that want to go online—onramp providers. There is a tremendous amount of capital and brainpower being devoted to online commerce. In the future, online purchasing will be commonplace, thanks to secure credit card transactions and better consumer awareness of Web benefits. Mastercard International has adopted the Secure Electronic Transaction system for use in conjunction with its credit cards. Microsoft and Visa will release new merchant software packages next year. The next version of Netscape will come with a built-in wallet. Online commerce will become an everyday occurrence when Web broadcasters devote more resources to their online advertising campaigns. The technology is already here for Web commerce to flourish. It just needs to be sold to the people.

Right now, the music industry mainly sees the World Wide Web as a marketing and advertising tool. Music sites are primarily locations to be visited, but there is little commerce taking place. Just wait. You will use the Web to listen to an album, purchase it, and have it delivered to your front door within a few days. Better still may be the day you receive your album electronically—either downloaded to your computer or stored in a third-party, "server jukebox" for you to access when you please.

The market niche is there. Mall stores in many parts of the United States are only carrying the top pop records that kids want to buy. The Internet is very effective for areas of the country where record stores don't stock an in-depth catalog, and where they choose not to carry slow-moving titles. Many titles that people in the older buying demographic prefer are no longer available in mainstream record stores. In a virtual store online, you can stock 150 thousand titles.

Now, think further into the future, when we have wider bandwidth and cable modems . . . where every online shopper has her own virtual shopping consultant. You'll never have to leave your computers for anything except fulfilling key bodily functions.

pricing

If you no longer have to go to a record store to buy an album, you're cutting out the middle man, you're also cutting out production costs. What will digital downloading do to the price of a CD?

"At the beginning the pricing is all going to be exactly the same," observes N2K's Larry Rosen. "The profit levels are going to be somewhat different. It's the same dollars, but who gets those dollars and how are they shifted around. It is a questionable thing how people would buy music, because you would have the ability to say, 'I want to buy one song from this guy, and one song from this guy, and one song from this guy and put it together that way.' There's a whole bunch of other ways that music could be sold than the way it is right now."

Society is changing. Teens and adults are used to having things and holding things. But five-year-olds are already nonlinear. They don't necessarily have the attachment to physical possessions the same way that we do. As purchasing power is part of the sociological experience, the concept of virtual ownership can be taught, just as citizens of the former Soviet Union learned to work only to meet quotas. If someone grows up knowing that the content they desire will always be available, they'll be less inclined to feel like they need to own it. We're coming upon a whole generation of thinking that will be happy enough with virtual ownership as opposed to actual ownership. The future is almost now. Now that they have finally figured out credit card encryption processes, copyright protection can't be far behind. In the perfect cyber universe, there will be mechanisms in place to protect a band's song copyrights and the whole nine yards. An artist will be able to sell product over the Internet and still be protected from duplication.

"People are arguing all kinds of cons against digital distribution," declares Michael Dorf, president and CEO of the Knit Media. "They say you're going to have no artwork to really be able to present a package. But, actually, that's to the contrary. The Internet gives you the opportunity to have an almost unlimited amount of music that can be digitally distributed directly to a consumer. You also have the opportunity to link to all kinds of visuals, or all kinds of hypertext links to the artist's life. Whatever the artist would like to share, whatever he wants to communicate, he can do over the World Wide Web. If he wants to share his list of the top one hundred musicians of all time, what he thinks is the best concert he ever saw, what is his favorite color, his favorite foods . . . whatever the artist is willing and wanting to share of himself can now be attached to his presentation. In that sense, the Web is the ultimate way for him to communicate with his fans."

The big question everyone is asking is: What is the consumer willing to pay for this opportunity? Should it be a paid service like cable television or something that's advertising subsidized, like normal network programming?

"As the music industry begins to realize the benefits of a wired consumer base, it will become more marketing savvy and less paranoid about stepping on the toes of distributors and retailers," observes Tony Winders, president of InterActive Agency, an online marketing and promotion firm. "Online media is about to turn the music industry on its head and anyone involved in 'traditional' distribution, who isn't thinking about an Internet strategy is already way behind the curve."

live on the net

At the moment, money is not the major concern of the record companies in regard to the Internet. They're already using the Internet as a form of marketing and promotion, assuming, like everyone else, that the profit model will fall into place. During the summer of 1996, the band Korn did a live Net broadcast of two songs from its second album *Life Is Peachy* followed by an online interview session. The exposure was tremendous. The band received 319,222 fan postings from twenty-eight countries . . . a far larger audience than they'd ever performed for. But did that translate into album sales? We'll see if *Life Is Peachy* sells more than the 700 thousand units their self-titled debut album scored.

When the Sex Pistols reunited for their world tour, a gig from the Hollywood Palladium was presented live over the Internet through the Rocktropolis site. The Palladium only holds 2,000 people, but 4,000 simultaneous Internet listeners were able to hear the entire uncensored live concert and view up-to-the-minute live stills and video segments. The concert was also tied into a competition called "Great Insults on the Internet" whereby entrants e-mailed their favorite put-downs and the most cynical were awarded Sex Pistols swag bags.

"It was as effective as it was offensive, which befits a band like the Sex Pistols," notes Ted Mico, special projects producer for Virgin Records. "You couldn't do a promotion like this with Julio Iglesias, but it works perfectly for this band. The Internet lets you cater to a group's attitude and vision."

The music industry seems to think that music fans will beg, borrow, and steal to get more information and music on their favorite bands. And there are probably several thousand people who will, but people throughout the world love the Web because it's free.

One of the musicians who is putting Internet potential to the test is David Bowie. In September 1996, he released the song "Telling Lies" exclusively on the Internet via his Web site at *www.davidbowie.com*. On January 8, 1997, for his fiftieth birthday celebration, Bowie let fans download five new songs.

"My first working encounter with the Internet was at the beginning of the *Outside* tour in Boston," offers Bowie. "It produced a great response, so I am only happy to take the whole thing to another level and actually release a song on the Web."

Could Virgin Records have charged an additional fee for access to this new Bowie song? Most definitely. But they didn't. It was a test. According to Nancy Berry, executive vice president of Virgin Records Worldwide, "Virgin is always looking for exciting and innovative ways of promoting our artists and getting the music to listeners. So clearly, we're keen to explore the potential of the World Wide Web."

Exclusive material may be one way to generate additional income in the future. Many are thinking that instead of charging Web sites money other than access time to be online, that they would offer customers cool items they can't get at retail. The Knit Media boasts that 10 percent of its revenues come from online services. Within moments, Internet browsers will come with wallets. Consumers are bracing themselves for a new buying experience.

empowering artists

Average artists, particularly ones without a record deal, are getting frustrated dealing with record industry people, radio people, and booking agents. If you have a tape, where do you send it to get a deal? Does your band send in promotional material to a radio station? Or to a record company? Or to a booking agent? Or do you just stick it up on IUMA, the Knit Media, or some Web site similar as such and see if anyone notices it?

People in the music industry have a right to be arrogant. It's a supply and demand thing. Radio airplay has a bandwidth problem. They don't have enough space for all the artists to get their messages across. Traditional record companies don't have enough money to develop all of the artists who want to record albums. Club bookers don't have enough clubs for all artists to play a date.

Guess what? The Internet doesn't have that kind of bandwidth problem. Online, any artist can get her message out to the people.

"The way for a band to use the Internet is to say, 'We're working on these demos . . . we're rehearsing for a live show at this location, and this is what it sounds like," offers Oded Noy.

In future years, visionaries such as Peter Gabriel and the Residents will be the norm; artists will conceptualize video, art, and music all at one time and one place. This concept is slow to catch on because many traditional artists still see themselves solely as musicians. The few musicians who are currently thinking multimedia are producing product that is outside of the mainstream. One of those artists is Thomas Dolby.

Q&A: thomas dolby

Musician Thomas Dolby first made a name for himself with the pop hit, "She Blinded Me With Science." Now he is focusing his efforts on virtual reality programming and multimedia. His company, Headspace, has scored and designed sound for various CD-ROM games and location based entertainment. Dolby attributes his interest in computers to his abilities as a keyboardist. He notes, "I'm not a very proficient keyboard player, so the computer became my instrument."

HOW HAS THE WORLD WIDE WEB AFFECTED YOUR CREATIVE PROCESS?

Thomas Dolby: It's put me a lot closer to my audience. It's effectively allowed me to compose and record a song, distribute it instantaneously to my fans, and get their feedback from it. They can tell me if they like it or don't like it, they can make comparisons and cross-references to other parts of my music or other artists. Anything it brings up for them, they can share with me on an individual basis. That's never before been possible. Even in its current, rather bandwidth challenged state the Internet is allowing an artist to get closer to his audience and therefore to his own art.

IS THE FEEDBACK YOU'RE GETTING FROM YOUR AUDIENCE AFFECTING YOUR CREATIVE PROCESS?

Thomas Dolby: Certainly. I no longer have to worry about first impressing the A&R man (artist and repertoire, the person who rewards an artist with a record deal), and then the radio programmer, and then the record store owner, before the public even gets a chance to hear it.

ONCE THE BANDWIDTH CHALLENGE IS SOLVED, WHAT DO YOU SEE HAPPENING WITH ONLINE POSSIBILITIES FOR MUSICIANS?

Thomas Dolby: The bandwidth problem will never be solved. We're on the slippery slide of thinking that we always need more bandwidth, which is actually perfectly true, there will never be enough. Economy and efficiency are always going to be absolutely crucial in this medium. The people who manage to find the loopholes, make the shortcuts, and make this year's technology perform like next year's technology are going to have a definite advantage in terms of capacity and the impact of what they can do. But it's all meaningless without good ideas and good images and sounds to begin with. That's something that can only be solved by making sure that the technology gets put into the hands of the best artists of our generation.

WHAT'S SOMETHING THAT YOU WOULD LIKE TO DO WITH MORE BANDWIDTH THAT YOU'RE NOT ABLE TO DO NOW?

Thomas Dolby: When I'm in my own studio, I am able to, in a completely nonlinear manner, compose music, cut and paste chunks of music around, change the key, the tempo of what I'm doing, have a large library or database of samples of real instruments played by musicians I have never even met that I can trigger from my computer. What we need is for every computer user to have the same facility on his or her machine that I have in my own recording studio. Then they will need to go into a virtual world, chat with their friends, or find out information, and my music will be playing in a fully interactive manner.

DO YOU HAVE ANY ISSUES WITH PEOPLE MANIPULATING YOUR ART, OR MANIPULATING YOUR MUSIC?

Thomas Dolby: I'm okay with it. There will always be times that I cringe, but that has always happened. You know, oh my God, I can't believe they used that photo of me, or I can't believe they just chopped five seconds of my song in with that music by those other people I don't like. The cringe factor will probably never go away. But the responsibility of a musician is to try and make things more beautiful, to make things look and sound better, and make the world a more beautiful place, really.

I can't imagine anything more ugly than just sort of random cacophony and noise in cyberspace. What my company is trying to do is provide a framework so that the author or the editor can intelligently plan the way media gets across to the end user.

internet/enhanced cd connection

For people creating Enhanced CDs and CD-ROMs, there is an obvious link to the Net. On the most rudimentary level, you can put up a Web site and tell people about what is happening with your CDs. Tell them about tour schedules or interesting news tidbits. It's an easy way to keep a lot of people aware of what's going on with an artist.

"To sell our band, we're going for a Net campaign. We're going to start using the Internet as a market and see how far we can go," announces Oded Noy about the *Onion* Enhanced CD. "We're planning to have material which appears on the Enhanced disc also appear as Shockwave applications on our Web site (*www.hotangels.com*). I'm writing a screen saver that people can download—a couple of images that will just run on the screen. If people like the imagery, then they can order the CD."

"Enhanced CDs don't have to have an Internet link, but we're all moving that way," confirms Elektra Record's John Mefford. "The future is in hybrid discs. Every one of our new discs will have some kind of link to the Internet."

"Our Web site is pretty important, we get hit a lot," observes Mark Waldrep of AIX. "Primarily because all the products we put out have our Web address on them."

Early on in the development of Enhanced product, Web sites were a secondary link. In the current market structure, the tide has turned. These days, Enhanced CDs are being seen as the link to the Web.

"We can provide a connection to the Internet on every disc that we do," confirms Todd Fearn of REV Entertainment. "So, not only do you have access to videos and bio materials, but you can click and jump right to the Web site of the band from the disc."

The CD/Internet model that everyone is gaga over at this moment is a CD with a simulation of the Web site's homepage and a built in Web browser. The band's site, which is designed in tandem with the CD, has all the current information, but the CD has the video and the audio. You can't really do video or audio on the Net at this point in time because it just takes forever to download a two or three mega-byte file—why wait an hour-and-a-half for ten seconds of video? The advantage of the Enhanced CD is that it plays video and audio well, but once the disc is commercially distributed, it's locked away from new information. On the Internet you can update easily.

Your mission is to find a way to integrate the two technologies seamlessly—by using a common interface that can be used as a Web page as well as an Enhanced CD interface—blurring the lines between the mediums.

For example, perhaps the Sting world tour schedule is not available when the new album is first released. But the information will be available by October. You program an area of the CD to sync with the computer's calendar. When the calendar reads October 1, 1998, that wing of the disc opens up and you have a tour schedule that you can access from the artist's Web site. On the disc, you create reasons for people go to the Web site. Perhaps the tour itinerary is linked to a diary that is updated regularly that can *only* be accessed through the CD screens. You'd download the tour diary, and view it from your hard drive. Perhaps it concludes with an interesting audio tidbit that is located on your Enhanced CD.

Many Enhanced CDs now come with a dial-up control that will link you directly to the Web page. From there, you'll find tie-ins to corporate America who help sponsor the product. Being a hotlink away from No Doubt, the Rolling Stones, or Soundgarden excites the money boys at Reebok and Levi's. Like it or not, corporate funding will most likely become an essential part of developing Enhanced CD/Web joint ventures.

"There's a huge tie-in to the Internet, which is causing a lot of fire as far as Enhanced CDs are concerned," observes Waldrep. "Enhanced

CDs are one prong in a multi-faceted approach of audio and new technology. As bandwidth expands, and the technology evolves, the Internet is playing a bigger part."

The Internet makes recouping costs a lot easier than trying to cover the expenses only through retail channel sales. By having access to the Internet, you have more leverage to work with advertisers and sponsors. Let's say Aerosmith's Joe Perry uses Gibson guitars. You have the Gibson section on your Web site where you find out more about the company's equipment. Then, link it to the Gibson site.

"We have to figure out a way to make the combination of the two greater than the sum of its parts," observes Highway One's Dave Antil. "The technology exists where we can put the front end of the CD-ROM on the Internet and put a fairly seamless hook on the CD to the Internet, so it's just a matter of connecting and putting all the pieces together."

Sell stuff. You've got a captive audience. They love you and want more. Offer them tour merchandise, a back catalog of music, other bands the management handles, or bands the record label wants to promote. You can even get esoteric with links to the group's favorite chocolate chip cookie company.

web promotion

"One of the inherent values of online communication is the ability to facilitate one-to-one, one-to-many, and many-to-many communication," notes Tony Winders of InterActive Agency. "This opens up tremendous possibilities for marketers because information about a product can be easily disseminated to the people who want or need it most."

In today's fast-paced digital age, lots of ordinary, intelligent people are spending hours and hours basking in the glow of their computer monitors. And, it's a phenomenon that's growing. Just think, the same sort of programming that is developed and broadcast to your televisions—sitcoms, quiz shows, soap operas—is being developed and broadcast to a computer screen near you.

Marketers have always known that word of mouth is incredibly powerful. There are opinion leaders out there among every group of friends, and if you can get to those opinion leaders and make them realize how cool your site is, word of mouth is going to spread like wildfire. "Oh, Chad says this is really cool. Let's check it out. He knows what he's talking about." Word gets out and then people explore. If the site really is good, they'll tell their friends. Word of mouth is one of the most important ways to promoting sites on the Internet.

Another extremely effective way of spreading the word is posting to Usenet newsgroups. Newsgroups are like giant bulletin boards where people from around the world congregate to blow off steam or share insights into their favorite subjects. There are also the search engines like HotBot, Alta Vista, and Webcrawler that are able to browse usenet newsgroups, Web sites, and gopher sites for key words like "alternative music." Search engines are powerful (and free) tools to point people to come visit your site. Off-line events drive people to online sites too. If you've got a football-themed Web site, then interest in the Super Bowl is going to make your site traffic increase simply due to an increased number search engine requests for football-related information.

"When you talk about grassroots or organic ways to promote a band, we can do that online," notes Capitol's Liz Heller. It's a great feeling of excitement and enthusiasm."

music on the web

The Internet is a great way to give a band exposure to a music-hungry audience. The World Wide Web displaces the importance of place and increases the importance of time. A lot of people would rather be at the concert virtually than see the concert later in a better manner.

"There's something magical about being in a live situation that will never be duplicated—I don't care how advanced the technology gets," notes Michael Dorf, president of the Knit Media (*www.knitmedia.com*), a company that specializes in setting up live concerts on the Net. "Everyone's time is getting so scarce, how many concerts a week can you go to? Concerts on the Web give you the opportunity to see something, sample it. To ask yourself, does this look like what I'd like to go to when the show comes to town?"

Online interviews, online concerts, online broadcasts are an interesting form of promotion that many groups have effectively utilized.

It's like giving music fans backstage passes and front row seats to their favorite event. It's a first rate experience, even though cybercasting is still a very young medium.

Sound on computers is still in its infancy, but sound technology is evolving at a rapid rate. Already, every computer can double as a musical instrument. This in large part is being facilitated by MIDI applications. MIDI stands for Musical Instrument Digital Interface. It was originally designed to allow various synthesizers from different manufacturers to talk to each other. Soundcards were put into computers to enhance the sound of games, and they used MIDI protocols to talk to the games. If you connected a keyboard to the joystick port on the soundcard, you could play that like any other type of general MIDI synthesizer. Several music software companies have identified a potential install base for people wanting to use their computers to play music. Companies such as the Hotz Corporation and Harmonix Music Systems, Inc., have devised realtime music composition and performance engines. These programs allow the users to generate original music in real time in a multitude of styles, and they feature low level mechanical components that are automated, making it easy for anyone to play music.

"In the short term, these technologies will prove to be a very entertaining and empowering medium for the masses," offers Bryan Biniak of Harmonix. "Utilizing a proprietary pro-audio software synthesis solution and streaming technologies which allow for consistent, reliable synchronization, companies like Harmonix are elevating today's music videos and concert netcasts into global jam sessions, allowing people to perform with their favorite artists and each other in real time."

Online jam sessions using MIDI are totally feasible at this point in time. The amount of information that MIDI needs to send down the pike is not too big for today's 28.8 modem to handle.

"There's a slightly more complicated issue involved with this," notes Oded Noy. "Having an open jam session online is like what a chat room feels like when you first walk into it. There's all kinds of people that just throw things from left field. Music is a very spiritual thing. There's a certain space and time that's being created by this sound and everybody needs to be really sensitive to that. Unless you have the total agreement of everybody involved, it becomes pretty chaotic."

Let's say Elton John is sitting in London with a monitor and a keyboard and Billy Joel is in New York with a similar setup. There's a big media thing and they're going to play a song together and all they have is a monitor linking the two of them. As opposed to just going ahead and playing, it would help a lot if they would coordinate before the media focused all their attentions on the event—they need to figure out what are we going to play that doesn't suck? In addition to having a path to follow, for Interactive jamming to become an effective method of making music, there needs to be a certain psychic communication between the artists. The big drawback with online jam sessions is that all musicians will tell you that making music is a very social experience; both for those making the music and the audience that's listening to the music. Let's say a group of musicians are making a song happen, they're listening to the universe giving them instructions as to what the song needs to be.

"If you're a really good musician, you're not playing what you want to play, you're trying as much as you can to play what the song wants you to play within the range of your understanding," states Oded. "In order to have a really high quality band there needs to be a certain mutual understanding of where things are and where things need to be, a certain spiritual connection while the music is being played. Technically it's possible to create that psychic connection between musicians across networks, but it's a very difficult process."

future of the net

There are already over 40 million people throughout the world with Internet access. That number will surely grow thanks to the market introduction of easy-to-use devices such as set top boxes and cable modems. These devices are already becoming standard fare in homes across America and it won't be long until streaming audio and video transmissions from the Net onto our TV sets are commonplace. Then anyone who wants to will be able to surf the Net, or launch her own television show by creating an episodic Web site.

"Before the World Wide Web becomes a true mass market phenomenon, it must become an dominant aspect of our everyday lives:

very much like the telephone, television, and radio," observes Bryan Biniak. "WebTV and other devices like network appliances will help mainstream the Web, creating an affordable vehicle for sending and receiving information whether it be data, graphics, audio, or video."

Corporate is dedicated to putting the television online. Sega and Nintendo have added Internet access to their video game machines. Bandai's Pippin and ViewCall America have designed set top boxes which plug into an ordinary television set. And Microsoft purchased WebTV. So the near future is going to prove to be a very exciting growth period for the Internet.

part three

business development

chapter 8

business development: licensing and clearances

Music is the brandy of the damned.

—**George Bernard Shaw**

the nature of the beast

You're sitting in the Big Record Company boardroom pitching ideas for multimedia projects. The decisive guitar disc project you've been wanting to develop gets a good response. You figure, why not go for broke. Out comes the pitch for your dream project—a comprehensive rock encyclopedia. Your eyes dance as you talk about putting in clips of The Beatles from "The Ed Sullivan Show" and rough Nirvana tracks which have been sequestered in the band's private vault. You have a vision of taking all of the music media assets that exist and presenting them in one entertaining and informative package.

You finish your pitch and look around, expecting everyone to be as excited as you over this idea. Instead, the CEO gives you a look as if you were a second grader who just broke a window.

"You're crazy," he gasps. "Think of the rights problems! You'd have dozens of different rights clearance issues. Perhaps thousands. That disc would eat up half a million dollars in legal fees alone!"

Many professionals involved with music and new technology have dreamed of creating a rock 'n' roll encyclopedia. But as of this writing, no one has successfully assembled such a project. The primary stumbling block are rights and royalty issues. Think of all the material you'd need to get permission to include in such a title: images, text, music, cover art, photographs, *Billboard* charts, music videos, film clips, interviews, and the like. Imagine the time, effort, and paperwork that would be necessary for securing permission to use these thousands of pieces of content . . . and how much money it will cost to assemble it.

Let's say you want to put clips from fifty songs on your disc—not an unrealistic number by any stretch of the imagination. If you have a prominent artist, like the Red Hot Chili Peppers, you may have problems. The nature of the entertainment industry is that your next deal has to be higher than your last deal, otherwise you're going to hell in a handbasket. Perhaps the last time the Chili Peppers sold rights to one of their songs, it went into a movie and they made $50,000. For your rock encyclopedia, the whole music budget for all fifty songs may be $10,000. Ten thousand divided by fifty comes out to $200 per song. Many artists aren't going to be very happy about trading their song rights for the cost of a night of drinking.

With multimedia, you can't pay the artists as much as they received the last time they licensed a song for a TV show, movie, or a compilation disc. Enhanced CDs and music CD-ROMs are still an uncertain market, and nobody wants to get involved with a losing deal.

This is where good negotiating skills come into play. You have to go out and make your best deal with everybody you can. People who are into new technology will let you do it. People who aren't, won't. Hopefully you will get enough of what you need to make the product that you want.

A hard and fast rule for using materials created by other people is: just clear everything. It's law that you must clear rights on any content made after 1963. It is expensive and will definitely get in the way of a lot of the creativity that you want to employ, but to be legally in the clear, you either have to create it yourself or clear it. Good luck. Your mission, should you choose to accept it, is to get proper clearance for every shred of content you choose to use.

"On any piece of material you use, you have to make sure everything is cleared," proclaims Fay Schreibman McGrew, consultant to Second Line Search stock house and clearance specialists. "If there's music, if there's a performer on it, a celebrity, sometimes certain buildings, trademarks, logos, the user has to go and clear the rights."

Once you make the decision to create a multimedia experience, your first duty should be to enlighten your friends and associates in affiliated industries whom you may be negotiating with in the near future. You'll need to get them up to speed on issues ranging from technology, to the product, to budget realities.

"Most people you're dealing with don't understand the market," notes Steve Gray of Om Records, which has released Enhanced titles like *Groove Active* and *Spiritual High*. "The people licensing stock photos from footage agencies are used to dealing with the print media, where the value of that photo might be $2,000 for its usage. You're trying to tell them the photo is just a tiny aspect of something that's a bonus on our product. Trying to convince people of the value that you bring and what it's worth is extremely difficult."

"The record labels are slow, they're extremely leery of this kind of stuff," observes George Bartko, chief operating officer of Second Line Search. "Some of them have very standardized forms that we can fill out, others piecemeal it. We did one job where they wanted four songs cleared and we were working on it for four weeks before we had numbers for them."

A successful Enhanced CD these days may move ten thousand to fifteen thousand units. Next year, there could be 100 thousand units flying off the shelves. A successful CD-ROM game is currently said to be selling more than 250 thousand units. When will that magic number jump to 750 thousand units? What about a Web site that pulls 100 thousand daily hits? How do you quantify the value of one small piece of content broadcasting from that site?

Content holders don't want to get shortchanged. That's why some are holding out for high licensing fees, while others are practically giving it away.

role of the attorney

Congratulations. You've made a handshake deal to acquire some content. Time to follow up with paperwork to seal the deal. You need a contract . . . or maybe three. . . .

"Every deal is unique, especially in multimedia," observes multimedia lawyer Michael Leventhal. "One of the questions frequently asked of multimedia lawyers is, 'Where can I get a good standard agreement?' The answer is you can't."

Boiler plate agreements are available. You may want to search the Internet, talk to friends, or buy a law book which tackles interactive media issues. One highly recommended source is the *Multimedia Law and Business Handbook,* by J. Diane Brinson and Mark F. Radcliffe. It comes bundled with sample contracts on disk which are very helpful to artists and developers who want to learn more about the specific deal points involved in clearing content for a multimedia project. Just keep in mind that a book or boiler plate agreement is no substitute for a qualified attorney. When you are dealing with legal issues, walk, don't run. And always proceed with caution.

"I sit down with the client and work out a deal proposal based on my knowledge of industry parameters and the information the client tells me about the particular project," comments Richard Thompson, a top interactive media attorney with the law firm of Bloom Hergott Cook Diemer & Klein. "Then I go and make the deal proposal to the company that's going to hire the client. Sometimes the company makes the initial proposal. Usually the company solicits one. Then I negotiate out the basic deal terms with the company. The company prepares the contract, which embodies the deal terms. I review the contract, make comments on it, negotiate my comments, the contract gets finalized, and everybody signs it."

Talented lawyers are expensive. A few enterprising developers have skirted this money problem by making their legal advisor a member of their development team. For a lower-than-usual, up-front fee, an attorney may choose to receive stock in your firm, thereby sharing the risk of your venture. That is, of course, if you can convince the attorney that your venture is worthwhile.

"What you do with a lawyer like me is have me oversee the whole project," observes Leventhal. "I make sure that every right is identified and that the contracts are drafted between the people creating the project and the people financing it. Lawyers are critical to success, but when it comes to strictly the mechanics of Rights Clearance, you're overpaying if you're paying your lawyer his hourly rate."

A lawyer's role in multimedia can really vary. Your lawyer can be the person who makes sure that your contracts are drawn up properly or that your intellectual property rights are covered. Some lawyers are more entrepreneurial and actually pound the pavement looking for deals. Your legal council can be somebody who guides you through the business angles of what you're doing and introduces you to investors. Or he may be the one who negotiates your deal and then disappears from view until there's another deal to be negotiated.

Lawyers are people (yes, I know this may be hard to believe). Each has her own personality and preferred set of business practices. Likewise, every law firm is unique. Before settling on the first lawyer you talk to, ask around about the firm's reputation and client list. The lawyer-client relationship should be more than a handshake business acquaintance. Ideally, it's a partnership.

Q&A: michael leventhal

Michael Leventhal is an attorney specializing in music and interactive media in Santa Monica, California.

MICHAEL, HOW DO YOU DESCRIBE WHAT YOU DO?

Michael Leventhal: I would describe myself as a multimedia and music attorney. My background is from the music business. I've been doing music business law for over ten years. I've been doing multimedia law for somewhere in the three-to-four-year range.

AS A MULTIMEDIA ATTORNEY, WHAT DO YOU DO?

Michael Leventhal: That involves representing artists and sometimes the money people, negotiating contracts, and protecting individuals' intellectual property rights . . . or a company's intellectual property rights.

HOW DO YOU PROTECT INTELLECTUAL PROPERTY RIGHTS?

Michael Leventhal: There are a lot of myths floating around about what's okay to use without clearance and all of that—they're all myths. The reality is that any unauthorized copying of anything—any copyrighted work, no matter how small—can subject you to a copyright infringement claim.

LET'S SAY I HAVE A PHOTOGRAPH OF AN ARTIST I WANT TO USE ON MY WEB SITE. IT'S MY PHOTOGRAPH. I TOOK THE PICTURE. DO I HAVE TO GET PERMISSION FROM THE ARTIST TO USE IT?

Michael Leventhal: Owning the photo doesn't mean you own the copyright to the photo. The photographer owns the copyright on that photo. With regard to copyright law, you would be the copyright holder of that photo, and probably everything in it depending on what's actually in the photo.

There are rights of publicity and rights of privacy which apply also. So, just knowing who the copyright holder is doesn't solve the whole problem. Let's say that it's a photo of an artist standing next to one of his paintings and both the artist and the painting are in the photo. You physically snap the photo, so you own the copyright to the photo you've taken. Now you have to find out who the owner of the painting is and get the rights from him to display the painting in whatever format you want. There can be two copyrights implicated in one photo, or more, depending on how many works of art may be in it. It gets pretty complicated, but all those things have to be dealt with.

music rights

If you plan on producing a multimedia project—whether it's an Enhanced CD, musical adventure game, or a virtual music studio online—you will need to learn more about the legal issues essential to developing and protecting your work.

We start with music, the most crucial element in a music-themed multimedia project. There are two basic copyright issues involved in any piece of music:

THE UNDERLYING COMPOSITION

Meaning the person who wrote the song. The publishing company, the publishers, the songwriters, or Michael Jackson usually own the words and melody that make up the song.

THE MASTER RECORDING

Meaning the person or band who recorded the song. This is also known as mechanical rights. Mechanical rights are the basic right to use a musical composition. With a standard song, the record company owns the master recording. Permission to use this song does not include the right to publicly perform the music, or to use the music with still or moving images.

All music has at least two sets of rights that have to be cleared.

"Sometimes it all goes through the record company," informs George Bartko. "They'll say, 'Well, we own all these rights.' Other times they'll say, 'Well, I can give you the publishing rights, but you've got to go to the artist on this and you've got to go to the writer of the song on this.' You've got three layers as opposed to one. Songs are very time consuming. It's a lot easier to sell a sunset than it is to go clear a song for a multimedia title."

Wait! Don't heave a sigh of relief on songs just yet . . . there may be more. You may find yourself with some issues on guild agreements for the musicians who played the songs. The guilds—like SAG, AFTRA, WGA—may have to be dealt with. As digital production is still a new medium, and not a particularly lucrative field, the guilds are to date an unknown quantity.

Another area that has yet to be clearly defined is rights usage for the new medium. Specific questions need to be asked, and an agreement formulated for those answers.

As of yet, there are no standard rules for questions such as the following:

- What kind of performance are you dealing with?

- What mediums are rights being cleared for?

■ What about reuse fees?

■ What are the rules about putting music you did not create on the Internet?

Guilds will raise these questions and others in an attempt to get the best possible situations for their clientele . . . and this is just for music. Or in the case of our rock encyclopedia, one of fifty pieces of music.

Rights must be determined and rates set before you can put any music you did not create on any piece of electronic media. There are two agencies that will help you facilitate this process. If you look at an album, you will notice that most songs are registered with ASCAP (Association of Songwriters, Composers, and Publishers) or BMI (Broadcast Music Inc). These conglomerates manage the fees involved with the use of music. Once a song is registered with ASCAP or BMI, royalties are collected automatically. The standard rate for music is 6.6 cents per song for each copy sold. This price is for the full song— less for a segment. Be advised, record companies may want a chunk of this money up front.

"Licensing costs all depend on the quality of music you're trying to license," observes Om's Gray. "Major labels can cost twenty-five to thirty thousand dollars in just music advances . . . ten to twenty thousand dollars for smaller artists."

What you will pay for the opportunity to use the material will differ. According to Bartko, "We're doing different multimedia projects, so we're dealing with almost every record label. None of their prices come in at the same rate, they're all over the map, everybody's making them up as they go."

When getting permission to use a song from the record companies, you will need what is called a "Master Use License" which is strictly a license that allows you to use the master recording in a certain format. This is just for the song. To attach the song to some visuals is going to require a different contract.

visual clips

If you want to use a clip from a television show or a movie for your project, start collecting your release forms now. To begin with, you're going to have to deal with the underlying music, so all previously mentioned clearances apply. You have the rights to the film clip that come from whatever studio created it. You might have the rights to the underlying script, which comes from some writer. There are the rights of the actors which need to be taken into account. If you're looking to license product that was created prior to this decade, it's highly unlikely that an actor granted the network or the studio the right to reuse this image on a computer disc or over the Internet, because these technologies were previously some sci-fi fantasy. (Many contracts from the sixties and seventies don't even account for home video.) Perhaps the script for the show you want to use was adapted from another medium, say a short story. That could be yet another right to clear.

stock footage

Television and movie clips are inevitably a morass of paperwork for one segment. An easier way to go may be to get stock video footage. The great thing about stock footage is that it comes with all rights already cleared. Practical, but this material is not particularly cheap. Stock video costs range from eight to twenty-five dollars per second. It can be acquired through companies like Footage Net and Second Line Search.

"A stock house is an agency that owns or represents collections. They have the right to structure the deals in multimedia, and sell bits and pieces for people to use to create other work," notes Schreibman McGrew. "When using stock footage, the most important thing is to be specific. Know what you need, have a budget in mind, and be very clear and specific."

synchronization rights

Let's say you're already making cool graphic stuff on your computer, and you want to use somebody else's music to create an Enhanced CD to promote your digital ability. Perhaps you want to use the song "High and Dry" by Radiohead. You can clear the rights on the song. The next question to ask is: do you have to get permission to use their music in conjunction with your visuals?

"If you're using your visuals and somebody else's music, you need to secure Synchronization Rights and a Master Use License," confirms Leventhal.

A Synchronization Right means getting permission from the composer to synchronize this composition with visuals. It's the paperwork you always need in order to do a music video or put a song into a movie.

Vice versa is a different set of rules. If it's your music and their visuals, first you must ascertain if the original visuals have a soundtrack. If this is the case, you must get permission to change the soundtrack. If the visuals are photographs, film footage, drawings, or anything else that's really cool that you want to work with . . . it's simple. You just license the freestanding content into the product.

public performance rights

Are you going to demo the product at a school or trade show? Then you need public performance rights. A performance is considered public if it is "open to the public" or at any place where a substantial number of persons outside of the "normal circle of family and social acquaintances" gather. Most music publishers permit either ASCAP or BMI to license their public performance rights.

fair use

Now that we've given you the basic rules, let's muddy the waters a bit. There are times that you don't need to clear something—when it falls under the guidelines of Fair Use. Before you leap for joy, be advised that there is no Fair Use case law for multimedia.

Fair Use is a section of the copyright code that deals with specific uses of some materials. For example, when you watch the nightly news and they show a picture of Michael Jackson dancing in conjunction with a news item about him and some thirteen-year-old boy, they didn't have to clear the rights to that stock footage because it's news. Editorial news can also fall under Fair Use.

According to Statute 17, Fair Use can be used "for purposes such as criticism, comment, news reporting, teaching (including multiple copies for classroom use), scholarship, or research . . ." Note that parody can fall under the "criticism" or "comment" categories.

Be advised, Fair Use is a very dangerous area and you had better be very careful about using material without clearing the rights.

"It's best not to assume Fair Use," confirms Schreibman McGrew. "Fair use was invented for educational applications, not for commercial use. For editorial use, there's one side of clearance that is not needed. You're allowed to use the image of that person—that's a First Amendment right—as long as it's not on the box or advertising what's featured in any way. As long as it is truly an editorial product and the personality is not being featured in the piece, you should be fine."

Sometimes people wonder, "Can I just do it and assume it's Fair Use?" The answer is no, you really can't without avoiding legal trouble.

Different courts have different views on Fair Use. Basically, Fair Use is a defense to copyright infringement. The defendant uses it as a scapegoat. The excuse is, "I know that I did this, I know that it was not an authorized use of this copyrighted material, but I get to use it because I'm performing one of these various functions: news, editorial, or reference." Fair Use doesn't mean you didn't use the material, it means that you have a defense as to why you used the material without permission. Be forewarned, Fair Use is an unreliable defense. You had better be absolutely certain of what you're doing before you decide to go off and not clear rights on something.

"You could really hang yourself if it's found not to be Fair Use, then you've infringed on the copyright," observes Leventhal.

rights clearance agencies

Your lawyer is your advisor, but he's not necessarily the person who would be the most cost efficient at Rights Clearance. If you're attempting a rock encyclopedia, you're going to have to clear all of the composers and all of the masters for each song. You're going to be clearing photos (and perhaps negotiating for the right to crop that photo). There are video clips, which could have a lot of different rights in them. You'll be clearing text out of already published books and newspapers for articles critiquing the work, or something that somebody just wrote. There will be so many types of clearances that it will make sense for you to engage the services of a clearance house such as Suzy Vaughn and Associates, Music Clearing House Limited, or Second Line Search.

"Closing these licenses and these agreements can be your biggest stumbling block," declares Om's Gray. "You can have a 95 percent finished piece, and you've not quite closed out this one piece of video and some label's stalling on it . . . they've agreed to give it to you, they've agreed on the price, but just getting that signed contract back can hold up everything."

If you can work it into your budget, using a Rights Clearance house may make life much easier and even more efficient than using lawyers. It's a clearance house's job to sit there all day long and talk to publishing companies and record labels and film clip libraries about the prices of this content, so Rights Clearance entities are going to know the prices for multimedia better than almost anybody else. They're also going to be able to make better deals because they may be clearing rights on 500 different items at the same time.

"Whether you clear the material yourself or go through a clearance house depends on time and money," observes Schreibman McGrew. "If you've got all the time in the world, then you can learn to do it yourself. But it's good to use a rights clearance person—especially for a big project—because they know the sources, they've done it before."

In the long run, a clearance house may prove to be less expensive. It may cost you $175 to clear a clip through a clearing house, whereas a lawyer's hourly rate will be closer to $225 an hour. It's going to take a lawyer $175 just to find the person to clear the rights through. The

Rights Clearance houses may have the necessary clearance people on their speed dial and they've talked to them twice today already.

Q&A: george bartko

George Bartko is the chief operating officer at Second Line Search, a stock footage agency and multimedia clearance house. Second Line Search understands the clearance business as well as anybody in multimedia.

GEORGE, HERE'S THE SITUATION. I'M WORKING ON A MULTIMEDIA PROJECT THAT'S GOING TO TAKE UP 200 MEGABYTES ON A DISC. IT'S GOING TO INCORPORATE VIDEO, STILL PHOTOGRAPHY, SONG LYRICS, EXCERPTS OF SONGS, AND INTERVIEWS WITH A BAND. WHAT PART OF THE BUDGET SHOULD BE ALLOCATED FOR RIGHTS CLEARANCE?

George Bartko: Rights Clearances on all this stuff is going to vary, it really depends on the sort of content you're going after. Prices will range depending on the artist and the record label we're dealing with to clear, so it's really difficult to give numbers without knowing the content you're trying to license.

WHAT ARE THE DIFFERENT RATES FOR FILM FOOTAGE?

George Bartko: Studios are giving me rates up to ten thousand dollars a clip. Some of them are giving me three thousand dollars a clip, others are given to me for one thousand dollars a clip. It ranges all over the map depending on how the studio values that title. If I'm buying footage from other stock libraries, I get a range at fifty dollars a second, three thousand dollars a minute. That's about our range, from fifteen hundred dollars a minute up to three thousand dollars a minute, depending on the type of footage we sell.

WHEN YOU SELL A FILM CLIP, DOES IT COME WITH RIGHTS CLEARED ON IT?

George Bartko: It's footage where there are no rights to deal with, it's free and clear. But, in certain instances like if you're going to be buying sports footage from me, I might have an athlete on some of my images that we'd have to pay. That's the game across the board when it comes to photography or video. You're going to get rights to the footage and then you've got to deal with what your other underlying rights are.

IS THERE A MINIMUM AMOUNT OF TIME THAT YOU HAVE TO PURCHASE?

George Bartko: It depends on the source. On our own material, we usually have a thirty-second or a one-minute minimum, depending on the collection. So, depending on how many sources you are buying from, that would vary.

allocating funds for clearances

There's no set percentage of your development budget that should be put aside for legal and Rights Clearance; as always, that has to be determined on a project-by-project basis. If we go back to our rock encyclopedia model, to do a compendium of rock 'n' roll would require photos and interviews with the artist, bios, critiques, and reviews, anything you can uncover about the musician. You could put a fabulous amount of information that will give you a sense of where and when and why and how social situations gave rise to specific genres of music. It's a tremendous project. Estimates for Rights Clearance, between the transaction cost of paying the lawyer and the actual payments to people for the rights, are going to be at least as much as all the rest of the production itself. So better than 50 percent of your entire budget will be allocated for this area.

Some of you out there may be going, "Well that's insane, I was able to pull this off for less." Maybe you can, good luck. Hassles of Rights Clearance are a big reason why a lot of the most compelling CD-ROMs that you see out there are totally original works.

"We don't have a clearance person, so we hire somebody," notes Liz Heller, senior vice president of New Media at Capitol Records. "We allocate what we think the cost is based on, whether they have controlled compositions or not, those kinds of things. We build it into the profit and loss statement, we just go through it on a case-by-case basis."

clearances: getting creative

Second Line Search devised an innovative approach to the rights and royalties issue when they were putting together an interactive version of the game *Trivial Pursuit*. In order to get around the accounting nightmare of paying royalties to all the celebrities involved, it was proposed that a donation be made in the celebrity's name to charity.

"We put $10,000 in a pool for that fund, and asked all the celebrities to sign on," recalls Bartko. "They didn't get paid anything, but it would be publicized that they contributed toward that $10,000 by giving us the rights to their image."

Second Line Search was able to clear a majority of the people for an interactive version *Trivial Pursuit* without paying individual royalties. Of course, some celebrities did have specific stipulations. Michael Jackson had to write his own question. Carl Lewis had to be on the packaging. Stephie Graff had to be playing with a certain racquet.

circumventing clearances

Whether it's on the World Wide Web or CD-ROM, any unauthorized use of material is copyright infringement. So if you don't have permission to use a piece of content, you can't use it. If you infringe a copyright, you can be sued in federal court. Even if there's no way to determine damage, you can be hit with statutory damages. Lawsuits are more than a hand slap. You get sued and you may spend one hundred thousand dollars defending yourself, or you may just turn around and file bankruptcy. But if somebody wants to make an example of you—and there are plenty of big companies out there who will—you're fried.

The area where you see people getting sued for copyright infringement on a regular basis is with sound samples in rap music, and they're losing. You cannot just sample music. And it doesn't matter if the existing material that's being borrowed is on another audio CD or CD-ROM or the Web. It doesn't even matter if it's for profit, if you use it, you're open to getting slapped with a lawsuit.

When you get hit for copyright infringement, the acts and responses may all be different. They may send you a letter saying "discontinue immediately or we'll hurt you." You discontinue and you're done. Or, the first thing you may hear about is a lawsuit, and then you're stuck defending this lawsuit for a long time to come. You never know what somebody wants.

"I've been in cases where we felt that we were right, where we hadn't committed any kind of infringement and the profit was minimal and we attempted to settle," relates attorney Leventhal. "We basically said, 'We're right, but we'll give you the money we've made just to get out of this lawsuit.' We could see what was coming, but we never got a response. And you sit there and you defend. There are attorney's fees provisions in some of these statutes that provide that the prevailing party is awarded their attorney's fees at the end of a lawsuit. So, the longer they prosecute against you, the more money you're going to have to pay at the end. It's ugly. You don't want to just put copyrighted information out there and go, 'Well, all right, if they get mad I'll take it off.' It's an extremely risky and fiscally unsound move."

net domain name rights

The following article has been reprinted by permission of the authors, Allen S. Melser and Becky Troutman of the Washington, DC law firm, Reid & Priest.

A company's trademarks and service marks are valuable intellectual property assets that enhance its marketplace recognition and reputation. Using your company's name or one of its trademarks or service marks as a domain name can be an important advertising tool. In addition, failure to police use of your company's name, trademarks, and/or service marks over the Internet by others may weaken your company's trademark rights or eliminate them altogether.

A trademark (or "mark") is any word, symbol, or slogan used in connection with a product to identify the source of the product and distinguish it from other products. Similarly, a service mark is a word, symbol or slogan used in connection with a service to identify the source of the service and distinguish it from others. Trademark protection is based on use of a mark in commerce. A federally registered mark is protected under federal trademark law. The trademark registration owner can prevent others from using any mark that is so similar to the registered mark as to cause a likelihood of consumer confusion as to the source or sponsorship of the goods or services of the parties. It is possible to register a domain name as a federal trademark or service mark. The U.S. Patent and Trademark Office's policy statement on federal registration of domain names as trademarks can be accessed at: *www.uspto.gov.*

It is important to note that even if a mark is not federally registered, it is protected under common law.

Each country has its own domain name authority that is responsible for registering domain names. These domain name authorities may or may not exercise control over domain name selection by applicants. The U.S. domain name authority, the Internet National Information Center (InterNIC), only recently began to consider third party trademark rights in granting domain names to applicants. Under InterNIC's current policy, the owner of a U.S. federal or a foreign trademark registration may, after notifying the domain name registrant, advise InterNIC that it is being injured by use of a domain name matching the trademark. If the domain name activation date is prior to the earlier of (1) the trademark registrant's date of first use of the mark or (2) the effective date of the trademark registration, then the domain name registrant will be allowed to continue using the domain name and the trademark registrant must seek its remedy in court.

If the domain name activation date is subsequent to the earlier of the trademark registrant's date of first use or effective registration date, InterNIC will request the domain name registrant to prove ownership of a federal or foreign trademark registration that was registered prior to the earlier of (1) the date of InterNIC's request for proof or (2) the date the trademark registrant notified InterNIC of the dispute. If the domain name registrant fails to provide such proof, then InterNIC will help the domain name registrant transfer to a new domain name and place the disputed domain name on "hold." Once a domain name is placed on "hold," no one can use the domain name until the parties submit to InterNIC a court order stating which party is entitled to use the domain name or other proof that the dispute has been resolved. This procedure prevents the domain name registrant from using the mark absent a court judgment in its favor or other resolution of the dispute. Thus, the domain name registrant must be willing to litigate or enter into a settlement arrangement in order to continue using the domain name. One significant problem with this policy is that it fails to take into account common law trademark rights that the domain name registrant may have.

If either party files a lawsuit before InterNIC places the domain name on "hold," then InterNIC will "deposit control of the domain name into the registry of the court." This means that InterNIC will turn the problem over to the court to decide which party has rights to the domain name.

Therefore, if a domain name registrant is using one of your company's federally registered trademarks or service marks as a domain name, InterNIC will prevent the domain name registrant or any other party from using that registered mark as its domain name unless InterNIC is presented with a judgment or settlement in the domain name registrant's favor. However, your company will also be prevented from using the mark as its domain name. Therefore, if your company wishes to use the mark as its own domain name, it will be necessary to litigate the matter and obtain a favorable judgment or settlement stating that your company is entitled to use the mark. InterNIC's domain name policy is posted at: *http://internic.net.*

It is unclear whether U.S. companies will be able to enforce an injunction or judgment against foreign domain name holders or vice versa. In a recent case, the U.S. District Court for the Southern District of New York allowed a U.S. plaintiff, Playboy Enterprises Inc., to enforce a prior injunction prohibiting distribution or sale of PLAYMEN magazines in the U.S. against an Italian defendant that had started using the PLAYMEN mark on an Internet Web site (*Playboy Enterprises Inc. v. Chuckleberry Publishing Inc.*, 39 U.S.P.Q.2d 1746 [S.D.N.Y. 1996]). The court ruled that making computer images on the PLAYMEN Internet site in Italy available to U.S. computer users qualified as "distribution" in the U.S. because users were able to download pictorial images from the PLAYMEN site onto their home computers. Therefore, the Internet site was an advertisement through which the Italian defendant distributed its pictorial images throughout the U.S. in violation of the prior injunction.

Copyright 1996 Allen S. Melser and Becky L. Troutman

Mr. Melser is co-chair of the intellectual property group of Reid & Priest, LLP, a law firm with offices in New York and Washington, D.C. He can be reached at: *amelser@reidpriest.com.*

Ms. Troutman is an associate in Reid & Priest's intellectual property group. She can be reached at: *btroutman@reidpriest.com.*

"Net Domain Name Rights" is provided with the understanding that it is not intended to provide legal services and that the authors are not rendering legal services. Because each situation is unique, if you have a legal problem, you should seek the advice of experienced counsel.

royalties

Once you've cleared the material for your production, another question arises: do you have to pay royalties? This question really depends on who the person is, what he wants, and what you're doing.

"In general, we haven't paid royalties to the actual creators of the content, like the video director, or the photographer," declares Capitol Record's Heller. "In all fairness to everyone who has provided content, I don't really feel like I can give them a royalty."

What you pay in royalties really depends on who you're dealing with. Some people are very cool and some people are very afraid. Some will just say "You know, give me a hundred bucks." Or, "You can have it for these uses." Or, "You agree to conduct yourself in a nice sort of way and I'll grant you the right to use these images or this sound byte."

If the involved parties insist on financial compensation, you can save the potential accounting nightmare and offer to donate a flat fee to a good cause such as Lifebeat or Rock For Choice.

who owns what

Let's say your team has cleared all the copyrights and put together a great Web site. Who owns the copyright on the Web site, and who owns the copyright on the materials in it? Where do intellectual property rights lie with regard to multimedia?

All that is contractual. Figure nobody's going to grant you the rights to the song just because you put it on the disc. The underlying concept behind copyright law is that if you create something, you own it—absent of several circumstances. You can give away your work. For this to be legitimate, copyright transfers have to be in writing. The other position would be an employment situation which would qualify the work as a "work-for-hire."

If you are an employee of a company and the work you are doing is within the course and scope of your duties at the company, then the company will own that work. If you've been asked to do work by a company and you're not an employee, it's not work-for-hire—unless there's a document executed before the job starts stating that all work done on this project is work-for-hire status and that you are merely entitled to compensation for that work.

"You hand somebody a box of content, and you say, 'Okay, create an interface using all this content,'" explains Heller about the process of creating a CD-ROM. "It's like a remix. And generally speaking, you don't get royalties on it if you're the remixer."

"On some of my discs, it's contractor work-for-hire, and people own the copyrights. They own the production," confirms Mark Waldrep of AIX Entertainment. "I can hang on to the materials in the assembled form. We copyright the screens, the contract doesn't give the label the right to them. The screens are not worth anything. I can't go off and sell those rights to somebody else because they're attached to the record company's rights. But, it does give me the right to promote using those screens in other things . . . although the Rolling Stones is a curious one. Every time I open my mouth about them I have to get some kind of clearance."

Q&A: liz heller

Liz Heller is the senior vice president in charge of new media at Capitol Records. She is one of the most forward thinking of all record company, new media executives. She was the first to institute the band Web site, using it to promote such groups as Megadeth, the Beastie Boys, The Beatles, and Duran Duran. In the Enhanced arena, she has spearheaded projects with artists like Yoko Ono and Bonnie Raitt.

IF YOU'RE CROSS UTILIZING ALREADY EXISTING ASSETS SUCH AS INTERVIEWS, PHOTOS, AND VIDEOS, DO YOU ALREADY HAVE THE CLEARANCES ON MATERIAL YOU'VE USED PREVIOUSLY?

Liz Heller: Not necessarily. Some things, yes, but it depends. It depends on the cameraman who shot the eight-millimeter film for the band in the studios. Half the time it's a fan or a friend of the band, so it's not difficult to get, but just because we've used it before doesn't mean we've got it for all those rights. In fact, a lot of stuff we don't.

WHEN YOU LICENSE MATERIAL FOR DIGITAL MEDIA, DO YOU HAVE TO PAY FOR IT AGAIN?

Liz Heller: We try not to, but it is a reality, definitely. With the Beastie Boys CD-ROM we are paying four or five people who contributed content. They were actually hired by the Beastie Boys.

HAVE YOU FIGURED OUT HOW MUCH YOU'RE GOING TO PAY FOR CONTENT?

Liz Heller: I didn't actually do the content clearance part of the Beasties. We gave them a budget, but I haven't heard back on how it's broken down. Everybody feels like this team should get paid a little bit of money because they created the content. Maybe they did it for fun, or they didn't get paid in the first place, I don't really know the history of the project.

PAYING FOR THE BEASTIE BOYS CONTENT IS A NEW PRECEDENCE FOR CAPITOL RECORDS.

Liz Heller: Exactly. You always want to try to own the content or control the content, which means paying for it to get done. It's expensive, so you add it on to some other projects. Like, if you're going to go and shoot an interview, you figure how many things can you use it for? MTV, the Enhanced CD, the Web site . . . you just keep utilizing your assets. But you also want stuff that's exclusive, so there's an added value. You always want to try to have some sort of new spin on it, because a lot of people that are really interested in a lot of the content are already fans. They want to see something they didn't see before. They want to see something that takes them to a new place with that artist. So you have to break it down into where it falls somewhere in between those two.

DO YOU PAY ROYALTIES FOR SONG BITS, PHOTOS, ANYTHING ON THE INTERNET?

Liz Heller: We have paid for some images that we've licensed from somewhere else to use on the Internet, but that's pretty rare. All that's changing now anyway. I'm not really sure what the impact is going to be. I don't think we fully know about the implications of the new regulations or how we fully resolve all the things that are going to happen on the Internet.

In terms of all the new areas where there might be money exchanged, we haven't gone down that path yet. Of course, we will try to hang onto the content rights for promotion as long as we possibly can.

chapter 9

business development: music publishers

Music is the timeless experience of constant change.

—Jerry Garcia

the power brokers

In the early days of commercial interactive media (1993-ish) the major record labels began to launch exciting "new media" divisions by transferring project managers and producers from other divisions to fill these thrilling new positions. These individuals did not necessarily have a multimedia "skill set," but they could walk-the-walk and talk-the-talk of a seasoned new media guru. When an artist would approach a label about producing a multimedia product, the corporate honchos could simply steer the artist to the appropriate department. The label didn't necessarily have to produce anything. At the time, it was more important to be in the *position* to produce multimedia product. That was then.

This is now. The labels have shaken off the cobwebs of the past and are making great strides toward making a business out of multimedia music. Warner Bros. Records released multimedia titles from the Barenaked Ladies, Mike Oldfield, Love in Reverse, and Randy Newman in the first half of 1996. By the end of that year, Columbia Records was releasing every audio CD with enhanced content, but not labeling the package with this information. Elektra released Jackson Browne, Tracey Chapman, and The Doors. Mercury's first interactive commitment is Kiss. Atlantic released the *Spew* collaboration, Hootie and the Blowfish, and the Pet Shop Boys. There's talk of Filter, the Red Hot Chili Peppers, and Joan Osbourne. The labels are just starting to get it together and take a chance on Enhanced product such as CDs or Web zones.

"With the compatibility problems and pricing issues that exist, it's hard to commit to one set way of producing Enhanced CDs," notes Bruce Hartley, senior director of new media at Mercury Records. "The possibilities are great though, and we're watching them closely."

As expected, each company has its own internal operating structure for multimedia. A&M has execs who make interactive decisions in conjunction with the band. Capitol Records approaches many of its groups direct, Columbia makes product for everything. MCA is developing specific tools. Epic and Geffen are kicking around some projects, but have yet to deliver product. Time/Warner is so big, they've got five different places to pitch product.

"Right now, multimedia production is an erosion of the value that they've worked so hard to create," observes Christopher Smith of Om Records. "Record labels control a huge chunk of the pie. They make so much money off their artists, and they're not backing any 'extras' that may cut into that profit margin. Many are reluctant to even touch something new."

Part of the problem is that the industry is still trying to agree on issues such as standards, royalties, price points, artist involvement, and all the rest of the issues crucial to successfully incorporating new media into its business mold. The industry needs solid business models to fully commit to new technology. And since most interactive music product is just now arriving on the retail shelves, we are a few years away from a business norm. If a few Enhanced titles "go platinum" in the next few months, that would definitely jump start things.

enhanced cd models

One other issue of concern to record labels are multimedia formats. We're not talking about the tired Mac versus PC format wars. Most of today's Enhanced music titles are hybrid Mac/PC discs. When we talk about formats, we're really talking about prevailing "models" for successful consumer price points.

Albhy Galuten, multimedia guru for MCA Records, sees three different types of "Enhanced" material evolving:

- *Audio with Promotional Package*. Something like the Rolling Stones *Stripped* album on Enhanced CD, or Kitaro's *An Enhanced Evening*. These titles are produced fast, with a template, in as little as two weeks. They generally use repurposed material and are often created with easy-to-use authoring tools such as Macromedia Director.

- *Paper Clip*. This is a CD-5 format like the Cranberries' *Doors and Windows* or Barenaked Ladies' *Shoebox* EP. The disc is an interim project, containing several new or live tunes with some deeper Enhanced material. Its purpose is to maintain the band's popularity while it records its new album. This format is also used to introduce new bands, such as Ardent Records did with Spot and Two Minute Hate. The product has the ability to link to the band or record label's Web site. The fixed medium becomes a dynamic force rather than simply an Enhanced archive.

- *Power to the Artist*. Tools which allow the artist to create the product by themselves, to better communicate their thoughts and ideas.

Currently, there are several different "models" of Enhanced CDs emerging in the marketplace. These include:

- Full-length Enhanced CD

- CD Single

- CD-5

- Two Sku

CD SINGLES

CD Singles are the nineties version of a 45 rpm record. This is a concept that was initiated by Trauma Records—one of the independent labels that was eating up a healthy percentage of the music market. Trauma came up with the concept of cultivating young artists such as Bush and No Doubt and making their material regularly available as Enhanced CDs. No Doubt's *Just A Girl* or *Spiderwebs* and Bush's *Glycerine* are prime examples. Trauma's lead in releasing CD Singles is now being picked up by other labels, such as Atlantic Records. The CD Single may actually revive the diminishing singles business.

Essentially, CD Singles are simple, low budget versions of Enhanced CDs. They retail in record stores for somewhere in the neighborhood of $3.50. These products tend to include the video, promotional materials, and whatever else happens to be lying around in the production studio.

In the case of *Glycerine*, production company Highway One had previously cleared video material from working on Bush's *Little Things* CD-5. They shared those assets and threw some of the remaining video material on *Glycerine*. On the CD Single for *Spiderwebs*, No Doubt played an integral role in the Enhanced CD process.

"We came up with ideas like incorporating other versions of the song: a demo version or maybe a couple of live versions," notes Tony Kanal, No Doubt's bass player. "We're also going to add stuff like interviews and snippets. It's going to be more personal."

CD-5

CD-5 is emerging as an interim project between albums. It's an Enhanced version of the EP—the extended-play album. A CD-5 features several tracks, usually from three to five songs. The tunes can be live, cover versions, album outtakes, or tunes that were originally intended for movie soundtracks. For fine examples of CD-5 product, check out Bonnie Raitt's *Burning Down the House* or Barenaked Ladies' *Shoebox* EP.

CD-5 is the type of product that independent labels, like the now defunct Ardent, offered with such artists as Spot and Two Minute Hate. These discs range in price according to material. They can go for as low as six to as much as twelve dollars. They are priced to give the listener the corresponding bang for her buck.

TWO-SKU

A few CDs, like Jackson Browne's *Looking East,* Randy Newman's *Faust,* and Metallica's *Load* were released in two versions: regular audio CD and Enhanced. The main reason for two-sku releases is that the record companies are commissioning the Enhanced content too late in the album's development cycle. The Enhanced product is missing the release date, but it's been paid for and the band is expecting the content on the disc. With *Faust* Enhanced, the release date was missed by a year.

Another reason for releasing a product two-sku is to allow for two different pricing structures. The traditional audio CD sells for $11.99 to $15.99. The Enhanced version can sell for up to three dollars more.

"This way of releasing titles is certainly confusing. It's difficult for the retailer to place and price two discs," confirms Georgia Bergman, vice president of Creative Enterprises for Warner Bros. Records. "The industry is still trying to determine what the pricing structure has to be. If the pricing structure has to be higher, the labels have to decide whether or not the audience for that artist is going to want to pay for it. It's easier releasing an Enhanced title one sku. But is it acceptable to the consumer if it's one sku at nineteen dollars? I don't know."

dealmakers

Truly successful businessmen—real estate tycoon Donald Trump, FedEx's founder Fred Smith, record mogul David Geffen—are not known so much for their creations as much as their business skills. In other words, it doesn't matter what kind of product you create or service you provide—unless you have a solid business foundation backing you up, success will be hard to come by.

In Hollywood, if you are a creative genius, agents will beat down your door for the chance of representing you. In the music industry, hot artists will sign ten-year management agreements worth millions of dollars. Of course, management will take a hefty percentage of your earnings in the process. But don't worry. They'll earn every dime of it.

In the exciting business of interactive music, you basically have two ways to rise to the top. Get in bed with the record companies or do it yourself.

"It's like just about anything else in Hollywood. It helps to know somebody," offers legal council Michael Leventhal. "It could be an agent. It could be a lawyer. It could be a manager. It could be just somebody you know who knows somebody who's one of the above. You need somebody to get your work in front of the person who's going to make that decision."

The music industry is definitely a game of who you know. At this moment in time, many software producers and publishers have little or no experience dealing with managers, agents, guilds, or unions. As the interactive media industry matures, this will, of course, change . . . music managers will inevitably sign multimedia producers to representation contracts. In the meantime, the producer must learn how to network with the industry "insiders."

"I'm a firm believer that not anybody can just do this," declares Leo Rossi, Highway One's technical wizard. "If you're not creative and you don't understand the business and logistics of entertainment, you're not going to jump right into this. You have to have a good entertainment background. You have to understand production. You have to know the psyche of an artist, and how managers, agents, and record companies work. It's a real 'who you know' business."

Getting your demo looked at is like sending in an album to the A&R (artist and repertoire) department. If you can get the record company to partake in what you've created, you're most of the way there.

"It's about having relationships within the industry. If you know the label and you've worked with them in the past, or you build a relationship, it can be very easy," reveals Om Record's Christopher Smith. "The more relationships we build, the quicker things happen. If you don't have relationships, you're not happening in the music business."

"Anybody who wants to get into the Enhanced industry, learn the technology end of it," declares Rossi. "There's always going to be room for someone who does great graphics."

Find the people who are heading up the new technology arms of each company and make friends. You need to educate yourself about who's who—then target the people in charge of your area of interest. Mind you, each record label has a different name for these divisions.

Often, they are called new media or new technology divisions, but other times, it's media services or marketing. You next need to find a way to get in with the company to demonstrate what you can do. Pitch yourself every chance you get, without becoming obnoxious, and take advantage of every opportunity to further your career.

reflections: rev entertainment

The lucky team at REV Entertainment got an exclusive contract to work with Atlantic Records on Enhanced CDs and music based CD-ROMs that was under Danny Goldberg's regime. There were modifications made to REV's contract when Mr. Goldberg left Atlantic Records in 1994. To date, they have released a compilation disc called Spew *and are working in conjunction with various labels on several other projects. According to REV's CEO Todd Fearn, the REV/Atlantic alliance came about by being at the right place at the right time, and having a demo handy.*

Fearn: We got hooked up with Atlantic at the NARM (National Association of Record Merchandisers) show in February 1994. We had put together an Eric Clapton demo for Polygram. People from Atlantic saw it and got all excited about it. They brought down people from A&R and A-Vision (the home video department, which is now known as Warner Vision). A couple weeks later, Atlantic Records' president Danny Goldberg showed up. Then they brought (former) CEO Doug Morris down. They got all excited and we did a deal.

reflections: aix entertainment

As you now know from reading this book, AIX is responsible for the Rolling Stones' Stripped *Enhanced CD, the largest selling Enhanced product to date. Mark Waldrep is the company's chief executive officer.*

Waldrep: AIX was started with the intent to be a content provider focusing on Enhanced CDs. Our other company, Pacific Coast

Soundworks, is a digital, multimedia facility and mastering studio. We perform the last step in the creation of CDs—perfecting the audio. That was our automatic "in" to the record companies.

Having had a background with multimedia positioned our studio as multimedia audio experts. We understood the file formats and a lot of the computer-based stuff. So it seemed like the natural marriage. We could afford to get into the interactive business because it didn't require a 600-thousand-dollar investment to produce one title or one game.

I put together a prototype of an artist on my label, Doug DeForest, with a band called Civilization. They already had audio tracks and video material. I made prototype product to demonstrate what I considered to be a multimedia music disc.

It was in October 1994, and some folks at EMI and Virgin—Joe Keiner, Cynthia Bryce, Liz Heller—invited a dozen companies to come to the Capitol tower and show what they were doing in this world of "combination technology" discs. AIX was the first and only company out of the twelve companies represented to actually put a disc in a machine and have it play music and multimedia. Most of the other companies, as I understand it, were just talking, "Well, if you give me money, or let us have the opportunity over the next six months, we'll create something for you that will be really cool."

This gathering was basically an information session. There was really no intent by any of the people in the room at the time to rush right out and hire a developer to produce Enhanced CDs. But it gave us a kick. It got us moving in the right direction.

studio deadlines

After months of sitting around the boardroom over a catered lunch that will be deducted from the budget of an artist that has yet to release his first album, the record company decides to make an Enhanced CD for one of its rising bands.

Examining the release schedule of the album, the execs realize that the marketing schedule dictates that the album will be released in exactly sixty days. You, the Enhanced CD developer, get called in on the project and the record company tells you that they have decided that the album does warrant Enhanced material and that they need the material immediately. That means you've got to have the Enhanced gold master completed and debugged in thirty-five days so that it can be pressed and shipped as part of the audio CD package. Can it be done?

"The Rolling Stones was completed in ten days for $20,000—start to finish," affirms Waldrep. "I got nine photographs, I was given transparencies and a videotape with some interview clips on it, and some of the video elements from the live *Voodoo Lounge* tour."

That's a worst case scenario, definitely. But when you finally get the gig, you're going to be at the mercy of record company schedules. Miss your deadlines once, and you won't work in the record business again.

"Enhanced CDs must be produced for very limited budgets in a very short time frame to match the model that the record companies are used to operating under. It's not the multimedia game model, where, if you need it, you can extend your deadline by another two months," affirms Waldrep.

To scare you even further, keep in mind that once you finish a project, it has to be cleaned up.

"If I take three or four weeks to build a project, it might take me two-and-a-half weeks just to debug the thing," reminds Highway One's Ken Caillat "It can be a horror."

corporate pov

"There are a few ways we decide who to work with," explains Liz Heller, who, on good days, is Capitol's interactive goddess. "Some developers come with the artist, like in the case of John Hiatt, Yoko Ono, or Dave Koz. In the case of Bonnie Raitt, Highway One had worked with artists that were like Bonnie in terms of her stature and the amount of things that'd be required in terms of management, clearances, and artist approval."

"It's up to the artist," notes Georgia Bergman of Warner Bros. "If you're an independent producer with the goal of developing a title, going out and negotiating with a label is a very big first step. If you have friends who are artists who you can get in on a collaboration, that's the easiest way to go. Get some experience before you leap into the joyous world of copyright clearances."

"You're better off dealing where you can be creative rather than being tied up by all the legal contracts that you would have with the label," confirms Om's Steve Gray. "Find a friend who has some quality music that you can make an Enhanced track to. That's the way to start."

All of the small labels—Om and Seventh Wave—put out a fair bit of material on unknown bands. The main reason being that they can create and clear content with a minimum of expense. The product is easier to develop and you've got something unique to show the labels.

"I need to see what sort of work people have done. I have to assume that somebody who's coming here has done something; it's having a disc, having a show reel, having something to show that you can actually create," informs Bergman. "It doesn't have to be a music project, but if it's not a music project, they have to have a lot of imagination, or they have to have some approach as to why they would be good at doing music. It doesn't necessarily translate that if you can do industrials, you can do music."

Another oddball way of doing things is going to the record company, and "tell them you'll do it for free," offers Tom McGrew. "The record company will approve of something if it can be completed for free. They just don't want to pay anybody. This is still all too new. It's a process that they've never been involved with before."

Q&A: liz heller

How will the record companies make a profit on Enhanced CDs? For that question, we've consulted Capitol's Liz Heller, a new technology executive straddling both sides of the enhanced challenge—empathizing with the artist while supporting a corporation's financial concerns.

HAS CAPITOL RECORDS FIGURED OUT HOW THEY'RE PRICING ENHANCED CDS?

Liz Heller: We're right in the middle of deciding. We haven't actually had the sales figures on a full-sku example yet, where the Enhanced version is the same exact thing as the audio album. We have yet to sort out if it should be just one sku or if it should be additional to the album. We're talking about it, but we haven't decided.

WHAT PRICE ARE YOU SELLING YOUR DISCS FOR?

Liz Heller: The Yoko Ono *Rising Mixes* CD is priced at $11.98. It's more of an EP price, yet it has sixty minutes of music on it as well. It's full of content, which we already had on hand. We avoided the clearance costs, so it wasn't very expensive to make.

Bonnie Raitt has about twenty-four minutes of music. It's priced at $5.98 which was something that we did because of the CD-5 aspect. I'm happy about the price because that means it's more visible as a "singles" product.

THAT'S A BIG DIFFERENCE IN PRICE!

Liz Heller: I don't know what the pricing is going to come down to be. I have very mixed feelings whether Enhanced should be the same price as an audio CD. There are like some very real hard costs that go into making these things. With the margins for CDs dropping daily, we're conceivably adding additional costs into a market and a margin that's not increasing. Maybe all that will change with DVD, but right now, Enhanced is a very tight fit. I think that's why the industry hasn't come together yet.

chapter 10

business development:
contracts

Music is the major form of communication. It's the commonest vibration, the people's news broadcast.

—**Richie Havens**

salad days, sleepless nights

Congratulations! After painstakingly screening dozens of music developers from around the globe, MegaMusic Interactive has decided to hire you. They want you to produce several items; an Enhanced CD for their new band, Pumping Red, a Pumping Red CD-ROM adventure game, and a Web site homage to the band and its music.

Now it's on to contract phase . . . where deal points are hashed out in an environment of honesty and cooperation. You hope.

A successful negotiation does not always conclude in a deal. Sometimes, negotiating parties agree to disagree and discontinue the deal. However, a written document that is deemed fair and equitable by both parties is the crowning achievement. Negotiating a contract can be a challenging "trial by fire" to those new to the negotiation process. Your first couple of interactive gigs may have gone smoothly, involving a simple handshake, your blood and sweat working on the project, and very few headaches or misunderstandings. However, for every handshake deal, there are ten nightmare deals. How can the simple act of negotiating a contract turn your sanguine, salad days into sleepless nights?

Although no two deals are exactly alike, contract problems usually arise when both sides interpret the same deal point differently. Developers are creative beings. They tend to avoid the business of this business at all costs. Psychologists call it conflict avoidance. But rather than looking at this character trait as a weakness, developers should recognize this trait as a sign that they need a strong business "player" on their team to help them through this process. That's where a good lawyer or agent comes into play. The great part about having professional representation during the negotiation process is that someone else can be the bad guy. As the creative genius, the last thing you want to be doing is fighting about money with your employer. Stay off the front line. Use your business representative as a shield. And remember to stay above the fray at all costs. That's why you pay ten to twenty percent of your deal to your representatives, isn't it?

Issues such as compensation, delivery, intellectual property and ancillary components are the foundation of any contract. Each of these areas must be discussed and agreed upon before you start work on a project.

It is important that the multimedia production team understand how each of these issues are addressed and how they interrelate.

compensation

How much money you and your team will get to produce a project is what compensation is all about. Compensation includes all up-front salaries (a flat fee or buy-out as opposed to a time-based rate), deferred payment, milestone bonuses, and royalties.

The following compensation questions should be raised during the negotiation process:

- When will the money be paid? In stages? What are the required milestones for payment? Immediately in full or partially based on milestones on development? What is a fair process for determining if the conditions are satisfied?

- How is the percentage royalty set? On what is the royalty based, gross revenue, adjusted gross revenue, or net revenue? If the royalty is a percentage of the adjusted gross or net revenue, how is the adjusted gross revenue or net revenue defined? What is deducted (marketing expenses, shipping, taxes, etc.) and how do you audit for fairness?

■ How are revenues from bundled products handled? How are refunds and returns handled?

■ When are royalties paid? Thirty days after the publisher sells the title? Thirty days after the publisher receives payment? Is it a monthly or quarterly payment? How is this audited?

■ How are the merchandising sales revenues from ancillary products such as T-shirts, online, and toys to be handled?

delivery

Setting the right delivery expectations and parameters for the creation of the product is crucial to a good working relationship.

"The constraints applied by the labels, because they feel they have the upper hand, can be enormous," notes Om's Steve Gray, "I don't know if the major labels quite see the value of the multimedia."

Realistic development time tables and a mechanism to resolve issues are the two key aspects in dealing with this area. Note that the record companies will not necessarily be realistic, but since they're paying the bills, that is their prerogative. Below are some of the delivery issues that should be addressed during the negotiation:

■ Establishing realistic development time schedules (milestones) with some back-up plans for delays; building in incentives to meet the schedule, preferably in the form of milestone bonuses; addressing the issue of change orders from the publisher, making sure not to penalize the production team unfairly for radical changes not foreseen;

■ Setting a realistic approval process (comment period) that doesn't delay development yet ensures a quality product;

- Establishing reasonable boundaries on the extent and amount of revisions that may be requested;

- Providing for a resolution process in the event of disagreement (a mutually trusted third-party familiar with the area could serve as an arbitrator or mediator).

intellectual property

The most important issue in the intellectual property area is ownership. Who will be the owner of the title and its associated rights? Most record company funded deals are based on the idea that the producer is an independent contractor providing a service, the end product of which is owned by the publisher. The outcome of who ultimately owns the product will depend on how involved the production team gets in developing the product (the more developed, the better the argument that the production team should retain more ownership) and how the product will be distributed.

For example, a record company may feel actual ownership is less important if it has exclusive rights to distribute the product in certain territories or through certain channels or for some time period.

The issues surrounding the intellectual property are central to the deal, especially the ownership of the produced title. If you as producer do not end up owning the developed title, do not despair. Many a novice producer has reached success by first creating a hit product for her first employer, then moving on to better deals because of the new-found reputation.

What follows are a number of additional intellectual property issues that may arise during negotiations:

- Has all the content for the title been approved through a Rights Clearance process?

- Who will own the copyright to the product and related intellectual property rights? Will this ownership be for all code or just characters and story line? Will the writer be able to retain de-

217

sign formats, software engines, and the like for use in other titles not related to the product?

- What about merchandising rights?

- Are there options/rights of first refusal on future titles for the production team? Is this an exclusive production agreement? Will the production receive first option to develop derivative and ported products?

- What about rights to repurchase the intellectual property through some buyout mechanism? (i.e., Will the production team have the right to repurchase the titles intellectual property rights if sales fall below a set figure?)

- To what extent will each party receive a grant of licenses for use of trademarks of the other?

ancillary components

Several ancillary deal points crucial to a production team's agreement should be addressed during negotiations as well:

- *Provisions for Paid Ads.* Will the production team receive credit other than on-screen credit (i.e., instruction manuals, box sleeve, poster, award submissions, etc.).

- *Provisions for Sequels and Remakes.* Does the production team retain the right of first refusal on all sequels and remakes? At what payment rate?

- *The Drop Dead Clause.* What happens if the publisher decides to terminate you from the project or terminate the project completely? Is the terminating party required to pay the other party some form of compensation?

■ *Complimentary Product.* Will the production team receive complimentary copies of the title upon general release?

■ *Localization Consultancy.* Will the production team be utilized as a consultant or intermediary should the title be localized into another market (i.e., German version, French version)?

■ *Confidentiality Provisions.* Will the publisher safeguard sensitive material provided by the parties (salaries, etc.) often referred to in deals as no-quotes?

■ *Provisions for Additional Expenses.* Will the producer pick up travel and lodging expenses for research, meetings and/or appearances? What about a travel per diem? Will the producer pay for necessary guild pensions and welfare payments?

budgets influence everything

Perhaps the greatest influence on the current state of the interactive music business is the budget. Three years ago, when the music industry was first learning about new technology, music publishers, like their cohorts in the gaming business, believed that 175 to 400 thousand dollars was a realistic budget range for an interactive title. David Bowie's *Jump* CD-ROM, Sting's *All This Time*, or interactive titles like *MTV Unplugged*, or *The Cranberries: Doors and Windows* are prime examples.

Many Enhanced CDs (with the exception of CD singles) now have multimedia budgets in the ten-to-fifty-thousand-dollar range. It should be no surprise then that an Enhanced CD, with limited disc space and limited production funding, looks and functions the way it does.

"We can't justify spending a lot of money on this," confirms Nikke Slight, the online editor/media services liaison for Atlantic Records. "we did Hootie and the Blowfish for fifteen thousand dollars, the Pet Shop Boys for ten thousand dollars, and we don't even want to spend that much. We want to keep the price as low as possible."

It the film world, you might mistake an Enhanced project for a low-budget feature film such as *El Mariachi* or *Clerks*. Consequently, employee salaries, milestone bonuses, points, royalties, and the like differ dramatically because of the media (CD-ROM, Enhanced CD, the Web) and their corresponding budgets.

"The most defining aspect of all this has been budget," notes Mark Waldrep. "To make a project much cooler, you have to spend more effort on it than the actual dollars that have been allotted."

"One thing that we do in the software business that we never did in the record business is a financial forecast," observes Ted Cohen from Philips Interactive. "In the software industry, you do have certain kinds of products. You know that games are selling 'X' amount of units. You know that music product is selling between twenty-five thousand and one hundred thousand units (depending on who you talk to). It's easy to create a budget for an artist that can sell one hundred thousand pieces, or for an artist that's selling around twenty-five thousand pieces. It can't be done in a vacuum anymore. You have to look at the project's potential."

"Budgeting Enhanced CDs is still a hot potato," notes Capitol's Heller. "The budget is determined by my conversations with the developer. The budget process is similar to how we budget a music video. The artist has this grand vision. He'll say, 'We need a hundred.' And I reply,' Well, I only have fifty.' The artist says, 'Well, what am I going to lose?' And I say, 'Well, what am I going to get for my money?' I determine budgets by what I think I can get from the production company behind the artist, or what I think is really going to be required to do what they want to do. That has to do with degrees of complexity."

Once a record company decides upon budget, it has to figure out which department should pay for the development. Is an Enhanced CD a form of marketing and promotion? Is it a publicity element? If the artist is an integral part of the project, should it be recouped as part of artist development? How do these same issues apply to a Web site or a full-blown CD-ROM title?

"Anything that's commercial has got some kind of recoupability, that means it's A&R driven as opposed to marketing and promotion," notes Heller. "If it's something that everybody thinks would be really cool and the manager isn't sure but would like to do it, then we try to see if it's a marketing and promotion expense. We're trying not to set too many precedents because we don't really know where this stuff is going to end up . . . either for the artist or for ourselves. So we try to just kind of look at each case as a unique deal."

royalties

The most often asked question about payment concerns royalties. Are artists, producers, or writers entitled to them? How are they determined? Can you retire on them?

On a music CD-ROM title, you may be able to negotiate a modest royalty deal if you are one of the content creators or producers. But for Enhanced CD or Web experiences, royalties are rare.

"All producers should insist on a royalty," states attorney Richard Thompson of the law firm, Bloom Hergott Cook Diemer & Klein. "However, there are situations when they can't get a royalty. For example, the producer is coming in on something that is a preexisting property or something that has a lot of design work already done on it. Many publishers don't want to pay royalties. The reality is, that once a producer who's any good gets involved in a project that is already under way, the whole thing often times must be substantially redesigned. It turns out to be a huge amount of work for the producer and that warrants a royalty. I don't know anybody who's gotten rich off of royalties. But a producer of a hit title can potentially see tens of thousands of dollars in royalties."

"The big companies that are managing interactive music projects, such as Enhanced CDs, have hard and fast rules as to how much of the back end they're going to give up to creators. Usually something like 15 percent of the pie can be divvied up to all the creative people," notes Michael Leventhal. "If you're talking about the multimedia artists who are creating the CD-ROM, you pay them a production fee as they go, and they may or may not be in the back end. If they're bringing you the content, it's a different kind of project and you're going to have to give them a back end."

Those lucky developers with hot content or ideas should seek the best deal based on potential profit to be made. The ultimate number should be agreed upon after considering the potential harvest and the level of risk involved for both sides.

"Those numbers really vary dramatically, depending on a lot of things," Leventhal illuminates. "One question is, which company is publishing or backing the project? Another is, how important is the content to the project? Another is, what kind of up-front do you get? Sometimes you get a higher up-front and smaller back-end, and others vary on the up-front with a larger back-end. It depends on the company. If you're Philips, you can spend money to avoid giving away the back-end. If you are a small-time producer lacking cash to create the project, you have to give away a share of the back-end."

When will a creator start seeing royalty statements in the mail?

"About nine months from the title's ship date at the earliest," notes Thompson. "For example, take a producer who is creating a title targeted for a Christmas release. The producer is hired in say, November of 1997 for a product that's intended for a Christmas 1998 release. Finally, she finishes. The title is completed and it ships in September of 1998. The title will have some sales in the third quarter of 1998, but the bulk of the title's sales will come in the Christmas quarter. A publisher won't be paid for its Christmas sales until the first quarter of 1999. Let's say that the first quarter sales for 1999 are also strong. The publisher won't be paid for those sales until the second quarter of 1999. The publisher won't account for your first royalties until sixty days after the close of the first quarter. So, you'll probably receive your first royalty statement in May of 1999 for a title you started in November of 1997. Your first statement will reflect substantial sales, but the first sales are going to go to recoup your advance against the royalty. In all likelihood, you're not going to get a check. In this example, you're more likely to see a check in August of 1999."

revenue after expenses

If royalties are based on net revenue, which is often the case, record companies and multimedia publishers will argue that royalties should be based on the cash they actually receive after expenses. The next critical step is defining what is deducted from gross revenue as part of the equation. Publishers will, of course, want as many deductions as possible and producers will argue that fewer deductions are appropriate. The ultimate deal should reflect the charges that actually apply to the product and some percentage of overhead including run rate. Christopher Smith of Om Records explains, "run rate is our monthly office overhead."

For example, your product should not be charged for all the advertising costs if other products are advertised as part of some group promotion. Net revenue deals can be difficult to monitor and excessive charges against revenues are commonplace. Whenever possible, the production team should negotiate a cap on expenses and a minimum royalty.

"The only reason that we've been able to draw royalties is because we were able to do something that somebody else couldn't," notes Mark Waldrep. "Any multimedia developer who goes in and expects to get royalties from the record companies on these things is fooling himself. It's only because for the longest period of time there was no other way to do it. If you wanted to go somewhere you went to me or you went to maybe Warners or you went to the guys down in Australia and you said, 'We need to make one of these pre-gap discs. Blue book isn't ready yet, can you help us?' There's a little bit more of an arm-twist on that. And since we run a successful CD brokerage here, I can make it painless to people because I can sell them a disc at less than they would pay by going to somebody else. I build in my royalty through that brokerage."

You can negotiate a back-end deal, but the record company is going to keep that percentage as low as it can. If it is already maxed out on budget, it'll probably give you a nice salary and say, "That's all you get."

performance milestones

If you're a developer negotiating a contract, how do you benefit from building performance milestones into the deal? In other words, if "X" number of units are sold, what bonus is appropriate?

The fact of the matter is that very few CD-ROMs succeed in the retail channel. If you built in performance milestones with bumps at fifty thousand and another bump at one hundred thousand units, that would be great. As long as you keep in mind that only a handful of titles will ever reach those sales figures.

"I used to urge all my clients to insist on as much money up front as possible," recalls former Hollywood talent agent, Jon Samsel. "I had to constantly remind my talent that if the money was not there, up front, in the initial deal, it wasn't there. Back-end cash, whether it's called a milestone bonus or a royalty, is the motivational carrot publishers dangle in your face when they're low-balling you on the up-front money."

Everybody's out there making predictions as to how many CD-ROMs will sell and what a hit is going to look like and what the market penetration is going to be. Sometimes they're right and sometimes they're wrong. This market has not evolved like anybody thought it would. Predictions are constantly proved wrong by that great unknown called the consumer.

What follows are two case studies of music CD-ROM titles—*Bob Dylan: Highway 61 Interactive* and *On the Road with B.B. King*. Both studies were written by writer/analyst Paul Palumbo and have been reprinted by permission.

case study:

BOB DYLAN: HIGHWAY 61 INTERACTIVE

Publisher: Graphix Zone (Ignite, Inc.)
Development Company: Graphix Zone (Ignite, Inc.)
Content Rights: Columbia Records
Budget: $650,000
Break-even units: 45,000
Units sold: 100,000+
Platforms: PC/Mac
Retail Price: $59.95

Description: Highway 61 Interactive is a compilation of the events and major works of singer/songwriter Bob Dylan woven into an exploration of Bob Dylan's music. The strategy behind the CD-ROM was to present the artist in a way that the user comes away with a greater appreciation for the artist's work.

Acquisition/Rights

The major issue with any music CD-ROM is to clear the publishing and performance rights. That was made slightly more complicated in the case of the Dylan CD-ROM because some concert footage had to be secured from private sources and agreements had to be secured for those properties based on the amount of material used, with an assessment of what that material might be worth in the format presented.

In the case of Dylan, however, most of the publishing and performance rights were held by Columbia Records, which made research much easier. Once given the "OK" by the artist and record label, it was then easy to go about determining what shape the licensing agreement would take.

Developer/Partner

Graphix Zone produced and published the Dylan title. In addition, the company produced original video for the project. Graphix Zone created everything but the music, which was compiled for the disc by Bob Dylan. The product was assembled using the Apple Media Tool and original source code.

Promotion/Marketing

The artist Bob Dylan is well known to music retailers, mass merchants, and consumers of all age groups. Therefore the title was easily positioned in a number of retail outlets (record stores, mass merchants, specialty video, and computer superstores). When a well-known artist is the basis of a CD-ROM title, marketing experts know how to exploit the artist's name to maximize press coverage and ultimately, sales.

The Dylan title was launched with a "premier" party at Bob Dylan's New York studio, which was attended by Roger McGuinn and Al Kooper (key channel partners). Launch parties were thrown in a number of cities with additional channel partners in attendance. The parties provided the "story" for the PR machine to kick into gear—churning out advance release "hype" for radio station promotions and music trade press coverage. This free publicity provided the sales force with the necessary "hook" to sell the title into the channel. By informing the press and key music organizations well in advance of the title release, Graphix Zone was able to sustain the press campaign until the title's natural release date. Graphix Zone was able to continue this PR push by entering the title in numerous multimedia contests—winning twenty-five of them. The most prestigious award won was *Byte Magazine's* Top 10 CD-ROMs of All Time award. The title went on to garner positive reviews in newspapers and periodicals across the country, helping to expand retail sales efforts.

case study:

ON THE ROAD WITH B.B. KING

Publisher: MCA
Development Company: MediaX
Content Rights: MCA
Budget: $625,000
Break-even units: 55,000
Units sold: N/A
Platforms: PC/Mac
Retail Price: $49.95

Description: B.B. King seemed a particularly good subject for a CD-ROM because of his personality—he is the quintessential story teller with southern charm. He is also an icon in the blues community. From a marketing perspective, it just doesn't get any better. His appeal flows across all genders, all races, and all ages.

Development

Alex Melnyk, VP of Interactive for MCA Music, helped launch the B.B. King title. Before deciding on B.B. King as the focus for MCA's first music CD-ROM title, she looked at several possible properties and characters upon which to enter the interactive universe. Her feeling was that the world wasn't quite ready for a full-blown online title, mainly because of bandwidth considerations. She felt that CD-ROMs which were based on strong musical identities with a body of work of which to draw upon would be the best bet for MCA's first time out of the interactive chute. Of all of the different properties that MCA owns, a B.B. King title seemed to have the most potential.

Acquisition/Rights
MCA has some very stable artists which are known as "bread and butter artists." They no longer sell millions of albums each year, but they generate a fair amount of sales revenue year-in and year-out. B.B. King, a legend in his own time, is one such artist. The acquisition of rights were a painless process since MCA and B.B. King had a long, healthy relationship doing business with each other.

Developer/Partner
MCA initially put together a production team, and was sorely disappointed by the team's first effort. After six months of disappointing results, MCA pulled the plug and started all over again with a new development team.

The new development team, MediaX, did something pretty remarkable. They took a miserable project and completely re-created everything. Alex Melnyk hired a writer named Michael Shaun Conaway, who wrote the treatment, the script, and the branching in five days.

The developers then arranged for the blue screen video shoots and other production details with B.B. King. B.B., a CD-ROM aficionado, was very involved in the whole development process. He was even involved in reviewing the projects scripts and treatments. MediaX and Melnyk sifted through every information resource they could find relating to B.B. King and his work, including museums and library archives. They gathered together the necessary material, then cleared all of the music, publishing, and media rights. In short, they went from inheriting a dismal project to delivering a finished gold master in less than six months, including new video shoots, content acquisition, and programming. MediaX really saved the day in terms of its ability to contribute to both the creative process as well as doing a bang up job putting the title together.

Promotion/Marketing
The B.B. King title was placed in music stores over software channels by a ratio of 60:40. One of the most prominent in-store displays was made possible through a deal with the Tower Records chain. The title also lent itself extremely well to the book channel since the disc contained a rich history of B.B.'s music, as well as a history of the early music scene. MCA did a truckload of audience research and found

out everything there was to know about B.B.'s fans, his record sales (where his music sold well and not so well), what kind of channels they sold through, and his concert demographics.

The company also worked very closely with B.B.'s manager (Sid Feinberg, who has been B.B.'s manager for thirty-odd years). MCA took the time to get to know B.B.'s audience and then utilized that knowledge to its advantage.

Working within a tight budget forced MCA to get creative with both its marketing campaign and marketing dollars. The music giant created stickers and slapped them on the bin cards in the B.B. King Blues and R&B sections of record stores. The stickers said things like "now available, B.B. King has gone interactive," pointing the customer to the CD-ROM.

Luckily for MCA, B.B. was ringing in a "big" year. He won the coveted Kennedy Award, appeared on "The David Letterman Show," celebrated his seventieth birthday year, and celebrated the twenty-fifth anniversary of his single biggest hit, "The Thrill is Gone." MCA even installed a Web site two weeks before product launch (*www.mca.com*).

web deals

The World Wide Web is another beast when it comes to negotiating deals for content producers. The main problem is to identify what type of deal you need. Are you a producer creating a Web site as a "work for hire?" Does a Web broadcaster want you to write a monthly column on the Enhanced CD industry? Are you a developer being hired to create a Web commerce site for a record label? Perhaps a local entertainment firm wants to broadcast some of your music as "background Muzak" for a contest on its Web site.

It doesn't take an expert to realize that in every instance mentioned above, a different contract would apply to the content creator or content provider. Some deals may resemble work-for-hire developer agreements. Other deals will resemble a book publishing deal or standard writer deals used in the magazine business.

Simply stated, most deals will mimic deals previously negotiated in similar industries because the Internet is the great melting pot of all media. Perhaps several years from now, standard Web contracts will be in place that the majority of Web broadcasters adhere to in an effort to streamline the contract process. Until that day comes, be creative and persistent as you negotiate in the wild, wired frontier.

web site development agreement

Diane J. Brinson and Mark Radcliffe, two enterprising attorneys in the Bay Area, assembled a boiler plate Web development deal in anticipation of potential legal chaos on the net. The following agreement has been reprinted by permission from Brinson & Radcliffe's book, *Multimedia Law and Business Handbook*, published by Ladera Press.

WEB SITE DEVELOPMENT AND MAINTENANCE AGREEMENT

This Agreement is made as of _____, 199__ (the "Effective Date") by and between_____ , a corporation with offices at _____ ("Corporation") and _____, Inc., a _____ corporation with offices at _____ ("Developer").

RECITALS

A. Corporation wishes to have Developer create a Web site and maintain such Web site for Corporation on the Internet. Corporation shall employ a separate entity to provide access to the Internet.

B. Corporation wishes to retain Developer to develop the Web site.

Now, therefore, in consideration of the premises and mutual covenants and agreements set forth herein, Corporation and Developer agree as follows:

SECTION 1: DEFINITIONS

1.1 Beta Version means a working version of the Web site recorded in executable form on the specified medium with any necessary supporting software and data, which has been fully tested by Developer prior to delivery and which Developer believes in good faith to be bug free and to fully implement all functions called for in the Specifications.

1.2 Corporation Content means the material provided by Corporation to be incorporated into the Web site.

1.3 Development Schedule shall be as set forth in Schedule "B" to this Agreement which lists the deliverable items contracted for ("Deliverables") and the deadlines for their delivery. "Payment Schedule" shall be as also set forth in Schedule "B."

1.4 Developer Tools means the software tools of general application, whether owned or licensed to Developer, which are used to develop the Web site.

1.5 Documentation means the documentation for the software and other material which implement the Web site.

1.6 Enhancement means any improvements to the Web site to implement new features or add new material. Enhancements shall include modifications to the Web site Content to make the Web site operate on a Server System of a new ISP.

1.7 Error means any failure of the Web site (i) to meet the Specifications and/or (ii) to operate with the Server System.

1.8 Final Version means a non-copy protected and unencrypted disk master of the final version of the Web site, recorded in executable form on the specified medium with any necessary supporting software and data, as to which all development work hereunder, and corrections to the Beta Version, have been completed and which meets the Specifications.

1.9 ISP means an Internet Service Provider which maintains the Web site on the World Wide Web portion of the Internet. The ISP may change from time to time.

1.10 Specifications for the Web site shall be as set forth in Schedule "A" to this Agreement.

1.11 Source Materials means (i) all documentation, notes, development aids, technical documentation, and other materials provided to Developer by Corporation for use in developing the Web site, and (ii) the source code, documentation, notes, and other materials which are produced or created by Developer during the development of the Web site, in such internally documented form as is actually used by Developer for development and maintenance of the Web site.

1.12 Server System means the hardware and software system owned or licensed by the ISP.

1.13 Web site Content shall mean (i) the graphic user interface, text, images, music, and other material of the Web site developed by Developer under this Agreement which is visible to World Wide Web browsers and (ii) software (including cgi scripts and perl scripts) developed by Developer under this Agreement to implement the Web site. Web site Content shall not include the Developer Tools.

1.14 Web site means the site to be developed for Corporation on the graphic portion of the Internet known as the World Wide Web which is described in the Specifications at the following address:_____.

SECTION 2: DEVELOPMENT AND DELIVERY OF DELIVERABLES
2.1 Development; Progress Reports. Developer shall use commercially reasonable efforts to develop each Deliverable in accordance with the Specifications. Developer shall first prepare a design for the Web site. This design shall include drawings of the user interface, a schematic of how to navigate the Web site, a list of hyperlinks and other components. All development work will be performed by Developer or its employees at Developer's offices or by approved independent contractors who have executed confidentiality and work-for-hire/assignment agreements which are acceptable to Corporation. Developer agrees that no development work shall be performed by independent contractors without the express written approval of Corporation. Each week following execution of this Agreement during which any development and/or testing hereunder remains uncompleted, and whenever else Corporation shall reasonably request, Developer shall contact, or meet with

Corporation's representative, and report all tasks completed and problems encountered relating to development and testing of the Web site. During such discussion or meeting, Developer shall advise Corporation in detail of any recommended changes with respect to remaining phases of development in view of Developer's experience with the completed development. In addition, Developer shall contact Corporation's representative promptly by telephone upon discovery of any event or problem that will materially delay development work, and thereafter, if requested, promptly confirm such report in writing.

2.2 Delivery. Developer shall deliver all Deliverables for the Program within the times specified in the Development Schedule and in accordance with the Specifications. All Deliverables shall comply with the Submission Guidelines set forth in Schedule "A."

2.3 Manner of Delivery. Developer agrees to comply with all reasonable requests of Corporation as to the manner of delivery of all Deliverables, which may include delivery by electronic means.

2.4 Delivery of Source Materials. Upon request by Corporation, but in no event later than the delivery of the Final Version, Developer shall deliver to Corporation all Source Materials.

SECTION 3 : TESTING AND ACCEPTANCE/EFFECT OF REJECTION
3.1 Testing and Acceptance Procedure. All Deliverables shall be thoroughly tested by Developer and all necessary corrections as a result of such testing shall be made, prior to delivery to Corporation. Upon receipt of a Deliverable, Corporation will, in its sole discretion either: (i) accept the Deliverable and make the milestone payment set forth in Schedule "B"; or, (ii) provide Developer with written notice of the aspects in which the Deliverable contains Errors and request that Developer correct said Deliverable.

3.2 Additional Quality Assurance. If Corporation requests that Developer correct the Deliverable, Developer shall within five (5) calendar days of such notice, or such longer period as Corporation may allow, submit at no additional charge a revised Deliverable in which such Errors have been corrected. Upon receipt of the corrected Deliverable Corporation may, in its sole discretion: (i) accept the corrected Deliverable and make the milestone payment set forth in Schedule "B"; or, (ii) request that Developer make further corrections to the Deliverable and repeat the correction and review procedure set forth in this Paragraph 3.2. In the event Corporation determines, in its sole discretion, that the Deliverable is still not acceptable after three attempts at correction by Developer, Corporation may terminate this Agreement.

SECTION 4 : OTHER OBLIGATIONS OF DEVELOPER

4.1 Web site Quality. Developer agrees that the Web site will be of high quality and will be free of defects in material and workmanship in all material respects. The Web site will conform in all respects to the functional and other descriptions contained in the Specifications. For a period of one year after the date of acceptance of the Final Version by Corporation, Developer agrees to fix at its own expense any Errors ("Warranty Period"). DEVELOPER DISCLAIMS ALL IMPLIED WARRANTIES, INCLUDING WITHOUT LIMITATION, THE WARRANTIES OF MERCHANTABILITY AND FITNESS FOR A PARTICULAR PURPOSe.

4.2 Web site Maintenance. Developer also agrees to provide Corporation with reasonable technical support and assistance to maintain and update the Web site on the World Wide Web during the Warranty Period at no cost to Corporation. Such assistance shall not exceed __ hours per calendar month. After the expiration of the Warranty Period, Developer agrees to provide Corporation with reasonable technical support and assistance to maintain and update the Web site on the World Wide Web for $_____ annual fee for five years after the last day of the Warranty Period ("Maintenance Period"). Such maintenance shall include correcting any Errors or any failure of the Web site to conform to the Specifications. Maintenance shall not include the development of Enhancements at the time of the notice.

4.3 Enhancements. During the Maintenance Period, if Developer wishes to modify the Web site, it may request that Developer provide a bid to provide such Enhancements. Developer shall provide Corporation a first priority on its resources to create the Enhancements over any other third party with the exception of obligations under contracts with third parties existing on the date of the notice. Such services shall be provided on a time and materials basis at the most favored price under which Developer provides such services to third parties.

SECTION 5 : PROPRIETARY RIGHTS

5.1 Corporation's Ownership Rights. Developer acknowledges and agrees that the Web site Content and Documentation, including but not limited to images, graphic user interface, source and object code, and any documentation and notes associated with the Web site are and shall be the property of Corporation. Title to all property rights including but not limited to copyrights, trademarks, patents, and trade secrets in the Web site Content and Documentation is with, and shall remain with, Corporation.

5.2 Assignment of Rights. Developer agrees to transfer and assign, and hereby transfers and assigns to Corporation its entire right, title, and interest worldwide, if any, including without limitation all copyright ownership therein, no matter when acquired, in the Web site Content and Documentation. Developer agrees to cooperate with Corporation in perfecting any such assignment of rights, including without limitation by executing and delivering such documents as Corporation may request. During and after the term of this contract, Developer will assist Corporation in every reasonable way, at Corporation's expense, to establish original ownership of all such rights on the part of Corporation. Developer hereby waives any and all claims that Developer may now or hereafter have in any jurisdiction to so-called "moral rights" with respect to the results of Developer's work and services hereunder.

5.3 License to Web site Content. Corporation grants to Developer a non-exclusive, worldwide license to reproduce and modify the Corporation Content to develop and maintain the Web site.

5.4 Internet Access. Corporation shall be responsible for obtaining access to the Internet through an ISP. Developer shall not be responsible for such access and shall not be considered a party to the agreement between ISP and Corporation. Although the Web site will be hosted by the ISP, the ISP will not be a party to this Agreement nor will it be a third party beneficiary of this Agreement.

5.5 Liability for Corporation Content. Developer shall not be liable for the modification, display, or other use of the Corporation Content.

SECTION 6: PAYMENT

6.1 Payment Schedule. The development fees set forth in Schedule "B" shall be paid as provided in such Schedule.

6.2 Maintenance Fees. Maintenance fees shall be due thirty (30) days prior to the commencement date of each year of the Maintenance Period.

6.3 Taxes. Developer shall be responsible for the payment of all sales, use, and similar taxes.

SECTION 7: CONFIDENTIALITY

7.1 Confidential Information. The terms of this Agreement, the Source Materials and technical and marketing plans or other sensitive business information, including all materials containing said information, which are supplied by the Corporation to Developer or developed by Developer in the course of developing the Web site is the confidential information ("Confidential Information") of Corporation.

7.2 Restrictions on Use. Developer agrees that except as authorized in writing by Corporation: (i) Developer will preserve and protect the confidentiality of all Confidential Information; (ii) Developer will not disclose to any third party, the existence, source, content, or substance of the Confidential Information or make copies of Confidential Information; (iii) Developer will not deliver Confidential Information to any third party, or permit the Confidential Information to be removed from Developer's premises; (iv) Developer will not use Confidential Information in any way other than to develop the Web site as provided in this Agreement; (v) Developer will not disclose, use or copy any third party information or materials received in confidence by Developer for purposes of work performed under this Agreement; and (vi) Developer shall require that each of its employees who work on or have access to the materials which are the subject of this Agreement sign a suitable confidentiality and work-for-hire/assignment agreement and be advised of the confidentiality and other applicable provisions of this Agreement.

7.3 Limitations. Information shall not be considered to be Confidential Information if Developer can demonstrate that it (i) is already or otherwise becomes publicly known through no act of Developer; (ii) is lawfully received from third parties subject to no restriction of confidentiality; (iii) can be shown by Developer to have been independently developed by it without use of the Confidential Information; or (iv) is authorized in writing by Corporation to be disclosed, copied, or used.

7.4 Return of Source Materials. Upon Corporation's acceptance of the Final Version, or upon Corporation's earlier request, Developer shall provide Corporation with all copies and originals of the Web site Content, Corporation Content, and Source Materials, as well as any other materials provided to Developer, or created by Developer under this Agreement. Not later than seven (7) days after the termination of this Agreement for any reason, or if sooner requested by Corporation, Developer will return to Corporation all originals and copies of the Confidential Information, Web site Content, Corporation Content, and Source Materials, as well as any other materials provided to Developer, or created by Developer under this Agreement except that Developer may retain one copy of the Web site Content and Source Materials, which will remain the Confidential Information of Corporation, for the sole purpose of assisting Developer in maintaining the Web site. Developer shall return said copy to Corporation promptly upon request by Corporation.

SECTION 8 : WARRANTIES, COVENANTS, AND INDEMNIFICATION
8.1 Warranties and Covenants of Developer. Developer represents, warrants, and covenants to Corporation the following:
   (a) Developer has the full power to enter into this Agreement and

perform the services provided for herein, and that such ability is not limited or restricted by any agreements or understandings between Developer and other persons or companies;

(b) Any information or materials developed for, or any advice provided to Corporation, shall not rely or in any way be based upon confidential or proprietary information or trade secrets obtained or derived by Developer from sources other than Corporation unless Developer has received specific authorization in writing to use such proprietary information or trade secrets;

(c) Except to the extent based on the Corporation Content, the Web site Content and Documentation do not infringe upon or misappropriate, any copyright, patent right, right of publicity or privacy (including but not limited to defamation), trade secret, or other proprietary rights of any third party.

(d) Its performance of this Agreement will not conflict with any other contract to which Developer is bound, and while developing the Web site, Developer will not engage in any such consulting services or enter into any agreement in conflict with this Agreement.

8.2 Developer's Indemnity. Developer agrees to indemnify, hold harmless, and defend Corporation and its directors, officers, its employees and agents from and against all claims, defense costs (including reasonable attorneys' fees), judgments, and other expenses arising out of or on account of such claims, including without limitation claims of:

(a) Alleged infringement or violation of any trademark, copyright, trade secret, right of publicity or privacy (including but not limited to defamation), patent, or other proprietary right with respect to the Web site Content or Documentation to the extent Developer has modified or added to the materials provided by Corporation;

(b) Any use of confidential or proprietary information or trade secrets Developer has obtained from sources other than Corporation;

(c) Any negligent act, omission, or willful misconduct of Developer in the performance of this Agreement; and

(d) The breach of any covenant or warranty set forth in Section 8.1 above.

8.3 Conditions to Indemnity. Developer's obligation to indemnify is conditioned on Corporation's notifying Developer promptly of any claim as to which indemnification will be sought and providing Developer reasonable cooperation in the defense and settlement thereof.

8.4 Corporation's Indemnification. Corporation agrees to indemnify, hold harmless, and defend Developer and its directors, officers, its employees and agents from and against all claims, defense costs (including reasonable attorneys' fees), judgments, and other expenses arising out of the breach of the following covenants and warranties:

(a) Corporation possesses full power and authority to enter into this Agreement and to fulfill its obligations hereunder.

(b) The performance of the terms of this Agreement and of Corporation's obligations hereunder shall not breach any separate agreement by which Corporation is bound.

(c) The Corporation Content does not infringe or violate any trademark, copyright, trade secret, right of publicity or privacy (including but not limited to defamation), patent, or other proprietary right.

8.5 Conditions to Indemnity. Corporation's obligation to indemnify is conditioned on Developer's notifying Corporation promptly of any claim as to which indemnification will be sought and providing Corporation reasonable cooperation in the defense and settlement thereof.

SECTION 9: TERMINATION

9.1 Termination for Non-Performance or Delay. In the event of a termination of this Agreement by Corporation pursuant to Paragraph 3.2 hereof, Corporation will have no further obligations or liabilities under this Agreement. Corporation will have the right, in addition to all of its other rights, to require Developer to deliver to Corporation all of Developer's work in progress, including all originals and copies thereof, as well as any other materials provided to Developer, or created by Developer under this Agreement. Payment of any Development Schedule milestones under Schedule "B" which have been met shall be deemed payment in full for all obligations of Corporation under this Agreement, including full payment for all source code, object code, documentation, notes, graphics, and all other materials and work relating to the portion of the Program which has been completed as of the time of termination.

9.2 Termination for Convenience. Corporation shall have the right at any time to terminate this Agreement on twenty-one (21) days written notice. In the event of such termination, Corporation's entire financial obligation to Developer shall be for then accrued payments due under the Development Schedule, plus the pro-rated portion of the next payment, if any, due with respect to items being worked on up to the time of termination.

SECTION 10: GOVERNING LAW AND DISPUTE RESOLUTION

10.1 Arbitration. The parties agree to submit any dispute arising out of or in connection with this Agreement to binding arbitration in San Francisco, California before the American Arbitration Association pursuant to the provisions of this Section 10.1, and, to the extent not inconsistent with this Section 10.1, the rules of the American Arbitration Association. The parties agree that such arbitration will be in lieu of either party's rights to assert any claim, demand, or suit in any court action (provided that either party may elect either binding arbitration or a court action with respect to a breach by the other party of such party's proprietary rights, including without limitation any trade secrets, copyrights, or trademarks). Any arbitration shall be final and binding and the arbitrator's order will be enforceable in any court of competent jurisdiction.

10.2 Governing Law: Venue. The validity, construction, and performance of this Agreement shall be governed by the laws of the state of _____ and all claims and/or lawsuits in connection with agreement must be brought in.

SECTION 11: MISCELLANEOUS PROVISIONS

11.1 Notices. For purposes of all notices and other communications required or permitted to be given hereunder, the addresses of the parties hereto shall be as indicated below. All notices shall be in writing and shall be deemed to have been duly given if sent by facsimile, the receipt of which is confirmed by return facsimile, or sent by first class registered or certified mail or equivalent, return receipt requested, addressed to the parties at their addresses set forth below:

If to Developer: If to Corporation:

_____   _____
_____   _____
_____   _____
Attn: _____   Attn: _____

11.2 Designated Person. The parties agree that all materials exchanged between the parties for formal approval shall be communicated between single designated persons, or a single alternate designated person for each party. Neither party shall have any obligation to consider for approval or respond to materials submitted other than through the Designated Persons. Each party shall have the right to change its Designated Persons from time to time and to so notify the other.

11.3 Entire Agreement. This Agreement, including the attached Schedules which are incorporated herein by reference as though fully set out, contains the entire understanding and agreement of the parties with respect to the subject matter contained herein, supersedes all prior oral or written understandings and agreements relating thereto except as expressly otherwise provided, and may not be altered, modified, or waived in whole or in part, except in writing, signed by duly authorized representatives of the parties.

11.4 Force Majeure. Neither party shall be held responsible for damages caused by any delay or default due to any contingency beyond its control preventing or interfering with performance hereunder.

11.5 Severability. If any provision of this Agreement shall be held by a court of competent jurisdiction to be contrary to any law, the remaining provisions shall remain in full force and effect as if said provision never existed.

11.6 Assignment. This Agreement is personal to Developer. Developer may not sell, transfer, sublicense, hypothecate, or assign its rights and duties under this Agreement without the written consent of Corporation. No rights of Developer hereunder shall devolve by operation of law or otherwise upon any receiver, liquidator, trustee, or other party. This Agreement shall inure to the benefit of Corporation, its successors, and assigns.

11.7 Waiver and Amendments. No waiver, amendment, or modification of any provision of this Agreement shall be effective unless consented to by both parties in writing. No failure or delay by either party in exercising any rights, power, or remedy under this Agreement shall operate as a waiver of any such right, power, or remedy.

11.8 Agency. The parties are separate and independent legal entities. Developer is performing services for Corporation as an independent contractor. Nothing contained in this Agreement shall be deemed to constitute either Developer or Corporation an agent, representative, partner, joint venturer, or employee of the other party for any purpose. Neither party has the authority to bind the other or to incur any liability on behalf of the other, nor to direct the employees of the other. Developer is an independent contractor, not an employee of Corporation. No employment relationship is created by this Agreement. Developer shall retain independent professional status throughout this Agreement and shall use his/her own discretion in performing the tasks assigned.

11.9 Limitation on Liability: Remedies. Except as provided in Section 8 above with respect to third party indemnification, neither party shall be liable to the other party for any incidental, consequential, special, or punitive damages of any kind or nature, including, without limitation, the breach of this Agreement or any termination of this Agreement, whether such liability is asserted on the basis of contract, tort (including negligence or strict liability), or otherwise, even if either party has warned or been warned of the possibility of any such loss or damage.

IN WITNESS WHEREOF, this Agreement is executed as of the Effective Date set forth above.

By: _____ By: _____
Name: _____ Name: _____
Title: _____ Title: _____

SCHEDULE A: SPECIFICATIONS

SCHEDULE B: DEVELOPMENT AND PAYMENT SCHEDULE

Item	Due Date	Payment Upon Acceptance
Contract Signing	_____	_____
Delivery of Web Site Design	_____	_____
Delivery of Beta Version	_____	_____
Delivery of Final Version and Source		
Materials	_____	_____
TOTAL	_____	_____

Acceptance of Final Version by:

Each of the foregoing milestone payments shall be payable upon Corporation's acceptance of an acceptable Deliverable.

Bonus. Corporation agrees to pay Developer a bonus of $_____ which shall be payable to Developer in the event Developer delivers a Final Version of the Web site which is acceptable to Corporation prior to

_____.

appendix

glossary

Access Times The access time is how long it takes to find and return data. The access time of an average CD-ROM is 300 milliseconds, while the access time for a hard drive is about 10-20 milliseconds.

Analog An electric signal emulating acoustic soundwaves detected by transducers.

Authoring Environment An authoring environment is the interface to programming, a library where you're able, to a certain degree, to link sets, objects, actions in a pre-organized fashion. It allows people that are more oriented to art or design to actually be involved in the sculpting of the product.

Authoring Program Authoring is the integration of various data types into the design via a commercial package that simplifies the process of programming by offering you preprogrammed procedures for brining these elements together without having to program.

Bandwidth The range of signal frequencies that can be carried on a channel. Data transmission capacity. Convention phones need very little; interactive digital video requires a great deal.

Binary A system of numbers comprised of two digits, 0 and 1. This is the system used by computers.

Bit A binary digit; either 0 or 1. The smallest measure of computer information.

Blue Book Enhanced CD is Blue Book standard. It's an offshoot of the Photo CD technology which has a separate session on a discreet portion—on the outside edge—of the disc. (Discs read from the inside out.) It was specified that the multimedia, video, 3-D and other graphic components would be on the outside track.

Broadband A large bandwidth which enables a greater amount of data to be transmitted. Broadband telecommunications could permit the interactive transmission of voice, data, and video. A narrow band system, conversely, has less capacity and might only be able to transmit voice and data communication (phone calls and faxes) with limited interactivity.

CD-DA Red Book CD for Digital Audio.

CD Plus Name coined by Sony and Philips to describe CDs using stamped multi-session technology.

CD-ROM The term CD-ROM stands for Compact Disc-Read Only Memory. CD-ROM is a massive information storage device that can be reproduced quickly and cheaply. A single CD-ROM can currently store 680MB of data. CD-ROM only plays on your computer.

CD-ROM/XA (CD-ROM Extended Architecture) This technology was proposed by Philips, Sony, and Microsoft in 1988 as an extension to Yellow Book. This specification stretches the Yellow Book standard and adds the most interesting idea from Green Book (CD-I), interleaved audio. Before this time, audio was confined to one track at a time.

Credit Job titles which serve as recognition for those people who worked on a project. Placement of credit may appear on-screen and/or off-screen.

DLL An algorithm for a set of procedures that do a certain function. A lot programming is grabbing pre-written libraries of codes so you can put in an algorithm process.

Download The transfer of information from one computer to another, typically from a centrally located large computer via modem to a personal computer. Upload is sending the information the other way.

DVD Digital Versatile Disc (originally Digital Video Disc). A collective term for the new generation high-density CDs.

ECMD Electronic Commercial Music Distribution.

Enhanced CD A hybrid disc format which merges the audio-only characteristics of Red Book and the visual data of Yellow Book enabling a computer to play both multimedia data and CD-quality audio.

EQ To equalize the sound by adjusting bass and treble to the particular needs of what you're doing, or correcting deficiencies in what somebody else did.

Green Book The Green Book CD-ROM is the basis for a special format called Compact Disc Interactive, or CD-I. Although CD-I using the Green Book standard is a general CD-ROM format with the bonus of interleaved audio, all CD-I titles must play on CD-I players. Only this piece of equipment can decode the CD-I formatted discs with a special operating system known as OS/9.

Hypertext A type of nonlinear writing by computer in which groups of text are linked to one another. In other words, the reader is able to jump from within one body of a text to another body of text.

Icon A graphic image on a computer screen that represents a command.

Install Information on a CD-ROM that is downloaded onto a computer's hard drive.

Interactivity The ability of the user to interact with a computer which can be used to control the flow, pace, and content of a program.

Interactive Multimedia Combines the interactivity of computers with access to multiple media sources. The viewer is able to participate in the program.

Interleaved Audio Allows the sound to be divided and intermixed with other content.

Interleaved Data The means of taking various forms of media, such as pictures, sounds, and movies, and programming them into one track on a disc. Interleaving is one way to make sure that all data on the same track is synchronized.

Internet A worldwide network of computer networks. Maintained by the National Science Foundation. Comprised of trunk lines, routers, dedicated access lines, software protocols, and data servers, linking some 20 million users.

IUMA Internet Underground Music Archive.

Jewel Box The protective case used to house CD discs.

M-Bone The backbone of a multicast, a way to move a lot of information to a lot of people without overloading the system.

Mechanical Rights Mechanical rights are the basic right to use a musical composition. They do not include the right to publicly perform the music. A mechanical license also does not permit the use of the music with still or moving images. Such use requires a "synchronization" license. Although copyright law provides a compulsory license for mechanical rights, most licensees prefer to obtain these rights commercially through a rights clearance agency. This preference is based on the very onerous payment and accounting requirements imposed on the "compulsory" license in the Copyright Act (taken from The *Multimedia Law Primer* by Ladera Press).

MIDI Musical Instrument Digital Interface.

Milestone Bonus Specific compensation for a pre-established amount to be paid at a preestablished date in time, used as an incentive/safeguard by two negotiating parties.

Mixed Mode When a CD has CD-ROM tracks and CD-Audio tracks it's called a "Mixed Mode" disc. To date, data cannot be read while sound is being played, so computer applications must use Mixed Mode in a staged manner. To get around these limitations and to obtain synchronization of multiple tracks, an interleaved style was added in the form of the CD-ROM/XA standard.

MMCD The trademark for the Sony/Philips proposed high-density disc described in the Gold Book, standards which are now built into DVD.

MPEG (Motion Picture Experts Group) A video format that permits for full-screen, full-motion video playback on a CD. Its lower data rate and quality of movie allows the user to have a transparent experience that's equivalent to what they see on MTV.

Multi-Session A format that allows a CD-ROM to be burned more than one time. It allows for incremental updates to the media, and for multiple standards to be applied to a single disc. It is key to the creation of Enhanced CDs.

No Quote One of the most overlooked and important clauses in a production agreement. A no quote agreement prohibits a production company from releasing the terms of the team's deal to future employers. Often times, a negotiating record company will reference a production company's fees with previous employers to determine "proper" compensation. This works against a production team that has previously worked below its rate and severely hampers a team's chance of raising its fees in the future.

Orange Book The Orange Book standard is used to define the writeable CD format. Part 1 of the standard covers the new magneto-optical which is completely revisable. Part 2 covers the CD-R (compact disc recordable) for compact disc write-once media that defines the Multi-Session format that allows for incremental updates to the media.

Paid Ads Credit which appears on nonstandard items such as a program's poster, box art, documentation guides, hint books, Online teasers, billboards, promotional flyers, demos, etc. Paid ads usually have to be spelled out in detail.

Programming Where you actually create procedures that are exclusive to the operation and functions performed by the Multimedia title.

Public Performance Rights Permission for a public performance because the multimedia work will be shown and demoed to audiences. A performance is considered public if it is "open to the public" or at any place where a substantial number of persons outside of the "normal circle of family and social acquaintances" gather.

QuickTime Apple's multimedia standard allowing users to edit or view video, music, and animations.

Red Book The original compact disc. The audio CD conforms to the Red Book standard. Anything you play on your stereo is Red Book. The technology limits the type of data that can be stored to only audio. The Red Book standard allows for up to seventy-four minutes of stereo music using Pulse Code Modulation (PCM) to compress two stereo channels into 680MB of space.

RIAA Recording Industry Association of America.

Royalty A payment based on a percentage of revenue generated by a program, often corresponding to the actual number of units sold. The production team should carefully examine how the production company defines the term "royalty" in a contract—is it based on "net" or "gross" proceeds. These terms also need to be defined in any agreement.

Run Rate A business' monthly office overhead.

Sample Rate Analog signal rate as it is measured and stored as a digital value.

Sequencer Software application for MIDI data; specifically utilitzed for recording, editing, and playing data.

Software Developer The person or company that develops software. The developer may license the software to others, in which case he may be referred to as a licensor, supplier, or vendor.

Sweatheart Deals Multimedia material that is offered free, or at a reasonable price with all rights cleared.

Synchronization License If the music is to be synchronized with still or moving images on a screen, the licensee must obtain a "synchronization" license.

Transfer Rate The transfer rate is the amount of data that is passed in a second. The transfer rate for CD-ROM is about 150 kilobytes per second, rooted in the technology designed to play a steady stream of digital CD music. (The transfer rate needed for noncompressed full-screen full-motion video is approximately 30MB per second.) Dual speed drives help improve performance by providing up to 300KB per second transfer rates.

Two-Sku When two similar products, such as a Red Book audio and Enhanced CD, are released into the market at different times and at different prices.

Yellow Book Computer CD-ROMs conform to the Yellow Book standard. This standard defines the proper layout of the computer data on a disc. Yellow Book takes the basic Red Book standard and defines two new track types—computer data and compressed audio or video/picture data. The format also adds better error correction (necessary for computer data) and better random access capabilities.

RIAA "Enhanced CD" Voluntary Specification

Version 0.9

Rev.100295

Overview

All "Enhanced CD" discs (including but not limited to Single Session, Multisession, "CD Plus") should be capable of playing on all CD audio players including home players, disc changers (jukebox, cartridge, carousel types, etc.), portable players, and car players. Currently some of these products may cause some CD audio players to have difficulties in mounting the disc. The primary purpose of this document is to define the disc-player interface needed to improve compatibility. A secondary purpose is to provide general recommendations for CD-ROM maders concerning these products.

By the establishment of a recommended specification, the RIAA wishes to encourage widespread use, compatibility, and consumer enjoyment from the Enhanced CD formats.

Assumptions

This document presupposes that the manufacturer has a current CD license with Sony/Philips to manufacture compact discs and/or compact disc players. It is also assumed that the manufacturer has access to the "Red Book," "Yellow Book," "Orange Book," "Green Book," and "Blue Book" specifications from Sony/Philips, as listed in the "Required Reference Documents" page, or other lawful alternatives.

Definitions

1. This document also defines a set of general parameters for manufactured Enhanced CDs, CDDA players, and CD-ROM readers. These parameters are not intended to supersede, preclude, or replace the existing Philips/Sony Compact Disc Specifications for CDDA, CD-ROM, CD-ROM XA, Multisession, CD-1, and "CD-Plus," but are intended to insure a compatible interface between an Enhanced CD disc and CDDA audio players.

2. The Enhanced CD, as employed in this document, is defined as a compact disc that combines "Red Book" audio and "Yellow Book" data on one manufactured disc and retains "Red Book" compatibility and compliance with audio players. This definition includes, but is not limited to, the following Format methods:

    (a) The Single Session Enhanced CD (sometimes referred to as "Pre-gap") format; [Tk 01, Ix 00 - "Yellow Book" data (CD-ROM data, with PVD at 00:02:16AbsoluteTime),

RIAA "Enhanced CD" Voluntary Specification courtesy of the RIAA. All Rights Reserved.

Tk 01, Ix 01 - "Red Book" audio, etc.] Refer to Figure 1.

(b) The Philips/Sony "Blue Book" specification, known as the "CD-Plus" format; [Two Sessions, first session: "Red Book" audio, second session: "Yellow Book" CD- ROM XA data] Refer to Figure 2.

(c) The Philips/Sony "Yellow Book" Multi-Session Compact Disc specification, known as the "Multi-Session" format; [Two or more sessions, containing: CD Audio, CD-ROM XA, CD-I] Refer to Figure 2.

Recommended Requirements

CD Audio Player

1. Analog Audio output muting is mandatory in all modes when the data type is not CDDA audio, rather than recommended, as in Item 14, on Page 5 of the "Red Book" Attachment document, titled "Attachment to the Description of the Compact Digital Audio System."

2. CD Audio players should not be able to perform an access prior to Track 01, Index 01, This includes not being able to directly Track 01, Index 00, or scan (<Reverse) to this Index.

3. CD Audio players must re-initialize if located in an index fm than Track 0l, Index 01.

Enhanced CD Format

The Enhanced CD disc format also conforms to, but is not limited to, the following:

1. Backwards compatibility with CD Audio players; refer to the CDDA "Red Book" specifications.

2. Disc playback on CD Audio players must begin at Track 01, Index 01, as outlined on Page 42 ofthe CDDA "Red Book" specification.

3. If the disc is a Single Session Enhanced CD format, the "Yellow Book" data within the gap (Track 01, Index 00) will be succeeded by "Red Book" audio (preferably unmodulated), being no shorter than three (3) seconds (00:03:00) and preferably no longer than two (2) minutes, two (2) seconds (02:02:00).

In the CD-ROM Program Area of this disc format (Figure 1), Track 01, Index 00, the data is typically in CD-ROM MODE 1 sector format. In this area, sector 0, absolute time of two (2) seconds (00:02:00), will contain the start of the Apple HFS file system information, (if an HFS volume is present) and sector 16, absolute time of two (2) seconds, sixteen (16) frames (00:02:16), will contain the ISO 9660 Primary Volume Descriptor, (if an ISO volume is present). The standard two (2) second (CD-ROM MODE 0)

Postgap, as required by the "Yellow Book," succeeds the CD-ROM data. The CD-ROM data is followed by audio information, in "Red Book" format.

The subcode control bits are set to 00xl (audio) in the Lead-In Track (Track 00). These change to 0lxl (data) during the data portion of Track 01, Index 00. The control bits return to 00x1 during the audio pause, which succeeds the CD-ROM Postgap and precedes the start of audio program in Track 01, Index 01.

The "P" flag subcode channel is coded according to "Red Book"; low (0) during Lead-In and Track 01, Index 00 (the data area); high (1) start flag, two (2) to three (3) seconds, preceding the first piece of music (Track 01, Index 01) and Lead-Out, and a two (2) second start flag preceding all other Tracks.

4. If the disc is formatted in accordance with the Philips/Sony "CD-Plus" ("Blue Book") specification, or the Philips/Sony Multi-Session ("Yellow Book") specification, the "Yellow Book" data must reside in a disc session other than the first session, as specified by the respective format specifications.

CD-ROM Readers and Platforms

It is encouraged that the CD-ROM data of the Enhancd CD be designed to play on multiple consumer platforms.

Hardware requirements should be determined by the individual product developer. Specifications may be available from the MPC Council, SPA, IDSA, etc.

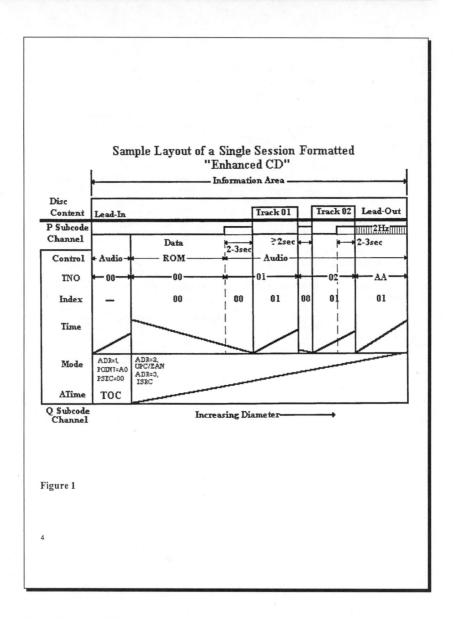

Figure 1

4

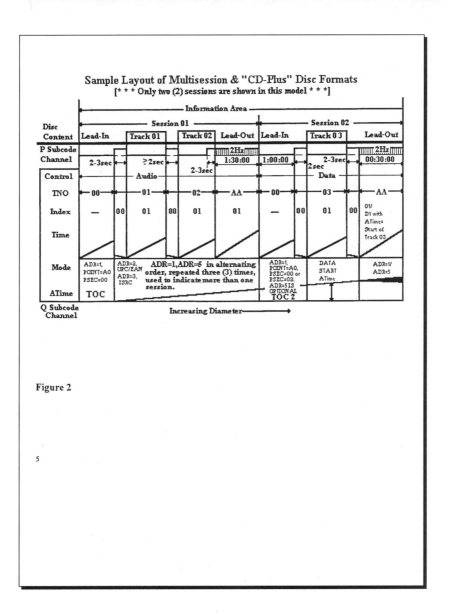

Figure 2

5

RIAA "Enhanced CD" Voluntary Specification courtesy of the RIAA. All Rights Reserved.

Required Reference Documents

Compact Disk Digital Audio Specification—"Red Book"

CD-ROM [Compact Disk Read Only Memory]—"Yellow Book"

CD-ROM XA [Compact Disk Read Only Memory Extended Architecture]—"Yellow Book"
Extension

CD-Write Once [Compact Disk Write Once, Recordable Compact Disk Systems Part 11,
Version 2.0]—"Orange Book"

Multisession Compact Disc—"Yellow Book" Extension

Enhanced Music Compact Disc "CD-Plus"—"Blue Book"

ISO 646—ISO 7-bit coded character set for information interchange.
Ref. No. ISO 646: 1983 (E)

ISO 2022—ISO 7-bit and 8-bit coded character sets—coded extension techniques.
Ref. No. ISO 2022: 1986 (E)

ISO 3166—Codes for the representation of names of countries.
ReE No. ISO 3166: 1988 (E/F)

ISO 8859-1—ISO 8-bit single byte coded graphic character sets. Part 1: Latin alphabet No. 1.
Ref. No. ISO 8859-1: 1987 (E)

ISO 9660—Volume and file structure of CD-ROM for information interchange.
Ref. No. ISO 9660: 1988 (E)

ISO 10918—Digital compression and coding of continuous-tone still images ("JPEG standard").
Ref. No. ISO 10918: 1992 (E)

ISO11172—Coding of moving pictures and associated audio for digital storage media up to about 1.5
Mbit/s ("MPEG-1 standard"). Ref. No. ISO 11172: 1993 (E)

General MIDI Specification—Musical Instrument Digital Interface (MIDI) File Format.
Specified by the International MIDI Association (IMA).

"Enhanced CD" Voluntary Specifications _Corrections_

Edits and/or Additions:

OVERVIEW—first paragraph, last sentence;

A secondary purpose is to provide general recommendations _for CD-ROM
readers_ concerning these products.

*This should be included so as to be clear to all hardware manufacturers that
this specification does, in fact, include CD-ROM reader manufacturers and
their related hardware and interfaces.

(2) DEFINITIONS—Item 1, first sentence;

This document also defines a set of general parameters for manufactured
Enhanced CDs, CDDA players _and CD-ROM readers._

*Again, for clarity of purpose and definition.

(3) Enhanced CD Format—Item 3, first paragraph;

If the disc is a Single Session Enhanced CD format, the "Yellow Book" data within the gap (Track 01,
Index 00) will be succeeded by "Red Book" audio (preferably unmodulated), being no shorter than _three
(3) seconds (00:03:00)_ and preferably no longer than two (2) minutes, two (2) seconds (02:02:00).

*This change was inspired by the "P Channel" switching time. By increasing this minimum value to three
(3) seconds, there would be no chance that the "P Channel" flag would be switching during the DATA
Information Area of the "GAP." This flag typically switches in approximately two (2) seconds and thirteen
(13) ATime sectors (00:02:13), therefore three (3) seconds would be adequate and more appropriate as a
specification.

(4) Figure 2—Information Area, Session 2, Track 03, line labelled TNO;
Originally read as "04," changed to correctly read "03."

RIAA "Enhanced CD" Voluntary Specification courtesy of the RIAA. All Rights Reserved.

Screen shots from Real McCoy's *One More Time* Enhanced CD courtesy of Minds Eye Media, San Francisco, and David Greene, president of Creative Spark. Copyright 1997. All Rights Reserved.

Screen shots from Real McCoy's *One More Time* Enhanced CD courtesy of Minds Eye Media, San Francisco, and David Greene, president of Creative Spark. Copyright 1997. All Rights Reserved.

Ever since I first touched a computer keyboard, I have been fascinated by its possible uses as a tool for so many different fields. When I was working as a photographer, I started using a computer to increase the output of some of my pictures. Years later, as a musician and producer, I found myself using computers once again. I jumped from Commodore to the Atari and, finally, ended up using a Macintosh.

As an artist, one of my major goals was to release an Enhanced CD/CD Plus title. I wanted to give the fans of Real McCoy a "Plus" of information about the group, in addition to giving consumers "more for their money." You see I always enjoy going through the booklet of an artist's album while listening to the music, and I'm disappointed if there is not enough background information or pictures included. Usually there isn't enough for me!

When it comes to finding the right person to work with and create something like a record, or in this case, an Enhanced CD version of the new Real McCoy album, it's always hard to know where to find the right person. In this case, Andy Kahan (a member of the band) told me about David Greene who he knew from a previous project. I looked at some of David's earlier work and decided to discuss the Real McCoy project with him. I talked with David a few times on the phone about our upcoming release and pretty soon I knew that he would be the right person to work with.

Although I didn't do the actual programming or the artwork for the release, I was still involved with the production of it in many different ways. It was kind of like a video production for one of our songs-- a rough idea at first ended up with a complex structure visualized in a thick storyboard. It felt much the same as being in the studio recording a new song-- the minute you start to forget about the emotions and try to find any kind of a logical answer, you get lost.

From the moment we started thinking about this CD project, I was also thinking about our Real McCoy Web site. I didn't want to end up just releasing an Enhanced CD without being able to update the information or be able to give more background details about some of the subjects on the CD. We designed the Enhanced CD as a general starting point for getting to know a little more about Real McCoy. We'll use our Web page to provide more details, updates and also have a way of being able to exchange questions and answers with our actual fans. Through the Web site, we'll be able to learn more about what our fans like and/or don't like. This feedback will
help us in our future projects. Although we make music the way we think it should be in our minds/ears/hearts, we always want to have a strong and close relationship with our fans. At the end of the day, the fans are the ones that are buying our records and making us successful all around the world.

As new technologies develop, consumers will expect more bang for their buck. As the future of music changes, Real McCoy will need to change to--becoming both music stars and visual stars. We look forward to fulfilling that goal.

O-Jay
Real McCoy

Worldwide Artist Management, Ltd.

This new format of CD Plus or Enhanced CD has recently emerged in the music industry, and in the next few years I feel that it will double or perhaps triple in terms of units sold. From the management perspective, there is really no reason *not* to release some sort of enhanced CD for a successful group like Real McCoy.

From the consumers point of view, the "perceived value" of a purchase is key. This applies to every purchase we make, whether it's a CD or a car. The relatively small investment that is spent on developing the enhanced portion of a CD is nothing compared to the added value (i.e. perceived value) that is passed on to the consumer. However, in order to take advantage of this added value feature of an enhanced CD, it's crucial that the purchase price remain the same as a CD without the enhanced feature.

For the Real McCoy enhanced CD, we decided early on that it should be visually based as opposed to text based. We felt that our fans would prefer to have fun exploring our 3-D world we have provided on this release rather than sit down at the computer and have to read all sorts of text. We have worked closely with David Greene in all aspects of this project, and fortunately he has welcomed our ideas with open arms. From the very beginning, we felt it was important to be given the opportunity to approve each element of the release.

As more and more consumers get computers with CD ROM players, I think we'll see more artists asking their record companies to include an enhanced feature upon the album's release. The possibilities are endless, and we're glad to be part of the growing curve.

Robert Wieger
Worldwide Manager for Real McCoy

about the author

Jodi Summers is an authority on entertainment content. She is the author of the *Interactive Music Handbook*, a guide to new technology and music, and she is the president of World View Media. This nine-year-old company supplies entertainment and new technology material to magazines, newspapers, Web sites, and online services throughout the world. Current clientele include more than one-hundred forty college newspapers in the United States and forty publications throughout the world. Additionally, World View Media contributes entertainment content to various interactive sites, including movie material to *www.filmzone.com*, and music material to *www.jitter.com*, among others.

Ms. Summers has twelve years experience in music industry journalism. Her work has been published in every leading music publication, as well as *Rolling Stone, Esquire, People, Time*, and *Penthouse*. She's been editor and photo editor for such renowned U.S. music publications as *Hit Parader, Rip, Rockbeat*, and *Hot Shots*. Domestically, she co-authored the book *Rock Dirt*, and has ghost written several others including *Queen Mother: My Life With 15 Miss Americas, The Thin White Line*, and *Black's Ten Keys to Success*.

index

The Source for
Desktop Music Information

Music & Computers is the *only* magazine dedicated to showing you how to make better music with your computer. Through extensive tips and tutorials, detailed columns (the Fat Man on composing multimedia music, Jim Aikin on MIDI), and feature articles by luminaries like Craig Anderton, Julian Colbeck, and Bob Safir, *Music & Computers* teaches *how to*, not just about.

Music & Computers is the newest title from the publisher of *Keyboard*, *Guitar Player*, and *InterActivity*. It is available at select book stores, newsstands, music stores, and computer stores worldwide. For more background, visit www.music-and-computers.com. To subscribe, call 303-678-0439. For advertising information, call Karin Becker at 415-655-4119.

Music & Computers 411 Borel Ave., Ste. 100, San Mateo, CA 94402  **Miller Freeman**
A United News & Media company